James C. Ha

MW00412046

School Violence:
From Discipline to Due Process

Section of State and Local Government Law /ABA American Bar Association

Cover design by ABA Publishing

The materials contained herein represent the opinions and views of the authors and/or the editors, and should not be construed to be the views or opinions of the law firms or companies with whom such persons are in partnership with, associated with, or employed by, nor of the American Bar Association or the Section of State and Local Government Law unless adopted pursuant to the bylaws of the Association.

Nothing contained in this book is to be considered as the rendering of legal advice for specific cases, and readers are responsible for obtaining such advice from their own legal counsel. This book and any forms and agreements herein are intended for educational and informational purposes only.

08 07 06 05 04   5 4 3 2 1

Library of Congress Cataloging-in-Publication Data

    School violence / James C. Hanks, editor.— 1st ed.
    p. cm.
    Includes bibliographical references and index.
    ISBN 1-59031-465-4 (alk. paper)
    1. School violence—Law and legislation—United States. I. Hanks, James C., 1950- II. American Bar Association. Section of State and Local Government Law.

KF4159.S364 2004
344.73'0793—dc22   2004023759

Discounts are available for books ordered in bulk. Special consideration is given to state bars, CLE programs, and other bar-related organizations. Inquire at Book Publishing, ABA Publishing, American Bar Association, 321 North Clark Street, Chicago, Illinois 60610.

www.ababooks.org

Contents

Chapter 6
Workplace Violence: School Liability *by Mark A. Lies II*   81

Foreword

For students to fulfill their potential in school, schools must be safe and secure places for all students, teachers, and staff members. Without a safe learning environment, teachers have difficulty teaching and students have difficulty learning. Unfortunately, violence has become a factor in our country, our communities, and even our schools. It is hard to gauge the extent of violence in our schools, since it presents itself in such a broad range of types and severity. We hear reports of name calling, bullying, theft, assault, murder, and even terrorist threats. A large amount of media attention is often devoted to isolated incidents of violence at the extreme end of this spectrum.

Annually, the National Center for Education Statistics releases a report on school violence. The report provides "indicators" of violence and trends. The most recent (2004) gives us some perspectives on this problem (http://nces.ed.gov/pubs2004/2004004.pdf).

- In each school year from July 1, 1992 to June 30, 2000, youth ages 5 through 19 were at least 70 times more likely to be murdered away from school than at school.
- Between 1992 and 2001, the victimization rate for students ages 12 through 18 generally declined for thefts, violent crimes, and serious violent crimes at school and away from school.
- The percentage of students in grades 9 through 12 who were threatened or injured with a weapon on school property has fluctuated in recent years without a clear trend.
- The percentage of ninth- through twelfth-grade students who reported being in a physical fight on school property has declined from 16 percent in 1993 to 13 percent in 2001.
- The percentage of students who reported that they had been bullied at school increased from 5 percent in 1999 to 8 percent in 2001.

- Seventy-one percent of public schools experienced one or more violent incidents [during the annual reporting period], while 36 percent reported one or more such incidents to the police.
- About 54 percent of public schools took a serious disciplinary action in the 1999–2000 school year. Of those disciplinary actions, 83 percent were suspensions lasting 5 days or more, 11 percent were removals with no services (i.e., expulsions), and 7 percent were transfers to specialized schools.
- Between 1993 and 2001, the percentage of students in grades 9 through 12 who reported carrying a weapon anywhere and at school declined.
- In 2001, 12 percent of students ages 12 through 18 reported that someone at school had used hate-related words against them, and more than one-third of students (36 percent) saw hate-related graffiti at school.
- In 1999–2000, more than one-quarter (29 percent) of public schools reported daily or weekly student bullying.
- In 2001, 29 percent of all students in grades 9 through 12 reported that someone had offered, sold, or given them an illegal drug on school property in the 12 months before the survey.

It is clear that if we are to be successful in reducing violence in schools and in our communities, schools must work together with other agencies, groups and individuals in their communities to prevent rather than react to violence within our schools. There are, of course, many legal issues that impact these cooperative efforts, making the attorney's role an important component of creating and maintaining safe schools.

Whatever measures schools take to prevent and respond to violence, they must ensure that they adhere to constitutional limitations and statutory mandates. The chapters in this book look at the many constitutional and statutory requirements involved in preventing and responding to school violence. Meant as a practical resource, the tone of this publication is frank and clear. The focus is prevention and safety for the entire community. It has achieved that difficult balance between commonsense safety and a lock-down mentality. The specific limitations of the First Amendment right to free speech, the Fourth Amendment prohibition against unreasonable search and seizure, and the Fourteenth Amendment requirements of due process are examined. In terms of statutes, a review and discussion of the

Gun-Free School Act, Section 504, the Individuals with Disabilities Education Act, the Family Education Rights and Privacy Act, and the Safe and Gun Free Schools Act is provided.

The attorneys who have contributed to this work are highly respected and experienced. They have offered their knowledge and perspectives and given of their time. This is truly a valuable resource.

Julie Underwood, J.D., Ph.D.
General Counsel & Associate Executive Director
National School Boards Association

While the information presented strives to be useful and accurate, it should not be construed as legal advice. Readers should consult a competent professional when specific questions arise.

About the Editor

James C. Hanks is a member of the Local Government Law and Employment Law and General Litigation departments of Ahlers & Cooney, P.C., in Des Moines, Iowa. He attended the University of Iowa and received his B.A. in 1972 and his J.D., with high distinction, in 1975. He is a member of Phi Beta Kappa and in 1972 was nominated by the University of Iowa for a Rhodes Scholarship. He is a member of the American Bar Association, which he serves as a council member and chair of the Public Education Committee for the Section of State and Local Government Law, and as a member of the Section of Labor and Employment Law. He is also a member of the Iowa State Bar Association and its Section of Labor and Employment Law, and the Nebraska State Bar Association (NSBA). He formerly chaired the National School Boards Association Council of School Attorneys, the Iowa Council of School Board Attorneys, and the Iowa State Bar Association Labor Law Committee. He has served as lecturer on education or employment law issues for the University of Iowa College of Law, the National School Boards Association, the National Organization for Legal Problems in Education, the American Bar Association, the National Association of State Boards of Education, and the Iowa, Nebraska, Kansas, and Michigan Councils of School Attorneys. He is the author of "Employment at Will," NSBA Council of School Attorneys Annual Proceedings, 1984; "Fair Labor Standards Act Amendments of 1985," *Inquiry and Analysis,* NSBA Council of School Attorneys, May 1987; and "Ethics and the School Board Lawyer," NSBA Council of School Attorneys Annual Proceedings, 1995.

About the Contributors

Edgar H. Bittle is a member of the Public Finance and Local Government Law and Employment Law departments of Ahlers & Cooney, P.C., in Des Moines, Iowa. During 1988 and 1989, he was co-chair of the Iowa Legislative Post Secondary Education Task Force, which developed a 20-year plan for higher education. He is an adjunct professor in the College of Education at Iowa State University. He is a member of the American Bar Association and was chair of the ABA Urban, State and Local Government Section's Public Education Committee from 1985 to 1989 and 1993 to 1995. He is past chair of the National School Board Association National Council of School Attorneys. As a member of the Iowa Bar Association, he has served as chair of Lawpac and the Labor Law and Administrative Law Committees. He was elected to the Iowa House of Representatives in the 65th and 66th General Assemblies. He is a member of the National Association of Bond Lawyers, the American Management Association, and the ABA Sections of Banking, Business and Corporation Law and State and Local Government Law. He is counsel to the Iowa Association of School Business Officials and has served as general counsel to the Des Moines Independent Community School District and the Des Moines Area Community College, the Iowa Dental Association, and the Iowa Association of Independent Insurance Agents. He was general counsel to the Iowa Association of School Boards for 24 years.

Andrew J. Bracken is a member of the Local Government Law and Employment Law Department of Ahlers & Cooney, P.C. He is a member of the National School Board Association Council of School Attorneys (Board of Directors since 2002) and a past president of the Iowa Council of School Attorneys. He serves as an adjunct professor of graduate courses in school law at Iowa State and Viterbo universities. He is author of *The Legal Handbook for Iowa School Administrators* (Omni Publishing Company, 1998).

Heather K. Brickman is a partner in the firm of Hodges, Loizzi, Eisenhammer, Rodick & Kohn, with offices in Arlington Heights and Springfield, Illinois. Ms. Brickman concentrates her practice in all phases of school law, including governance and transactions, personnel, and school issues. She is a member of the Illinois State Bar and serves on the Executive Committee of the Illinois Council of School Attorneys.

Julie Devine practices in the education section of Tharrington Smith in Raleigh, North Carolina. Prior to joining the firm, she was a staff lawyer for the Kathryn A. McDonald Education Advocacy Project at the Legal Aid Society of New York.

Benjamin Ferrara is a member of Ferrara, Fiorenza, Larrison, Barrett & Reitz, P.C., in central New York, where he specializes in labor relations law, employment law, education law, and broadcasting law. He is an adjunct professor in the School of Education at Syracuse University. He was listed in *The Best Lawyers in America,* 1999–2000.

Sara E. Groom is an associate at Hodges, Loizzi, Eisenhammer, Rodick & Kohn. She is a member of the Illinois State Bar and the Illinois Council of School Attorneys.

Danielle Jess Haindfield is a member of the Local Government Law and Employment Law Department of Ahlers & Cooney, P.C. She is a member of the National School Boards Association, the Council of School Attorneys, the Iowa Council of School Attorneys, and the American, Iowa State, and Polk County Bar Associations. She is a member of the Order of the Coif and an honorary member of the Order of the Barristers. She is a contributing author of *America's Children at Risk* (American Bar Association, 2000).

Jeff Horner is a partner and head of the Public Law Section of Bracewell & Patterson, L.L.P., in Houston, Texas. Over the past 20 years, he has represented numerous Texas school districts in litigation involving student discipline, civil rights, construction disputes, condemnation, and other issues. In addition, he has authored approximately 40 articles and monographs related to school law. He is a 1983 graduate of the University of Virginia School of Law.

The Levin Legal Group, P.C. is an eight-lawyer firm in suburban Philadelphia, Pennsylvania, concentrating its practice on the representation of public school entities, civil rights litigation, insurance defense litigation, labor and employment law, and workers' compensation. Lawyers at the firm regularly speak at national and state seminars on all aspects of public school and labor and employment issues. The firm represents public school entities across Pennsylvania and is general counsel to the Pennsylvania School Boards Association, the School Boards Insurance Company, Ltd., and the Pennsylvania School Boards Insurance Trust.

Mark A. Lies II is a lawyer and partner with the national law firm of Seyfarth Shaw. He practices in the areas of employment, occupational safety and health, and tort litigation.

Ann Majestic is a partner in the Education Section of Tharrington Smith in Raleigh, North Carolina. Over the past 20 years she has represented numerous North Carolina school districts in litigation involving special education, student assignment, school accountability, student testing, free speech and freedom of religion, search and seizure, employment law, and teacher tenure. In addition, she is a frequent speaker at national, regional, and state conferences for lawyers and educators and has published articles in many education law publications.

Wade Norman practices in the Public Law Section of Bracewell & Patterson, L.L.P. in Dallas, Texas. He is a 2001 graduate of Harvard Law School.

David M. Pedersen is a lawyer with Baird Holm Attorneys at Law in Omaha, Nebraska. He received his law degree, magna cum laude, from the University of Michigan in 1973. While in law school, he served as both associate editor and Note and Comment editor of the *Michigan Law Review*. He is a member of the National School Boards Association Council of School Attorneys, the Education Law Association, the Nebraska Council of School Attorneys, and the North American Association of Educational Negotiators. He served as chairman of the National School Boards Association Council of School Attorneys in 1988-1989 and as president of the Nebraska Council of School Attorneys in 1979-1980 and again in 1999-2000. He is also a member of the Omaha Bar Association, the Nebraska

State Bar Association, and the Iowa State Bar Association. He is admitted to practice before the United States Supreme Court.

Ronald L. Peeler is a member of Ahlers & Cooney, P.C.'s Local Government Law and Employment Law departments. He is a member of the National School Boards Association Council of School Attorneys, the Iowa Council of School Attorneys, the Education Law Association, and the American, Iowa State, and Polk County Bar Associations.

Lisa L. Swem earned her J.D. from the University of Notre Dame School of Law and joined Thrun Law Firm, P.C., Lansing, Michigan, that same year. She is a member of the National School Boards Association and the Michigan Council of School Attorneys, the Education Law Association, and the National Association of College and University Attorneys, as well as the American Bar Association and the State Bar of Michigan. Ms. Swem gives numerous presentations on school law topics. She has published many articles on school law and authors the monthly "Law Column" for the *MASSP Bulletin*.

Carolyn Waller practices in the education section of Tharrington Smith. She is a member of the North Carolina Council of School Attorneys and the education section of the North Carolina Bar Association.

Student Violence and Harassment

1

Jeff Horner
Wade Norman

A. INTRODUCTION

Student violence and harassment is a broad category encompassing a variety of acts: simple schoolyard brawls, sexual harassment, hazing, bullying, gang violence, rapes, or even the highly publicized Columbine-style shootings. The effort to combat student violence is fought on different fronts. In the same vein, a school district's effort to avoid legal liability for student violence is multifaceted. For example, an incident of sexual assault could produce several different causes of action alleging: (1) that the school board was negligent in failing to adopt proper policies; (2) that a teacher negligently supervised the students; (3) that the school violated the victim's constitutional rights; and/or (4) that the school's response to the sexual assault is a form of gender discrimination. A school district must understand all of the different legal theories to protect itself from the lawsuits that often accompany acts of student violence.

B. TORT LAW LIABILITY

When a student commits an act of violence against a fellow student, the victim will often sue, asserting claims of negli-

1

gence or negligent supervision against the school district and/or its employees. The ability of a student to recover in such suits will vary widely depending on the jurisdiction, but a brief look at some representative cases will highlight the typical issues raised in these tort actions.

Many jurisdictions have imposed upon schools some level of duty to protect students from violence, including by third parties or fellow students. The typical legal standard for student violence cases was articulated in *Mirand v. City of New York*.[1] In *Mirand,* a student reported to her teacher that a fellow student had threatened her, but the teacher failed to take any action. The student was attacked at the end of that school day. In determining the level of duty owed by the school to its students, the court stressed that schools are not "insurers of safety" and should not be held liable for "every thoughtless or careless act by which one pupil may injure another."[2] However, the court held the school liable here for its failure to respond to the threat, because the school officials had a "duty to adequately supervise the students in their charge" and could be "held liable for foreseeable injuries proximately related to the absence of adequate supervision."[3]

The foreseeability of any violent act serves as an essential element in the typical student violence tort suit. In a more recent New York case, *Brown v. Board of Education,*[4] a high school softball player was injured by members of an opposing team in a violent melee that followed their game. The plaintiff alleged that her own school district and the opposing team's district had negligently supervised the students, but the court upheld the trial court's granting of summary judgment for the school districts, because they "had no actual or constructive knowledge of dangerous conduct on the part of the . . . plaintiff's attackers, and they could not have reasonably foreseen the sudden unprovoked attack on the . . . plaintiff."[5]

Courts will often find that violent acts that erupt suddenly were not foreseeable, but often student disputes simmer for hours, days, or weeks before reaching the boiling point. In the latter cases, the foreseeability of harm becomes a difficult inquiry. In *Kindred v. Memphis City Schools*, a high school student was shot and killed by a former student of the high

---

1. Mirand v. City of New York, 637 N.E.2d 263 (N.Y. 1994).
2. *Id.* at 264.
3. *Id.* at 265.
4. Brown v. Bd. of Educ. of the Glen Cove Public Schools, 700 N.Y.S.2d 58 (N.Y. App. Div. 1999).
5. *Id.* at 59.

school while leaving a school-sponsored student-faculty basketball game.[6] Earlier in the evening, school officials had broken up a fight between the shooter and the victim. As the shooter was being escorted off campus, he threatened the victim and vowed that he would return. The school officials took no further action to prevent the eventual shooting. The court ruled that the shooting was not foreseeable because school officials constantly heard students make similar threats, but none had been carried out before.[7]

When addressing students with known histories of violence, courts are more willing to find that harm was foreseeable. Some courts have even imposed upon schools the duty to inform teachers of a student's violent past. In *Ferraro v. City of New York*, a problem student was transferred to a new school because of violent acts committed at her former school.[8] The student continued to cause trouble at her new school and eventually assaulted a fellow student on a day when a substitute teacher was supervising the class. The court upheld a jury's finding of negligence because the administration had not warned the substitute teacher of the student's known violent behavior.

On the other hand, *Skinner v. Vacaville Unified School District* held that a failure to warn teachers of a student's known violent proclivities was not negligent.[9] In *Skinner*, the student's gym teacher was not aware of the student's prior violent acts. The problem student punched a female classmate, breaking her jaw. The court denied the victim's claim, holding that the failure to warn the gym teacher was not negligent because the gym teacher had adequate opportunity to observe the student on her own and discover any violent tendencies.

A school's duty to protect its students is generally limited to acts that occur while the students are in the school's custody, but some cases have extended the duty slightly beyond the school day. In *Broward County School Board v. Ruiz*, the court held that a "school's duty to provide supervision does not end when the bell rings."[10] The victim in *Ruiz* was severely beaten

6. Kindred v. Bd. of Educ. of Memphis City Schools, 946 S.W.2d 47 (Tenn. Ct. App. 1996).
7. *Id.* at 49.
8. Ferraro v. Bd. of Educ. of the City of New York, 212 N.Y.S.2d 615 (N.Y. App. 1961).
9. Skinner v. Vacaville Unified Sch. Dist., 43 Cal. Rptr. 2d 384 (Cal. Ct. App. 1995).
10. Broward County Sch. Bd. v. Ruiz, 493 So. 2d 474, 477 (Fla. Dist. Ct. App. 1986).

on school grounds while waiting for a ride home just after the end of the school day. The school admitted that no employee was charged with supervising that area of the campus in the hour after school ended. The court noted that "[i]f anything, the time period immediately after the end of school presents the greatest danger of misconduct by students who have been restrained all day in a disciplined setting."[11]

The existence of proper safety policies also becomes an issue in cases of school violence. In *John Doe v. City of New Orleans*, the parents of a nine-year-old who was sexually molested in a school restroom sued the teacher, principal, and the school board.[12] The teacher and principal testified that the campus usually followed an unwritten policy that young children should go to the restroom in pairs; however, the victim had been allowed to go alone at the time she was molested. The trial judge denied recovery against the teacher and principal, but found the school board itself negligent because the board "had a duty to formulate and properly promulgate an official policy against allowing young children to leave the classroom alone and use the bathroom during school hours."[13]

Just as schools can be faulted for not adopting proper safety policies, failure to follow existing policies can serve as evidence of negligence and foreseeability. In *Garcia v. City of New York,* a five-year-old was sexually molested in a school restroom, presumably by an older student in the school.[14] A jury held that the potential harm to the victim was foreseeable, and the school had acted negligently when the teacher sent the victim to the restroom alone, despite two written policies that pupils under third grade should go to the restroom only with a partner.

1. Immunity Doctrines—School Districts

The foregoing principles of negligence are not applicable in many states in which public schools and their employees are protected by some form of governmental or sovereign immunity. Immunity doctrines may have their basis in the common law, statutory provisions, or a combination of the two. The state of Texas serves as an example of a jurisdiction in which schools and school employees are heavily protected from tort suits. The

---

11. *Id.*
12. John Doe v. City of New Orleans, 577 So. 2d 1024 (La. Ct. App. 1996).
13. *Id.* at 1025.
14. Garcia v. City of New York, 646 N.Y.S.2d 508 (N.Y. App. Div. 1996).

Texas courts have applied the immunity doctrine to a variety of common law tort claims, including negligence, defamation, intentional infliction of emotional distress, malicious prosecution, tortuous interference with contractual relations, wrongful discharge, and invasion of privacy.[15] As a result, school districts in Texas are nearly totally immune from liability under state tort law.

Many states have carved out exceptions to their sovereign immunity doctrines by passing tort claims statutes. For example, the Texas Tort Claims Act allows tort claims against schools in one category of cases: where the negligence of an officer or employee of a school district arising from the operation or use of a motor vehicle causes injury or death to an individual.[16]

2. Immunity Provisions—Employees

Individual board members, administrators, and teachers who are acting within the scope of their duties or employment on behalf of a school district likewise enjoy a cloak of immunity in many jurisdictions. Under Texas law, for example, school employees are granted statutory immunity from tort suits:

> A professional employee of a school district is not personally liable for any act that is incident to or within the scope of the duties of the employee's position of employment and that involves the exercise of judgment or discretion on the part of the employee. . . .[17]

The statutory definition of "professional employee" includes "any person whose employment requires certification or the exercise of discretion."[18]

The only exceptions to the immunity statute are for motor-vehicle–related incidents[19] and for "circumstances in which a professional employee uses excessive force in the discipline of students or negligence resulting in bodily injury to students."[20] The ambiguously located "negligence result-

---

15. *See, e.g.*, Williams v. Conroe Indep. Sch. Dist., 809 S.W.2d 954 (Tex. App.—Beaumont 1991, no writ); Brown v. Indep. Sch. Dist., 763 F. Supp. 905 (S.D. Tex. 1991).
16. Texas Civ. Prac. & Rem. Code §§ 101.021, 101.051 (Vernon 1997).
17. Tex. Educ. Code § 22.051(a).
18. Tex. Educ. Code § 22.051(c)(4).
19. Tex. Educ. Code § 22.051(b).
20. Tex. Educ. Code § 22.051(a).

ing in bodily injury" phrase has been limited by interpretation to refer *only* to the discipline of students (e.g., excessive corporal punishment). Courts have also held that the "discipline exception" in the statute does not support recovery for a teacher's failure to discipline a student. Therefore, in *Pulido v. Dennis*, a lawsuit against a schoolteacher and principal filed by a student injured in a classroom fight, the appellate court upheld the trial court's granting of summary judgment.[21] The court held that the "failure to discipline" claim asserted by the plaintiff did not abrogate the employee's immunity under the Texas Education Code.[22]

Given Texas's strong school-employee immunity statute, it is safe to say that all of the various negligence and negligent supervision suits against school employees detailed in the first part of this section would have been dismissed by Texas courts had the defendants been employed by Texas school districts.

3. Limitations of Immunity

Immunity provisions for school districts and employees vary widely from state to state. The strong protections found in Texas are not necessarily the state of the law nationwide. Even among states that have immunity statutes, some have broadened the definition of "ministerial" (as opposed to "discretionary") duties or conduct from which employees are often not entitled to immunity.[23] Other states have created exceptions to their immunity doctrines if the school or employee has committed "willful and wanton misconduct."[24] Furthermore, it should be noted that private schools are generally not protected by the doctrine of sovereign immunity. Many states have a corresponding doctrine of charitable immunity, but charitable immunity doctrines have undergone significant pruning as nonprofit institutions have become larger players in local economies.

---

21. Pulido v. Dennis, 888 S.W.2d 518 (Tex. App.—El Paso 1994).

22. *Id.* at 521.

23. *See, e.g.*, Doe v. Escambia County Sch. Board, 599 So. 2d 226 (Fla. Dist. Ct. App. 1992) (holding that, because school boards and teachers have a statutory duty to supervise students, their supervisory actions are not discretionary; consequently, student who was raped could go forward with suit).

24. Dedes v. Asch, 521 N.W.2d 488 (Mich. 1994).

C. LIABILITY UNDER 42 U.S.C. SECTION 1983

Although public schools in some states enjoy widespread protection against traditional tort causes of actions, their status as state actors can create claims that their failure to protect a student amounted to a violation of the victim's constitutional rights. The typical federal constitutional claim brought in the school violence context alleges that the victim's Fourteenth Amendment right to due process was violated by the school's conduct.[25] Lawsuits to enforce federal constitutional rights are filed under 42 U.S.C. Section 1983.[26]

These suits have been largely unsuccessful in the school violence context because of the U.S. Supreme Court's decision in *DeShaney v. Winnebago County*.[27] The *DeShaney* decision held that the government's failure to protect an individual against a third party's violent act does not present a violation of the Fourteenth Amendment. The *DeShaney* opinion hinted, however, that liability could be proper in two situations: when the victim stands in a "special relationship" with the government entity, and when the affirmative acts of the government entity produced a "state-created danger."[28]

1. The Section 1983 Special Relationship Doctrine

A long line of cases involving prisoners and mental patients have flushed out the "special relationship" doctrine of Section 1983 liability. Courts

---

25. Under the Fourteenth Amendment, government entities may not "deprive any person of life, liberty, or property, without due process of law." U.S. CONST. Amend. XIV, § 1. The student claims are usually grounded in the concept of "substantive due process," through which courts have "recognized a variety of interests which are difficult of definition but are nevertheless comprehended within the meaning of either 'liberty' or 'property' as meant in the Due Process Clause." Paul v. Davis, 424 U.S. 693, 710 (1976).

26. Reading, in pertinent part: "Every person who, under color of any statute, ordinance, regulation, custom or usage, of any State or Territory, subjects, or causes to be subjected, any citizen of the United States or other person within the jurisdiction thereof to the deprivation of any rights, privileges, or immunities secured by the Constitution and laws, shall be liable to the party injured in an action at law, suit in equity, or other proper proceeding for redress."

27. DeShaney v. Winnebago County Dep't of Soc. Servs., 489 U.S. 189 (1989).

28. *Id.* at 201–02.

have ruled that victims of third-party violence in these institutions should be able to recover under Section 1983, because the state's restriction of the occupants' liberty has made them unable to care for themselves, thus creating a special relationship between the individuals and the state.

Attempts to extend these rulings to the educational setting have failed. The nation's appellate courts now unanimously refuse to hold school districts liable for violence committed by third parties under Section 1983's "special relationship" doctrine. Some judges have lamented this state of the law, noting the perverse truth that students harmed at school are unable to recover under Section 1983, while "those who find themselves in the care, custody, and control of the State because they are criminals are wrapped in the protective cloak of the constitution."[29] Despite the objections of some dissenting judges, the cases have unequivocally protected schools from Section 1983 liability, even in situations involving egregious harm to students coupled with arguably negligent acts by school officials.

In *Stevenson v. Martin County Board of Education,* the plaintiff was a sixth-grade student who was repeatedly assaulted by the same group of fellow students over a period of months.[30] The school was unable to stop the beatings, which culminated in a final incident that began in the school classroom. When the plaintiff asked the teacher for help, he was told, "There's nothing I can do . . . you probably deserved it anyway." The plaintiff fled the classroom, running to the principal's office, but two classmates followed him out of the room and continued to punch and kick him out in the hallway for 10 minutes. The plaintiff suffered numerous contusions, lacerations, and temporary eye dysfunction. The Fourth Circuit ruled, in an unpublished opinion, that the lack of a "special relationship" between the school and the student prevented the Section 1983 suit from going forward.

Student deaths have not shaken the resolve of the courts. In *Graham v. Independent School District,* the Tenth Circuit considered two consolidated cases, one involving a student shot and killed on campus, another involving a student stabbed on campus.[31] Both plaintiffs alleged that the

---

29. Walton v. Alexander, 44 F.3d 1297, 1310 (5th Cir. 1995) (Parker, J., concurring).

30. Stevenson v. Martin County Bd. of Educ., No. 99-2685 (4th Cir. Feb. 6, 2001) (per curiam), *available at* http://pacer.ca4.uscourts.gov/cgi-bin/getopn.pl?OPINION= 992685.U, *cert denied,* 534 U.S. 821 (Oct. 1, 2001).

31. Graham v. Indep. Sch. Dist. No. I-89, 22 F.3d 991 (10th Cir. 1994) (hereinafter *Graham*).

schools in question knew the victims were in danger of being harmed by fellow students but failed to take appropriate actions. The court ruled that the absence of a special relationship between the schools and the students prevented the Section 1983 suit from going forward.[32]

Even residential schools—perhaps one step closer to the prisons and mental institutions covered by the special relationship doctrine—have been protected from Section 1983 liability. The plaintiff in *Walton v. Alexander* was a student living at a state residential school for the deaf who was raped by the same classmate on two separate occasions.[33] The school's status as a residential facility charged with 24-hour custody of the students did not create a special relationship, according to the Fifth Circuit, because the students voluntarily chose to live at the school.[34]

The fact that school attendance is mandatory under state compulsory education laws has not altered the view of the courts. In *J.O. v. Alton Community Unit School District 11*, the Seventh Circuit ruled that laws requiring children to attend public schools do "not render . . . schoolchildren so helpless that an affirmative constitutional duty to protect arises."[35] Even severely disabled students that one might assume to be helpless are not covered under the special-relationship doctrine. The case of *Dorothy J. v. Little Rock School District* involved a mentally retarded male high school student who was sexually assaulted by a fellow male high school student in the gym shower.[36] The Eighth Circuit denied Section 1983 liability, even for a disabled student, because "public school attendance does not render a child's guardians unable to care for the child's basic needs."[37]

2. The Section 1983 State-Created Danger Doctrine

The second exception to the general *DeShaney* rule is the "state-created danger" doctrine. This doctrine asserts that a state actor can be liable under Section 1983 for harms committed by another, if the state's own affirmative actions placed the victim in danger. These claims also have been largely unsuccessfully in school violence cases, but a few recoveries against school districts do exist.

---

32. *Id.* at 995.
33. Walton v. Alexander, 44 F.3d 1297 (5th Cir. 1995) (en banc).
34. *Id.* at 1305.
35. J.O. v. Alton Cmty. Unit Sch. Dist. 11, 909 F.2d 267, 272 (7th Cir. 1990).
36. Dorothy J. v. Little Rock Sch. Dist., 7 F.3d 729 (8th Cir. 1993).
37. *Id.* at 732.

In *Maxwell v. School District of the City of Philadelphia,* the victim was a special education student who was attacked and raped in her classroom by fellow students.[38] The district court allowed the child's parents to recover under the Section 1983 state-created danger doctrine, because the school had taken an affirmative act that placed the child in harm's way. The school officials had locked the door to the classroom, blocking the child's only means of escape from her attackers.

A truly affirmative act by the school is essential to a state-created danger recovery. In *V.R. v. Middle Bucks Vocational Technical School,* the plaintiffs were female school children who allegedly had been sexually, verbally, and physically abused in a school bathroom and photography darkroom.[39] The affirmative acts alleged by the parents were the failure of the teacher and principal to report the misconduct to authorities and parents, and the placement of the class under the control of an inadequately trained student teacher. The Third Circuit considered it an "extremely close" case, but refused the Section 1983 claim because the plaintiff's allegations were of passivity and nonfeasance, rather than an affirmative act that placed the students in danger.[40]

The proposition that a "failure to act" cannot trigger the state-created danger doctrine was underscored in *Graham v. Independent School District.* As noted earlier, *Graham* was the consolidation of a student shooting case and a student stabbing case in which the parents claimed the school officials knew of the risk of harm, but failed to act. The Tenth Circuit rejected any "state-created danger" liability because the plaintiffs could not "point to any affirmative actions by the defendants that created or increased the danger to the victims."[41]

Even if the plaintiff can point to an affirmative act on the part of the defendant school district, that act must rise to a culpable level much greater than mere negligence. In *Leffall v. Dallas Independent School District,* a high school student was killed by another student who fired random gunshots in the parking lot at a school dance.[42] Dances at this particular school

---

38. Maxwell *ex rel.* Maxwell v. Sch. Dist. of City of Philadelphia, 53 F. Supp. 2d 787 (E.D. Pa. 1999).

39. D. R. v. Middlebucks Area Vocational Technical Sch., 972 F.2d 1364 (3d Cir. 1992) *cert denied*, 113 S. Ct. 1045 (1993).

40. *Id.* at 1376.

41. *Graham, supra* note 31, at 995.

42. Leffall v. Dallas Ind. Sch. Dist., 28 F.3d 521 (5th Cir. 1994).

were considered dangerous events, sometimes ending in gunfire. As a result, the Dallas Police Department had requested that the school not sponsor such functions until adequate police security could be provided. The plaintiff asserted that the school's decision to hold the dance over police objections and to assign only two unarmed security guards provided the "affirmative act" necessary to support Section 1983 liability. But the Fifth Circuit determined that, even assuming gross negligence on the part of school officials that might have "increased the danger of harm from third parties," the conduct did not violate Section 1983 because it "did not rise to the level of deliberate indifference."[43]

D. LIABILITY FOR GENDER-MOTIVATED ACTS UNDER TITLE IX

Although the law requires an affirmative act on the part of a school district to establish a Section 1983 violation, a district's inaction in the face of sexual harassment in some cases is enough to support a violation of Title IX. Title IX of the Education Amendments of 1972, 20 U.S.C. Section 1681 (Title IX), mandates that no educational institution that receives federal funds may discriminate on the basis of gender. The recent U.S. Supreme Court case *Davis v. Montgomery County Board of Education* determined that students who are sexually harassed by classmates can recover against their school districts under Title IX if the school district was "deliberately indifferent" to the harassment.[44]

Davis involved a female student who was taunted and harassed by a male classmate. Over a period of months, the male student made numerous suggestive statements to the victim and touched her inappropriately on several occasions. He eventually pled guilty to sexual battery. The victim reported each of the incidents to her teachers when they occurred, but no significant action was taken to correct the problem. The Court ruled that the plaintiff could recover money damages against the school district under Title IX. The legal standard adopted in *Davis* was high: It allowed Title IX recovery only against schools that are deliberately indifferent to known incidents of sexual harassment that are so severe, pervasive, and objectively offensive that they have the systematic effect of denying the student an equal educational opportunity.[45]

---

43. *Id.* at 531.
44. Davis v. Montgomery Cty. Bd. of Educ., 526 U.S. 629 (1999).
45. *Id.* at 653.

Because *Davis* is a recent case, the law regarding student-on-student harassment is still being developed. But in *Vance v. Spencer County Public School District,* the Sixth Circuit elaborated on *Davis*'s "deliberate indifference" standard.[46] The victim in *Vance* was a seventh-grade female student who presented allegations that took place over three school years. Some of her male classmates repeatedly called her sexually suggestive names, grabbed her buttocks, and pulled her bra strap. In one incident, she was approached by several male students who backed her up against a wall, held her, grabbed her hair, and started yanking off her shirt, while at the same time one student stated he was going to have sex with her and started taking off his pants. The victim asserted that she was constantly harassed at school, and that the school's response was usually limited to verbal reprimands of the students involved. The Court in *Davis* had been careful to state that districts had no duty to actually eradicate harassment, only to respond in a way not clearly unreasonable in light of the circumstances. But the *Vance* court found that the Spencer County schools had been deliberately indifferent, noting that "[w]here a school district has actual knowledge that its efforts to remediate are ineffective, and it continues to use those same methods to no avail, such district has failed to act reasonably in light of the known circumstances."[47]

Davis and *Vance* involve female students being singled out by male students for inappropriate sexual attention—the textbook example of sexual harassment. But other recent Title IX cases show that courts are willing to treat a school's response to any sexual assault as a potential violation of Title IX, regardless of whether the victim was targeted on the basis of gender. For instance, in *Wilson v. Beaumont Independent School District,* a district court considered a male 12-year-old student's alleged sexual assault of a mildly retarded male classmate.[48] Although the court denied the Title IX suit because the district had responded reasonably, the court clearly considered the assault to be a potential violation of Title IX, even though the victim was most likely singled out because of his mental handicap, not because of his gender. Similarly, in *Father v. Marriott,* a court ruled that one female first-grader's scratching and digital penetration of another female first grader's vagina, coupled with her urging the victim to lift her

46. Vance v. Spencer County Pub. Sch. Dist., 321 F.3d 253 (6th Cir. 2000).
47. *Id.* at 261.
48. Wilson v. Beaumont Ind. Sch. Dist., 144 F. Supp. 2d 690 (E.D. Tex. 2001).

dress and show her panties to the boys in the class, presented actionable sexual harassment under Title IX.[49] Here, instances of inappropriate sexual acting-out and exploration by a child most likely too young to have prurient motives for her actions gave rise to a potential violation of Title IX. These cases demonstrate that schools should not rely on traditional notions of what constitutes sexual harassment when considering Title IX liability, but should respond reasonably to *any* incident of sexual conduct.

Questions will be raised about the related application of Title IX (a statute intended to remedy gender discrimination in schools) to harassment on the basis of sexual orientation. The U.S. Department of Education's Office for Civil Rights (OCR) has stated in its latest Title IX Policy Guidance that "sexual harassment directed at gay or lesbian students that is sufficiently serious to limit or deny a student's ability to participate in or benefit from the school's program constitutes sexual harassment prohibited by Title IX."[50] OCR states that only *sexual* harassment of homosexual students (inappropriate touching, sexual propositioning, etc.) is actionable, whereas harassment that is not sexual in nature (e.g., shouting "no gays allowed" at the lunch table) is not covered by Title IX. While the OCR's policy guidance does not have the force and effect of law, a federal district court in *Ray v. Antioch Unified School District* ruled that Title IX covers sexual harassment on the basis of sexual orientation.[51] The *Ray* case involved a male student who was harassed and eventually assaulted by fellow male students because they assumed he was homosexual. The district court refused to grant summary judgment for the school district, finding "no material difference" between gender-based sexual harassment and sexual orientation–based sexual harassment.[52]

E. CONCLUSION

The vision of the school district defendant walking into court ensconced in an armor of protection is somewhat accurate, at least in the context of student violence cases. School districts in many states enjoy immunity

---

49. K.F.'s Father v. Marriott, 2001 U.S. Dist. LEXIS 2534 (S.D. Ala. 2001).

50. U.S. Dept. of Educ., Office for Civil Rights, *Revised Sexual Harassment Guidance: Harassment of Students by School Employees, Other Students, or Third Parties* (Jan. 19, 2001) at 3.

51. Ray v. Antioch Unified Sch. Dist., 107 F. Supp. 2d 1165 (N.D. Cal. 2000).

52. *Id.* at 1170.

from most negligence and negligent supervision claims. Attempts to hold schools accountable in federal court through Section 1983 actions have been, by and large, unsuccessful. A small chink in the armor of school district defendants has been exposed in the recent Title IX cases, but it applies only to cases of sexual harassment and requires a standard of liability extremely difficult to meet. Critics thus complain that the current state of the law provides no incentive for school districts to protect their students from violence. Despite the strong legal protections afforded school districts, the prevention of school violence remains a top priority in school districts across the country. Perhaps a genuine concern for the well-being of children serves as just as strong a motivator as the threat of legal action.

Weapons in Schools

2

James C. Hanks

A. INTRODUCTION

Congress enacted the Gun-Free School Zones Act[1] in 1990 and the Gun-Free Schools Act[2] in 1994. The Gun-Free School Zones Act makes it "unlawful for any individual knowingly to

---

1. 18 U.S.C. § 922(q)(2)(A) (2000). In 1995, the Supreme Court held the Gun-Free School Zones Act unconstitutional, as exceeding Congress's power under the Commerce Clause. United States v. Lopez, 514 U.S. 549 (1995). As it read at the time, the statute "made it a federal offense 'for any individual knowingly to possess a firearm at a place that the individual knows, or has reasonable cause to believe, is a school zone.'" Id. at 551 (quoting 18 U.S.C. § 922 (q)(1)(A) (1988 ed., Supp. V)). After Lopez, Congress amended the statute to include its findings as to how the presence of guns in school zones affects interstate commerce. See 18 U.S.C. § 922(q)(1) (2000). In addition, the statute now contains a jurisdictional requirement, which prohibits only knowing possession of "a firearm *that has moved in . . . interstate or foreign commerce*" in a school zone. Id. § 922(q)(2)(A) (emphasis added). The amended Gun-Free School Zones Act has been upheld as a constitutional exercise of Congress's commerce power. See, e.g., United States v. Danks, 221 F.3d 1037, 1039 (8th Cir. 1999).

2. 20 U.S.C. § 7151 (Supp. 2003). The Gun-Free Schools Act, as Spending Clause legislation, is not subject to the same constitutional vulnerability as the pre-*Lopez* Gun-Free School Zones Act.

15

possess a firearm that has moved in or that otherwise affects interstate commerce at a place that the individual knows or has reasonable cause to believe, is a school zone."[3] The Gun-Free Schools Act requires states receiving federal funds for education to enact state laws that require "local educational agencies to expel from school for a period of not less than 1 year a student who is determined to have brought a firearm to school, or to have possessed a firearm at school."[4]

These two laws laid the groundwork for subsequently enacted state statutes regulating weapons in and around schools. Specifically, states have made it illegal to possess a weapon within a particular distance of a school, as proscribed in the Gun-Free School Zones Act.[5] In addition, because federal funding is contingent upon it, states have enacted laws that mandate expulsion of students possessing a firearm on school grounds, as required by the Gun-Free Schools Act.[6]

1. The Gun-Free School Zones Act

The Gun-Free School Zones Act makes it a federal offense to knowingly possess a firearm in a school zone.[7] A "school zone" is defined as the area in or "within a distance of 1,000 feet from the grounds of a public, parochial or private" elementary or secondary school.[8] A violation of the Gun-

---

3. 18 U.S.C. § 922(q)(2)(A).

4. 20 U.S.C. § 7151(b)(1).

5. *See, e.g.*, CAL. PENAL CODE § 626.9(b) (West 2003) (prohibiting the possession of a firearm in a school zone); FLA. STAT. ch. 790.115 (2002) (prohibiting the possession of any weapon "at a school-sponsored event or on the property of any school, school bus, or school bus stop," and prohibiting the exhibition of any weapon within 1,000 feet of a school during school hours or activities); GA. CODE ANN. § 16-11-127.1 (2002) (prohibiting the possession of specified weapons in "school safety zones"); IOWA CODE § 724.4B(1) (2003) (prohibiting the possession of a firearm on the grounds of a school); LA. REV. STAT. ANN. § 14:95.2 (West 2003) (prohibiting the possession of firearms and "dangerous weapons" on "a school campus, on school transportation, or at any school sponsored function . . . , or within one thousand feet of any school campus"); WIS. STAT. § 948.605(2) (2003) (making it a felony to possess a firearm in a school zone).

6. *See* Kathleen M. Cerrone, Comment, *The Gun-Free Schools Act of 1994: Zero Tolerance Takes Aim at Procedural Due Process*, 20 PACE L. REV. 131, 165–75 (1999) (providing a table of state legislation enacted pursuant to the Gun-Free School Zones Act).

7. 18 U.S.C. § 922(q)(2)(A).

8. *Id.* § 921(a)(25).

Free School Zones Act is punishable by a fine and up to five years' imprisonment.[9]

2. State Statutes

The examples of state laws that impact weapons possession in and around schools vary in terms of both scope and punishment. For example, in Iowa, a person who commits a public offense that involves a weapon within a "weapons free zone" is subject to a fine that is double "the maximum amount which may otherwise be imposed for the public offense" if the offense had been committed outside a weapons-free zone.[10] A "weapons free zone" is within 1,000 feet of "the real property comprising a public or private elementary or secondary school."[11] In addition, simply carrying a firearm on school grounds in Iowa is a class "D" felony.[12] A class "D" felony is punishable by up to five years' imprisonment and a fine between $750 and $7,500.[13]

California's statute is similar to Iowa's in that it is illegal to possess a firearm within 1,000 feet of a public or private school that provides instruction in kindergarten or grades one through 12.[14] The punishment for this crime ranges from a three-month sentence in county jail to a five-year sentence in state prison.[15] However, California's statute is more expansive than Iowa's in that it also includes institutions of higher learning.[16] Carrying a firearm onto the grounds of a university or college is punishable by imprisonment in state prison for one to four years.[17]

In Georgia, the law is stricter both in its punishment and in its scope.[18] The Georgia statute extends not only to "school safety zones," which are

---

9. *Id.* § 924(a)(4).

10. Iowa Code § 724.4A(2) (2003).

11. *Id.* § 724.4A(1).

12. *Id.* § 724.4B(1).

13. *Id.* § 902.9(4).

14. *See* Cal. Penal Code §§ 626.9(b) (West 2003) (prohibiting the possession of a firearm in a "school zone"), 626.9(e)(1) (defining "school zone" as "an area in, or the grounds of, a public or private school providing instruction in kindergarten or grades 1 to 12, inclusive, or within a distance of 1,000 feet from the grounds of the public or private school").

15. *Id.* § 626.9(f).

16. *Id.* §§ 626.9(h)-(i).

17. *Id.*

18. Ga. Code Ann. § 16-11-127.1 (2002).

defined as the area within 1,000 feet of an elementary or secondary school, technical school, vocational school, college, university, or other institute of post-secondary education,[19] but also to school transportation and areas where school functions take place.[20] Thus, in Georgia, in contrast to California, a school safety zone includes the area surrounding colleges and universities, not just the campus grounds themselves.[21] Carrying or possessing a weapon within a school safety zone, at a school function, or on a school bus is a felony punishable "by a fine of not more than $10,000, by imprisonment for not less than two nor more than ten years, or both."[22]

3. Exceptions

There are obvious exceptions in these statutes for peace officers, military personnel, and school security officers.[23] In addition, there are other exceptions that must be noted. In particular, the federal Gun-Free School Zones Act does not apply to an individual who is licensed to possess the firearm by the state where the school zone is located.[24] In some states, the minimum age to obtain a permit is 18,[25] but there is a trend toward increasing it to 21.[26]

In states in which the minimum age to obtain a permit is 18, the "permit exception" to the Gun-Free School Zones Act has drawn criticism that guns are, in fact, allowed in schools.[27] Specifically, there is concern that there are students who are at least 18 years old attending school who there-

19. *Id.* § 16-11-127.1(a)(1).

20. *Id.* § 16-11-127.1(b).

21. *Id.* § 16-11-127.1(a)(1).

22. *Id.* § 16-11-127.1(b).

23. *E.g.,* 18 U.S.C. § 922(q)(2)(B)(vi) (2000); CAL. PENAL CODE § 626.9(*l*) (West 2003); GA. CODE ANN. § 16-11-127.1(c) (2002); IOWA CODE §§ 724.4B(2)(a), 724.4(b)-(f), (j) (2003); LA. REV. STAT. ANN. § 14:95.2(C) (West 2003); WIS. STAT. § 948.605(2)(b) (2003).

24. 18 U.S.C. § 922(q)(2)(B)(ii).

25. *E.g.,* IOWA CODE § 724.8(1) (2003).

26. *See* GA. CODE ANN. § 16-11-129(b)(1) (2002) (stating that no license may be issued to an individual under the age of 21; 18 PA. CONS. STAT. ANN. § 6109(b) (2003) (declaring that a person must be 21 to apply for a license to carry a firearm); N.Y. PENAL LAW § 400.00(1) (McKinney 2001) (noting that no license shall be issued or renewed to an individual under 21).

27. *See* Jessica Portner, *Loophole Seen Allowing Guns in Schools*, EDUCATION WEEK (Aug. 2, 2000), *available at* http://www.edweek.org/ew/ewstory.cfm?slug=43gun.h19&keywords=gun.

fore can legally carry a weapon to school.[28] Of course, in states in which a person must be 21 to obtain a permit, concern over students being allowed to legally carry a gun in school is minimized. However, critics are concerned that teachers, administrators, and other school employees may also take advantage of the permit exception to the Gun-Free School Zones Act.[29]

In actuality, however, this exception has a minimal impact. This is because many state laws go a step further than the federal law to disable the exception. For example, in Iowa, while there are several exceptions to the Code section that makes it illegal to carry a firearm on school grounds, carrying a weapon with a permit is not one of them.[30] In contrast, Florida allows persons who have weapons licenses to carry weapons to school; it is only a crime for a license holder to "unlawfully discharge" a weapon on school property.[31]

The federal Gun-Free School Zones Act contains another exception for unloaded firearms that remain in locked containers or firearm racks on motor vehicles.[32] Many state statutes also contain this exception.[33]

Georgia's statute, for example, tracks the federal law as applied to teachers and school personnel who are licensed to carry weapons.[34] However, as applied to licensed persons other than school personnel and students, Georgia only allows possessing guns in school safety zones if the license holder is dropping off or picking up a student, and the weapon is kept in a vehicle in transit or is kept in a locked compartment of a motor vehicle or locked firearm rack.[35]

The state statutes enacted pursuant to the Gun-Free School Zones Act are penal statutes with criminal penalties. These statutes may be applied to any individual, regardless of whether he or she is a student.

---

28. *See id.* ("[M]ost adults in those states are legally free to carry handguns and rifles into school classrooms, through crowded hallways, and to football games.")

29. *Id.*

30. *See* IOWA CODE §§ 724.4B, 724.4(b)-(f), (j) (2003) (listing exceptions to the prohibition of weapons possession in and around schools). *See also* LA. REV. STAT. ANN. § 14:95.2(C) (West 2003) (listing exceptions to the prohibition of possessing a weapon in school, but not including carrying it with a permit); VA. CODE ANN. § 18.2-308.1(B) (Michie 2003) (same).

31. FLA. STAT. ch. 790.115(2)(e) (2002).

32. 18 U.S.C. § 922(q)(2)(B)(iii) (2000).

33. *See, e.g.*, CAL. PENAL CODE § 626.9(a)(2) (West 2003); WIS. STAT. § 948.605(2)(b)(3).

34. GA. CODE ANN. § 16-11-127.1(c)(17) (2002).

35. *Id.* §§ 16-11-127.1(c)(7)–(8).

4. The Gun-Free Schools Act

There are additional penalties created by the Gun-Free Schools Act that apply only to *students* who bring weapons to school. The Gun-Free Schools Act compels states to enact statutes requiring local educational agencies to expel for at least one year any student "who is determined to have brought a firearm to school, or to have possessed a firearm at school."[36] The Act also conditions educational funding on local educational agencies implementing "a policy requiring referral to the criminal justice or juvenile delinquency system of any student who brings a firearm or weapon to a school served by such agency."[37] However, the Act mandates that the state statutes "shall allow the chief administering officer of a local educational agency to modify such expulsion requirement for a student on a case-by-case basis if such modification is in writing."[38] The Act also contains exceptions for firearms that are lawfully stored inside a locked vehicle on school property and for firearms that are "for activities approved and authorized by the local educational agency," as long as the agency "adopts appropriate safeguards to ensure student safety."[39]

States have enacted statutes to carry out the Gun-Free Schools Act.[40] Like the federal statute,[41] many state statutes indicate that the term "weapon," as used in the statutes, means "firearm," as defined in 18 U.S.C. § 921.[42] However, some states have defined weapon more broadly, making students subject to expulsion for bringing any "dangerous weapon" to

---

36. 20 U.S.C. § 7151(b)(1) (Supp. 2003).

37. *Id.* § 7151(h)(1).

38. *Id.* § 7151(b)(1).

39. *Id.* § 7151(g).

40. Cerrone, *supra* note 6, at 165 (providing a table of 42 state statutes enacted pursuant to the Gun-Free Schools Act). *See also* CAL. EDUC. CODE § 48915(a)(2) (West 2003) (stating that the principal or superintendent "shall recommend the expulsion of a pupil" for possessing "a knife or other dangerous object of no reasonable use to the pupil," "unless the principal or superintendent finds that expulsion is inappropriate"); FLA. STAT. ch. 1006.13(2)(a) (2002) (requiring district school boards to adopt a policy of zero tolerance, which requires expulsion for at least one year of students who bring a weapon or firearm to school).

41. 20 U.S.C. § 7151(b)(3).

42. *See e.g.,* ALA. CODE § 16-1-24.3(b) (2003); GA. CODE ANN. § 20-2-751(4) (2002); IOWA CODE § 280.21B (2003).

school.[43] As discussed in the following section, state definitions of the term "weapon" are far from uniform.

B. WHAT IS A WEAPON?

Schools come into contact with weapons that fall into three categories: true weapons, such as knives or guns; look-alike weapons, which resemble true weapons but cannot inflict physical injury; and inadvertent weapons, that is, items that were not created or brought to school to look or function like weapons but may be used to cause physical injury.

1. True Weapons

Weapons that fall into the category of "true weapons" are usually described or named explicitly in state statutes. In Georgia, the state legislature has listed approximately 20 weapons, including guns, knives, razor blades, metal knuckles, "bats, clubs, or other bludgeon-type weapon[s], or any flailing instrument consisting of two or more rigid parts connected in such a matter as to allow them to swing freely," such as "nun chahka, nun chuck, nunchaku, shuriken, or fighting chain."[44] Colorado, which makes expulsion mandatory for possessing a "dangerous weapon" at school, defines dangerous weapon to include: firearms, pellet or BB guns, spring-loaded knives, fixed-blade knives with blades longer than three inches, pocket knives with blades longer than three and one-half inches, and "any object device, instrument, material, or substance, whether animate or inanimate, used or intended to be used to inflict death or serious bodily injury."[45] Florida's statute lists only six specific weapons but contains a "catch-all" provision that brings many more weapons within its purview: "any dirk, metallic knuckles, slingshot, billie, tear gas gun, chemical weapon or device, or any other deadly weapon except a firearm or a common pocketknife."[46]

---

43. *See e.g.*, COLO. REV. STAT. §§ 22-33-106(1)(d)(I) (2003) (requiring expulsion of students possessing a "dangerous weapon" at school); MASS. GEN. LAWS ch. 71 § 37H (2003) (subjecting a student in possession of a "dangerous weapon, including, but not limited to a gun or a knife" to expulsion). *See also* CAL. EDUC. CODE. § 48915(a)(2) (subjecting a student in possession of "any knife or other dangerous object of no reasonable use to the pupil" to expulsion).

44. GA. CODE ANN. § 16-11-127.1(a)(2).

45. COLO. REV. STAT. § 22-33-106(1)(d)(II)(A)-(D).

46. FLA. STAT. ch. 1006.13(2)(a) (2002) (requiring expulsion of a student bringing a firearm or "weapon" to school), ch. 790.001(13) (defining "weapon").

Parents, students, and administrators would likely agree that students who bring true weapons to school should be punished. Possession of such dangerous instruments can clearly disrupt the education process and may result in serious bodily injury or death to other students.

2. Look-Alike Weapons

When a student brings a "look-alike" weapon to school, the need for auto-matic expulsion is less clear. A look-alike weapon is an item that resembles a weapon but is not designed to be used to cause serious bodily injury. Some states have included look-alike weapons in their expulsion statutes. For example, in Utah, "the actual or threatened use of a look-alike weapon with intent to intimidate another person or to disrupt normal school activi-ties" can result in expulsion for at least one year.[47] Based on this language, mere possession is not enough to result in expulsion; the student must use the look-alike weapon to intimidate or disrupt.[48]

In contrast, Illinois has defined weapon to include "'look-alikes of any weapon."[49] A student may be expelled for "a period not less than one year" for bringing a look-alike to school or a school-related function, regardless of whether it is used to intimidate others or disrupt school activities.[50]

Most states have not enacted statutes that include look-alike weapons. However, many school districts have included look-alike weapons in their weapons policies.[51] School districts take differing approaches to dealing with look-alike weapons. For example, the school district policy in Fed-eral Way, Washington, prohibits look-alike weapons "if the item is in-tended to be used as a weapon or would reasonably perceived to be a weapon."[52] The South Salem School District in Salem, Virginia, makes it

47. UTAH CODE ANN. § 53A-11-904 (2)(a)(i)(B) (2002).

48. *Id.*

49. 105 ILL. COMP. STAT. § 5/10-22.6(d) (2003).

50. *Id.*

51. *See e.g.*, Federal Way Public Schools, Rights and Responsibilities: Section VIII–Consequences for Student Misconduct, *available at* http://www.fwsd.wednet.edu/info/rr/sec8.html (last visited August 12, 2003) (hereinafter "Federal Way Policy"); Inver Grove Heights Community Schools, School Weapons Policy, *available at* http://www.invergrove.k12.mn.us/policies/501.pdf (revised Jan. 21, 2003); Turtle Lake School District, Possession or Use of Weapons, *available at* http://www.turtlelake.k12.wi.us/Policies_and_Codes/weaponsonschool. htm (last visited Aug. 12, 2003) (here-inafter "Turtle Lake Policy").

52. Federal Way Policy, *supra* note 51.

an offense to carry, bring, use, or possess a look-alike *gun* on school property, but does not proscribe other look-alike weapons.[53] Blair High School in Silver Spring, Maryland, states that "bringing facsimiles (model Uzis, water pistols, etc.) to school may result in a ten (10)-day suspension and *recommendation for expulsion.*"[54]

Look-alike weapons policies can be difficult to enforce and can enrage the parents of students against whom the policies are enforced. For example, in West Deer, Pennsylvania, a five-year-old kindergarten student was suspended for one day because he wore his Halloween costume, which contained a five-inch plastic axe, to school.[55] The boy was dressed as a firefighter and the axe was attached to his costume.[56] In Seattle, a sixth-grader was suspended for possessing a water pistol, which had been painted black, and fell out of his book bag.[57] In Jonesboro, Arkansas, an eight-year-old boy was suspended for three days because he pointed a chicken finger at his teacher and said, "Pow, pow, pow."[58]

Another consequence of look-alike weapons policies is that they affect legitimate school activities. For instance, a school in Loudoun County, Virginia, required the drama club to use wooden staffs instead of fake swords in its production of William Shakespeare's *Twelfth Night* because using fake swords would violate the district's weapons policy.[59] On its face, this prohibition of look-alike weapons in theater productions seems extreme. However, the administrators and teachers responsible for this decision explained that allowing students to possess weapons, even if they

---

53. South Salem School District, Parent Handbook: Weapons Policy, *available at* http://www.salem.k12.va.us/south/ParentHandbook/weapons.htm (last visited Aug. 12, 2003).

54. Blair High School, Montgomery Blair Discipline Policy, *available at* http://mmm.mbhs.edu/resources/teacher/DisciplinePolicy.pdf (last visited Aug. 12, 2003) (emphasis in original).

55. Carmen J. Lee, *School Suspends Kindergartner Whose Costume Violates Weapons Policy*, Pittsburgh Post-Gazette, Nov. 3, 1998, *available at* http://www.post-gazette.com/regionstate/19981103ax2.asp.

56. *Id.*

57. Dick Lilly, *District Won't Back Down on Strict Policy over Weapons*, Seattle Times, Oct. 7, 1998, *available at* http://seattletimes.nwsource.com/news/local/html98/gunn_100798.html.

58. *Child Suspended for Brandishing Chicken*, L.A. Times, Feb. 1, 2001, at A16.

59. David Nakamura & Susan Saulny, *Shakespeare, Without a Sword to Draw*, Wash. Post, Oct. 12, 1998, *available at* http://www.washingtonpost.com/wp-srv/local/daily/oct98/plays12.htm.

are fake, weakens the message that students must not bring weapons (real or look-alike) to school.[60]

Some parents and administrators may believe that look-alike weapons policies should be abandoned altogether; however, there are reasons to have these policies in place. Many schools describe the reasons for adopting the policies in their handbooks. For example, the Federal Way School District has determined that look-alike weapons may cause a substantial disruption to the education process.[61] In addition, a student who sees an item that looks like a weapon may be psychologically affected, regardless of whether the item actually is a dangerous weapon.[62] Accordingly, the Loudoun County, Virginia School District policy bans "'toy' or 'look-alike' weapons" that could "injure, harm, endanger, or induce fear in another person."[63] While it may seem that some schools have taken an extreme approach to look-alike weapons through these policies, they may help protect the educational experience and psychological well-being of students.

3. Inadvertent Weapons

Schools and parents have a difficult time determining what discipline, if any, a student should receive for bringing "inadvertent weapons" to school. The category of inadvertent weapons is best explained through example. In one case, an 11-year-old Cobb County, Georgia, girl was suspended for 10 days for bringing a 10-inch-long chain attached to a Tweety Bird wallet to school.[64] The school later rescinded the suspension.[65] The Cobb County School District's weapons policy includes "chains" within a lengthy list of prohibited weapons.[66]

---

60. *Id.*

61. Federal Way Policy, *supra* note 51.

62. *See* Lilly, *supra* note 57 ("Toy guns look just like real guns. . . . When a kid takes a toy gun and points it at another kid and says, 'Bang bang, you're dead,' that's malice.") (quoting John Stanford, superintendent of the Seattle School District).

63. Loudoun County Public Schools, Policies and Regulations Manual § 8-32(b)(4), *available at* http://www.loudoun.k12.va.us/policy/8-32.pdf. (revised Feb. 8, 2000) (hereinafter "Loudoun County Policy").

64. *Georgia School Lifts Suspension of Girl with Tweety Bird 'Weapon,'* at http://www.cnn.com/2000/US/09/29/wallet.suspension.01/ (Sept. 29, 2000).

65. *Id.*

66. Cobb County School District, Weapons Policy, *available at* http://www.cobbk12.org/Departments/HR/HRBoardPolicies/J_Policies/jcdac_p.htm (revised May 23, 2002).

In another example, a Michigan teen was suspended for one term when he dressed in full Scottish Highland regalia, including a small dagger known as a *skean-dhu* in his sock, for his high school prom.[67] The student, who spent two years planning his costume, could have been suspended for an entire year under Michigan law.[68]

In 1998, a kindergarten student found a butter knife while walking to school.[69] When he was discovered with the knife, he was suspended for five days, although, according to the school principal, he could have been expelled under the weapons policy. Similarly, many students have been suspended for possessing objects such as nail clippers and bottle openers at school.[70]

In each of these situations, the objects the disciplined students possessed *could have* been used to inflict physical injury on another, and thus fell within the schools' weapons policy. Schools often treat weapons policy violations as strict liability offenses and punish violators for possessing objects that are *capable* of inflicting physical injury, even absent a showing of knowledge or intent to do so.[71] In contrast, some weapons policies

---

67. Duncan Campbell, *Scots Zealot Sets off Alarm Bells at U.S. High School*, THE GUARDIAN, July 26, 2001, *at* http://www.guardian.co.uk/Print/0,3858,4228388,00.html.

68. *Id.*

69. Pat Carome, *Beloit 5-year-old Suspended for Bringing Butter Knife to School*, BELOIT DAILY NEWS, June 3, 1998.

70. *See, e.g.*, Michael McLeod, *Zero Tolerance Makes Zero Sense, Some Say; Opponents Questioned Disciplinary Actions of the Hard-Line Policy, but Educators Said Students' Safety Is the Smart Choice*, ORLANDO SENTINEL TRIB., June 14, 2001, at A1 (reporting the ten-day suspension and threatened expulsion of a high school student who brought a nail clipper to school); Anand Vaishnav, *Trinket's Knife Earns Suspension; School Says Key Chain Is a Weapon; Sixth-Grader Kicked Out for Rest of Year*, NEW ORLEANS TIMES-PICAYUNE, Dec. 27, 1998, at B1 (reporting the six-month suspension of a sixth-grader for possessing a key chain that contained a one-inch knife, nail file, and bottle opener).

71. *See, e.g.*, McKeesport Area School District, Weapons Policy, *available at* http://www.mckasd.org/weapons_policy.htm (revised Dec. 13, 1995) (prohibiting possession of "any tool, instrument or implement capable of inflicting serious bodily injury"); Loudoun County Policy, *supra* note 63, at § 8-32(b)(4) (prohibiting possession of "any instrument, device, or substance . . . which could injure, harm, endanger, or induce fear in another person").

only prohibit inadvertent weapons if the object is *actually* used to threaten or harm another.[72]

C. CULPABLE MENTAL STATE

Another issue that arises in enforcing weapons policies is the culpable mental state, if any, that is required to punish a student possessing a weapon at school. The answer depends on the statute that is being enforced.

1. The Gun-Free School Zones Act

The federal Gun-Free School Zones Act does contain a culpable mental state requirement.[73] In order to be convicted for possessing a firearm in a school zone, an individual must "knowingly" possess the firearm.[74]

However, many state statutes based on the Gun-Free School Zones Act do not contain the "knowingly" requirement and thus read like strict liability statutes. For example, Georgia, Louisiana, and Virginia all make it a crime to possess a weapon on school grounds without any requirement that the weapon was knowingly possessed.[75]

However, when faced with a statute that is silent on the issue of the requisite level of intent, some courts will read a requirement of knowledge into the statute. For example, in *In re the Welfare of C.R.M.*,[76] the Minnesota Supreme Court examined a case in which a teacher discovered a folding knife with a four-inch blade in a student's coat pocket.[77] C.R.M. was convicted of possessing a "dangerous weapon" on school property, in violation of a Minnesota statute that was similar to the Gun-Free School Zones Act but that did not contain a "knowingly" requirement.[78] On appeal,

---

72. *See, e.g.*, Press Release, San Diego City Schools, Zero Tolerance Policy for Weapons, Violence Continues to Ensure Safer Schools (Aug. 13, 1997), *available at* http://www.sdcs.k12.ca.us/news-releases/news-releases/1997/nr.970813) ("Any object used in a threatening manner, even if it is not normally considered a weapon, will be considered a weapon under the zero-tolerance policy."); Turtle Lake Policy, *supra* note 51 (classifying as a weapon "[a]ny item used by a student to inflict harm (ie: pencil, scissors, pen, letter opener, etc.)").

73. 18 U.S.C. § 922(q)(2)(A) (2000).

74. *Id.*

75. GEORGIA CODE ANN. §§ 16-11-127.1(b) (2002); LA. REV. STAT. ANN. § 14:95.2(A) (West 2003); VA. CODE ANN. §§18.2-308.1(A)-(B) (Michie 2003).

76. *In re* the Welfare of *C.R.M.*, 611 N.W.2d 802 (Minn. 2000).

77. *Id.* at 803.

78. *Id. See also* MINN. STAT. § 609.66(d) (2003) (making it a felony to possess a dangerous weapon "while knowingly on school property").

C.R.M. argued that he should not be punished because he simply forgot to take the knife out of his pocket after the weekend, when he was using it to whittle.[79]

The court held that because it was a felony-level crime and the "nature of the weapon here—a knife—was not so inherently dangerous that appellant should be on notice that mere possession would be a crime, respondent was required to prove that [the student] knew he possessed the knife on school property."[80] The court reasoned that "strict liability statutes are generally disfavored,"[81] and that "great care is taken to avoid interpreting statutes as eliminating mens rea where doing so criminalizes a broad range of what would otherwise be innocent conduct."[82]

Similarly, in *Washington v. Peart*,[83] the Washington Court of Appeals interpreted Washington's gun-free school zones statute, which contained no culpable mental state element.[84] Reasoning that the statute "could criminalize a broad range of innocent behavior if it were treated as a strict liability crime," the court held that the statute prohibited only "knowing" possession of a firearm on school premises.[85]

2. The Gun-Free Schools Act

Unlike the federal Gun-Free School Zones Act, the federal Gun-Free Schools Act does *not* mandate that students expelled due to firearms possession possess any level of intent.[86] Rather, the statute simply states that states shall "requir[e]" local educational agencies to expel students who possess a firearm at school for at least one year.[87] Although it initially appears to require school districts to enact "zero-tolerance" or strict liability weapons policies, the Act contains a proviso mandating that state stat-

---

79. *C.R.M.*, 611 N.W.2d at 803.

80. *Id.* at 810.

81. *Id.* at 805 (citing Staples v. United States, 511 U.S. 600, 606 (1994)).

82. *Id.* at 809 (citing *Staples*, 511 U.S. at 609).

83. Washington v. Peart, No. 20882-6-III, 2003 WL 116162 (Wash. Ct. App. 2003) (unpublished op.).

84. *See* WASH. REV. CODE § 9.41.280(1) (2003) (stating that it is unlawful to possess a firearm or other dangerous weapon on school grounds).

85. *Peart*, 2003 WL 116162, at *3. *But see In re* M.A., 729 N.Y.S.2d 597, 599 (N.Y. Fam. Ct. 2001) (holding that possession of a box cutter on school grounds is a strict liability offense that requires no culpable mental state).

86. 20 U.S.C. § 7151(b)(1) (2000).

87. *Id.*

utes enacted pursuant to the federal Act "shall allow the chief administering officer of a local educational agency to modify such expulsion requirement for a student on a case-by-case basis if such modification is in writing."[88]

Although the federal Act does not require a showing that the student "knowingly" possessed the weapon, several state statutes enacted pursuant to the federal Act do contain such a requirement. In Nebraska, for example, only students "determined to have *knowingly and intentionally* possessed" a firearm on school grounds are subject to expulsion.[89] Similarly, under the Iowa statute, students are expelled only for "knowingly" possessing a weapon at school.[90]

In contrast to these statutes, many other state statutes do not contain culpable mental state requirements. For example, Alabama, Colorado, Florida, New York, and Pennsylvania all have statutes that subject students to expulsion for weapons possession regardless of their culpable mental states, subject only to the proviso that the school superintendent has the authority to modify the expulsion requirement if the particular student's circumstances so warrant.[91]

Statutes that subject a student to expulsion without any showing that the student knowingly possessed a weapon at school have been challenged as violative of students' constitutional rights. For example, in *Seal v. Morgan*,[92] the Sixth Circuit Court of Appeals addressed a case in which Dustin Seal, a Tennessee high school student, was expelled from school when a friend's knife was found in the glove compartment of Seal's car.[93] Seal's friend had placed the knife in the glove compartment when Seal left the vehicle to go to his girlfriend's door to pick her up.[94] The Tennessee statute that authorized Seal's expulsion subjects students to expulsion for possessing knives and guns, among other things, but allows the superintendent to modify the expulsion decision on a case-by-case basis.[95] Seal

---

88. *Id.*

89. Neb. Rev. Stat. § 79-263 (2002) (emphasis added).

90. Iowa Code § 280.21B (2003).

91. Ala. Code § 16-1-24.3(a) (2003); Colo. Rev. Stat. § 22-33-106(1)(d)(I) (2003); Fla. Stat. ch. 1006.13(2)(a) (2002); N.Y. Penal Law § 3214(3)(d) (McKinney 2001); 24 Pa. Cons. Stat. §§ 13-1317.2(a), (b) (2003).

92. Seal v. Morgan, 229 F.3d 567 (6th Cir. 2000).

93. *Id.* at 571–73.

94. *Id.* at 571.

95. Tenn. Code Ann. §§ 49-6-3401(a)(7)–(8), (g) (2003).

challenged his expulsion, claiming that it was a violation of his substantive due process rights.[96] When the district court denied the school board's motion for summary judgment on Seal's substantive due process claim, the board took an interlocutory appeal from that decision, with the permission of the district court and the Sixth Circuit.[97]

The Sixth Circuit held that because the right to attend public school is not a fundamental right,[98] "[i]n the context of school discipline, a substantive due process claim will succeed only in the 'rare case' when there is 'no rational relationship between the punishment and the offense.'"[99]

The court concluded that "suspending or expelling a student for weapons possession, even if the student did not knowingly possess any weapon, would not be rationally related to any legitimate state interest."[100] Although schools "have an unquestionably powerful interest in maintaining the safety of their campuses and preserving their ability to pursue their educational mission,"[101] disciplining students who did not knowingly possess weapons was not rationally related to that interest. The court explained that "[n]o student can use a weapon to injure another person, to disrupt school operations, or, for that matter, any other purpose if the student is totally unaware of its presence."[102]

In a case reaching the opposite result, *Enterprise City Board of Education v. C.P.*,[103] school officials found a gun in C.P.'s car.[104] C.P. maintained that her mother placed the gun in the car and C.P. was unaware that it was there.[105] The school board expelled her for eight weeks, but the trial court held that this punishment was "shockingly disparate to the offense."[106] However, the Court of Civil Appeals reversed the trial court, noting that the trial court could not substitute its discretion for that of the school

96. *Seal*, 229 F.3d at 573.
97. *Id.* at 573–74.
98. *Id.* at 575 (quoting San Antonio Indep. Sch. Dist. v. Rodriguez, 411 U.S. 1, 33–37 (1973)).
99. *Id.* (quoting Rosa R. v. Connelly, 889 F.2d 435, 439 (2d Cir. 1989)).
100. *Id.*
101. *Id.* at 574 (citing Goss v. Lopez, 419 U.S. 565, 580 (1975)).
102. *Id.* at 575.
103. Enterprise City Bd. of Educ. v. C.P., 698 So. 2d 131 (Ala. Civ. App. 1996).
104. *Id. at* 131–32.
105. *Id.* at 132.
106. *Id.*

board.[107] The court held that because C.P. could have been suspended for an entire year, eight weeks was not shockingly disparate.[108] The court opined that letting C.P. go unpunished would send the wrong message, that is, that "some students will be allowed to violate school board policy and state law with impunity, but that others will be expelled for as long as one year for the same behavior."[109]

D. CONCLUSION

Since the 1990s a mass of legislation has been enacted on both the federal and state levels to combat the problem of weapons in schools. As a result of this legislation, not only may students be expelled for bringing weapons to school, but any individual in possession of a weapon on school grounds is subject to serious criminal penalties. Because the definition of weapon and the culpable mental state required to commit a weapons infraction vary greatly among statutes, states, and policies, school administrators must be diligent in each case in consulting the laws and policies that apply to their schools.

Moreover, in enforcing policies enacted pursuant to the Gun-Free Schools Act, it must not be forgotten that administrators have the discretion to temper harsh penalties with written modifications if the particular student's circumstances so warrant.[110] If administrators utilize the common sense and fairness that the law entitles them to utilize, weapons policies can achieve the goals of ensuring students' safety and maintaining decorum in schools without the extreme and sometimes absurd results that litter the media and outrage the public. As Justice O'Connor stated in commenting on zero-tolerance policies: "'Implementation always must leave room for us to adjust to the circumstances.'"[111]

---

107. *Id.* at 133.
108. *Id.*
109. *Id.*
110. 20 U.S.C. § 7151(b)(1) (mandating that state laws enacted pursuant to the Gun-Free Schools Act "allow the chief administering officer of a local educational agency to modify [the] expulsion requirement for a student on a case-by-case basis if such modification is in writing").
111. Justice Sandra Day O'Connor, Address at a meeting of the Minnesota Women Lawyers (July 3, 2001), *quoted in* J. Kevin Jenkins & John Dayton, *Students, Weapons, and Due Process: An Analysis of Zero Tolerance Policies in Public Schools*, 171 EDUC. L. REP. 13, 33 (2003).

Searching Students in Schools 3

The Levin Legal Group, P.C.

A. INTRODUCTION

School violence can take a variety of forms, but perhaps the most serious kind involves the use of weapons. One obvious tool to stop this violence is to get rid of weapons in schools, but to do that, it would help to be able to search for those weapons. Of course, any search at least implicates the Fourth Amendment's prohibition on unreasonable searches and seizures. While school officials need to be cognizant of the Fourth Amendment's protections for students, that Amendment probably does not impair the schools' abilities to protect themselves against weapons by, for instance, the use of metal detectors, or to search for weapons it has a reason to believe a student possesses.

The Fourth Amendment, which governs searches and seizures, has never been considered a model of expressive clarity.[1] That amendment reads:

---

1. *See, e.g.*, the discussion in Akhil Reed Ahmar, The Bill of Rights, ch. 4 (1998).

CHAPTER 3

The rights of the people to be secure in their persons, houses, papers, and effects against unreasonable searches and seizures, shall not be violated, and no Warrants shall issue, but upon probable cause, supported by Oath or affirmation, and particularly describing the place to be searched, and the persons or things to be seized.

The protection against unreasonable searches and seizures extends well beyond the law-enforcement context, but its core protection is against those unreasonable searches and seizures that take place for law-enforcement and criminal investigation purposes. In other words, the core protection is against a police officer searching someone in an improper, unjustified way, and using what he or she finds in your pockets to arrest you and turn you over to the criminal justice system for trial. Still, it extends beyond the criminal law situation to all state officials. As the Supreme Court has said, "It is now beyond dispute that the Federal Constitution, by virtue of the Fourteenth Amendment [which incorporates the Fourth Amendment], prohibits unreasonable searches and seizures by state officers."[2] It is equally clear that public school officials fall under this category of "state officers."[3] Searches that teachers and administrators make of students in schools, however, are not judged by the same high standard as searches by police officers directed against suspects. One reason, according to the U.S. Supreme Court, is that students have a lower expectation of privacy. Another reason is that schools have an interest in the safety and well-being of their students that "is custodial and tutelary, permitting a degree of supervision and control that could not be exercised over free adults."[4]

B. TYPES OF SEARCHES

To sum up where the law of searches in school stands, it is useful to divide searches into searches of the students' persons and searches of places over which they may lay claim, like lockers. Further, searches of the students' persons—literally, such as a drug test, or simply of their purses or pockets—need to be divided into searches based on individualized suspicion and general, random searches. When a student's person is searched be-

---

2. New Jersey v. T.L.O., 469 U.S. 325, 334 (1985).
3. *Id.*
4. Vernonia Sch. Dist. 47J v. Action, 515 U.S. 646, 655 (1995).

cause that particular student is suspected of violating a disciplinary rule or of something more serious, all that is required to justify the search are reasonable grounds to suspect the search will turn up evidence that a rule has been broken. All that is required to justify the manner of the search is that its scope be reasonably related to the search's legitimate objective and "not excessively intrusive in light of the subject's age and sex."[5]

On the other hand, generalized searches not based on individual suspicion are permissible when there is a special need "beyond the normal need for law enforcement," a need "other than crime detection."[6] These special-needs searches must be carefully weighed, however, not to be too intrusive and to be based on a legitimately strong government interest.[7] So far, the Supreme Court has found the special needs search justifies general drug testing based on an announced policy that gives students notice. This justification, to date, has been extended only to students participating in any and all extracurricular activities, but the Court's reasoning appears to invite application to the entire student body.

1. Weapons Searches

The same special-needs searches ought to be applicable to at least some kinds of searches for guns and other weapons. Although the Supreme Court has not addressed the issue, state and federal courts throughout the nation have approved the use of metal detectors in schools. If the metal detectors are not used for the purpose of "catching crooks,"[8] but rather to deter the possession of weapons in school, they probably will be found acceptable. If the metal detectors are used as part of an announced policy that gives students prior notice of their use, they almost surely will be found acceptable.

2. Other Searches

Finally, searches of other areas over which students exercise some private control, such as lockers, have never been addressed by the U.S. Supreme

---

5. New Jersey v. T.L.O., 469 U.S. 325, 342 (1985).

6. Chandler v. Miller, 520 U.S. 305, 314–15 (1997) (striking down Georgia statute that required candidates for state office to submit to drug testing).

7. *Id.*

8. *See* Edmond v. Goldsmith, 183 F.3d 659, 664 (7th Cir. 1999) (discussing the requirement that the special need be unrelated to law enforcement during opinion striking down police roadblocks used for drug interdiction).

Court. It seems clear that where there is individual suspicion of a student's rule-breaking, a search based on reasonable grounds to suspect the locker will reveal evidence of that rule-breaking would be upheld. Some courts, however, have upheld much more—a general search of all lockers without any basis for suspicion. These courts often find that, in fact, students have no legitimate expectation of privacy in the contents of school lockers, at least if the school notifies the students that the school maintains joint control of the locker.

C. SUPREME COURT RULINGS: *T.L.O*

The Supreme Court's few forays into school searches have established (1) that students do have Fourth Amendment rights in the school, but (2) that students' rights do not afford them as much protection as is available outside the schoolhouse doors. Specifically, in *New Jersey v. T.L.O.*, 469 U.S. 325 (1985), the Court first held that school officials are bound by the Fourth Amendment, but that amendment does not require that the official have "probable cause" to search a student, as is generally required in most contexts (including law-enforcement searches). In *T.L.O.*, an assistant vice-principal at Piscataway High School searched the purse of a freshman girl who, after being caught smoking in the girls' bathroom, denied smoking at all. The assistant vice-principal found a pack of cigarettes, which proved she was lying, but he did not stop there. Instead, he continued the search and found marijuana, a pipe and rolling papers, and index cards with what could have been records of drug sales she had made. He called the police, and ultimately the girl was adjudicated delinquent and sentenced to a year of probation. Throughout the delinquency proceedings, the girl challenged the search as a violation of the Fourth Amendment.

The Supreme Court's decision in *T.L.O.* established both that the Fourth Amendment applies to school searches and that the demands of this amendment require less in a school context than in other contexts. The Court explained, first, that the "underlying command of the Fourth Amendment is always that searches and seizures be reasonable," but "what is reasonable depends on the context within which a search takes place."[9] To determine what is reasonable requires a balance between, on the one hand, "the individual's legitimate expectations of privacy and personal security" and, on the other hand, "the government's need for effective methods to deal

---

9. New Jersey v. T.L.O., 469 U.S. 325 (1985) at 336.

with breaches of public order."[10] Normally, when striking the balance under the Fourth Amendment to determine what counts as a reasonable search, the government must show probable cause to search a particular individual. This is particularly the case in the criminal context, upon which, of course, search and seizure law primarily is focused.

In *T.L.O.*, however, even though the ultimate use of the fruits of the search was in a criminal context, the Court applied a lesser standard, because in its view, "[i]t is evident that the school setting requires some easing of the restrictions to which searches by public authorities are ordinarily subject."[11] In other words, a school official does not need to have probable cause to search a student. Rather, all a school official needs to search an individual student "are reasonable grounds for suspecting the search will turn up evidence that the student has violated or is violating either the law or the rules of the school."[12] The facts of *T.L.O.* illustrate the difference between probable cause and this lesser standard. Just because the girl in that case had been seen smoking did not give rise to probable cause to believe that looking in her purse would provide evidence of a crime. After all, it was neither a crime nor a violation of school rules to possess cigarettes. On the other hand, it was reasonable to suspect that her purse would provide evidence that she smoked (smokers often carry cigarettes), and that in turn would be evidence that she was lying when she denied smoking in the girls' room, although she was in fact caught doing so.

Once the school official has a reasonable suspicion, the search can proceed as long as the scope of the search is "reasonably related to the objective of the search and not excessively intrusive in light of the age and sex of the student and the nature of the infraction."[13] In other words, searching T.L.O.'s purse was reasonable, but a strip search most likely would not have been.

Perhaps the most notable thing about *T.L.O.*, at least in hindsight, was the fact that the Court almost reached out to raise the question of whether school officials could search students without "individualized suspicion." After all, in the case before it, the Court was dealing with a particular individual who was suspected of breaking school rules. Yet in a footnote,[14] the Court specifically reserved the question of whether "individualized

---

10. *Id.*
11. *Id.* at 340.
12. *Id.* at 342.
13. *Id.* at 342.

suspicion" is an essential element for a reasonable school search. It took a number of years for the Court to return to that question, but in recent years the Court has approved general, suspicionless searches in the form of drug testing, at least for everyone participating in extracurricular activities. Moreover, it has left the door clearly open to such searches for all students irrespective of their participation in anything more than their compelled attendance.

1.   Suspicionless Searches: *Vernonia* and *Earls*

Searches undertaken without individualized suspicion are justifiable when the government has a special need unrelated to law enforcement.[15] In the school context, that special need arises from the school's custodial and tutelary responsibility to provide a safe environment for the children entrusted to that school. Until recently, the key decision in analyzing the limits of suspicionless school searches was *Vernonia School District 47J v. Action*, 515 U.S. 646 (1995). In that case, the Court approved a program of random drug testing of all student athletes. The *Vernonia* decision remains good law, but it is no longer the last word. The boundaries of suspicionless searches were pushed still further in the Court's end-of-term decision on June 27, 2002, *Board of Education of Independent School District No. 92 of Pottawatomie County v. Earls*, 122 S. Ct. 2559 (2002), allowing drug testing for all students in extracurricular activities. In that decision, the Court shows a special concern for drug use in schools, which it calls "this evil . . . being visited not just upon individuals at large, but upon children for whom [the schools have] undertaken a special responsibility of care and direction."[16] Although the Court's perception of the harm drugs create may affect the way it struck a balance in that case, the factors that the Court places in that balance would apply to all search and seizure cases. Specifically, the reasoning in *Earls* can easily be applied to justify at least certain kinds of generalized weapons searches.

---

14.   469 U.S. at 342 n.8.

15.   *See Chandler*, 520 U.S. at 314.

16.   Board of Educ. of Indep. Sch. Dist. No. 92 of Pottawatomie County v. Earls, 122 S. Ct. 2559 (2002) at 2567, *quoting* Vernonia Sch. Dist. 47J v. Action, 515 U.S. 646, 662 (1995).

In *Earls,* the Court held that a requirement at Tecumseh High School of submission to drug testing in order to participate in any extracurricular activity, such as choir, band, athletics, or Future Farmers of America, was constitutionally permissible. The Court recognized that such testing was, of course, a search, and one that was conducted without probable cause or even individualized suspicion. Yet it upheld the policy, as it "reasonably serves the School District's important interest in detecting and preventing drug use among its students."[17] The Court found that the School District's interest arose separate from any law enforcement activity, but rather from the special need schools have to protect their students. The school's interest arose not just from the problem drug testing was intended to address (the illegal use of drugs), but also from the relationship a school needs to have to its students.

This Fourth Amendment analysis in which the Court engaged balanced the intrusion on the students' privacy interests against the state's legitimate interests to determine if a search was reasonable.[18] On the students' side of the balance were their legitimate privacy interests, the intrusiveness of the search, and the consequences to the students that might flow from the search. On the school's side of the balance was "the nature and immediacy of the government's concerns and the efficacy of the Policy in meeting them."[19] Moreover, the school's concerns showed a "special need[], beyond the normal need for law enforcement."[20] The public schools' "custodial and tutelary responsibility for children" meant there is a special need arising from that responsibility inherent in public schools.[21] This special need is particularly relevant when issues of safety for the children are implicated, such as the substantial safety concerns raised by drug use.[22] That means in striking the balance described above, the "nature and immediacy of the government's concerns" might show a special need that will cause the Court to replace the probable-cause requirement with something less stringent.

17. 122 S. Ct. at 2562.
18. *Id.* at 2564.
19. *Id.* at 2567.
20. *Id.* at 2564.
21. *Id.*
22. *Id.* at 2568.

In other words, the Court did not say that the scourge of drugs created a special need, but rather that the nature of the relationship between school and pupil did. That means that any school search and seizure outside the criminal law context, when weighed in the balance, must recognize the special need that schools' custodial and tutelary responsibilities create. That special need means probable cause probably is never required in a school search outside of the criminal context when the school's interest in providing a safe environment is implicated.

The *Earls* Court did not approve a student-body–wide testing program, but then it was not asked to do so. In striking the balance in *Earls,* the Court appeared to give weight to the fact that those subjected to testing were not just students, but students who chose to be in choir or band or other extracurricular activities. The first factor in the balance is, again, the legitimate privacy interests of the persons searched. The Court noted that extracurricular activities are regulated in a number of ways and, although never explicitly relying on this fact, did mention several times that participation in these activities is voluntary. These factors "further diminish[] the expectation of privacy among schoolchildren."[23]

2. General Drug Testing

How would this balance be struck if a general school drug-testing program were instituted? One suggestion comes from the Court's use of the phrase "further diminishes the expectation of privacy. . . ."[24] First, one must realize that the Court's clear rule is that a "student's privacy interest is limited in a public school environment where the State is responsible for maintaining discipline, health, and safety."[25] Second, the Court already had ruled that drug testing is acceptable for student athletes in *Vernonia School District 47J v. Action*, 515 U.S. 646 (1995). In that decision, the Court stated that "[l]egitimate privacy expectations are even less with regard to student athletes."[26] In *Earls,* the Court characterized the words "even less" as showing the "supplemental nature of this factor [being an athlete]." It was the school context that was the "most significant element"—a "hefty weight on the side of the school's balance. . . ."[27] If the words "even less" in the *Vernonia*

---

23. *Id*. at 2566.
24. *Id*.
25. *Id*. at 2565.
26. 515 U.S. at 657.
27. 122 S. Ct. at 2565 n.3.

opinion are just supplemental, the words "further diminishes," applied to other extracurricular activities besides athletics in *Earls,* also could be seen as "just supplemental" to the "hefty weight" of the school context. That in turn means when the Court said suspicionless drug testing "may" be allowed for all students, it might in fact mean "is" allowed.

Whatever impact voluntary participation in activities has on the first factor in the balance—the student's legitimate privacy interest—the other factors are not affected by that status of voluntary participation. The Court found that urine testing is not that intrusive (the second factor), even though a faculty monitor actually stands outside a restroom stall and listens for the "normal sounds of urination."[28] Also, of course, drug testing at Tecumseh High School was an announced policy, not used to catch people red-handed so much as to deter drug use in the first place. Because it was announced in advance, it was not as intrusive as a surprise search would be.

Finally, the Court also mentioned that the test results do not lead to the imposition of discipline or academic consequences, nor are they turned over to law enforcement (thus avoiding the criminal context that will obviate any "special need").[29] All a bad urine test means is restriction from participation in extracurricular activities (and the inevitable result that the whole school will know there is some reason the student is not in choir anymore). This fact emphasized the "special needs" justification of drug testing; it was testing outside the context of criminal proceedings.

On the other side of the balance, the Court found that within the school context, itself the source of a special need, the government's interest was in stopping "the drug abuse problem among our Nation's youth."[30] The Court did not require Tecumseh to show any particular or pervasive drug problem in its schools. Finally, the Court found drug testing was "a reasonably effective means of addressing the School District's legitimate concerns in preventing, deterring, and detecting drug use."[31] The Court gave no reason for that finding.

3. Effects of *Vernonia* and *Earls*

Interestingly, Justice Breyer, whose concurrence was needed to form a majority for upholding the drug-testing policy, emphasized the serious-

28. *Id.* at 2566.
29. *Id.* at 2567.
30. *Id.*
31. *Id.* at 2569.

ness of the drug problem. Given the Court's obvious concern with drugs, what impact does the *Earls* decision have on other school-based searches and seizures? In particular, what impact does it have on schools that initiate suspicionless metal detector searches to find guns and other weapons that fuel violence in the schools?

We could begin to answer that question by looking closely at the elements in the Court's balancing equation. In turn, that examination can begin with the nature and immediacy of the school district's concerns, and whether those concerns can be seen as arising from a special need outside the context of law enforcement. Although the Court has emphasized the concern over drug use among students, in the wake of incidents like Columbine in an affluent school district and the less well-publicized but equally horrific daily risk of violence in some urban districts, no one could say that preventing violence is not an immediate serious concern for schools. Moreover, the public schools' "custodial and tutelary responsibility," which is especially implicated in matters of safety, gives rise to a "special need that inheres in the public school context."[32]

The safety concerns raised by weapons like guns and knives are certainly more immediate than those caused by illegal drugs. Cocaine may kill, but usually not nearly as quickly as a bullet. Thus, a search for weapons to prevent violence and deter students presents a special need arguably as strong, if not stronger, than the special need arising from the prevention and deterrence of illegal drug use. Although the Supreme Court has not addressed that special need, many other courts have done so, and have uniformly found the prevention of violence to present an overwhelming governmental interest not only in schools but in many other public places.[33] On the other side of the balance between students' privacy and government's needs, the Court in *Earls* made it clear that all students have a diminished expectation of privacy because they are under the schools' "custodial and tutelary" capacity; but the Court also did not rely on the general student diminution of privacy interests alone. The *Earls* Court could and did rely

---

32. 122 S. Ct. at 3564. Special needs, however, must arise outside of the context of law enforcement and criminal sanctions.

33. *See, e.g., Justice v. Elrod,* 832 F.2d 1048 (7th Cir. 1987) (upholding metal detectors at state courthouse); *Day v. Chicago Board of Educ.,* 1998 WL 60770 (N.D. Ill. 1998) (upholding metal detectors at the entry to administration building). The use of metal detectors in schools is discussed further below.

to some extent on the fact that those students in question also effectively chose to give up some privacy rights by voluntarily participating in extra-curricular activities. The language can be found in the *Earls* opinion that might allow a later court to call voluntary participation merely a "supple-mental factor." Should a court do that, it could rule that all students have no more expectation of privacy than, for instance, a football player who must allow drug testing before playing for the team. However, the U.S. Supreme Court has not gone that far yet.

One factor in both the *Vernonia* and *Earls* decisions is that in both cases the schools announced the testing program in advance. This fits, of course, with the special need unrelated to law enforcement or criminal investigation. Rather than a search that is intended to catch someone with evidence—a search best done by surprise—the drug testing in these cases was intended to deter and prevent drug use. Undoubtedly, both schools would be quite pleased if all the students passed the drug tests without incident, and both schools would probably view the testing program as a success in that event.

The "special needs" justification for drug testing in schools could readily be extended to a form of generalized weapons searching in schools that is much less intrusive than urine sampling. That form of general, suspicionless searching for weapons would be the use of metal detectors. This sort of search has survived largely without controversy and is highly relevant to preventing the use of weapons in schools.[34] Of course, requiring persons to pass through metal detectors constitutes a search for purposes of the Fourth Amendment.[35] Such a limited, warrantless search of people seeking to enter sensitive facilities is permitted, however, if the search is conducted as part of a general practice and is not associated with a criminal investigation to secure evidence.[36]

---

34. *See, e.g.,* United States v. Epperson, 454 F.2d 769 (4th Cir. 1972) (upholding use of metal detectors in airports); People v. Pruitt, 278 Ill. App. 3d 194, 214 Ill. Dec. 974, 662 N.E.2d 540 (Ill. App. 1 Dist. 1996) (upholding use of metal detectors in schools).

35. Wilkinson v. Frost, 832 F.2d 1330, 1340 (2d Cir. 1987), *cert. denied,* 485 U.S. 1034, 108 S. Ct. 1593, 99 L. Ed. 2d, 907 (1988).

36. Klarfeld v. United States, 944 F.2d 583, 586 (9th Cir. 1991) (allowing metal detectors at federal courthouse entries).

4. Metal Detector Searches

Courts have consistently upheld the constitutionality of metal detector searches for such deterrent and preventive purposes, rather than for criminal investigation.[37] These courts have noted that use of a metal detector involves "the absolutely minimal invasion of privacy."[38] On the other side of the balance, courts have taken judicial notice that threats of violence have been directed to public buildings, as well as their occupants.[39] The conclusion invariably has been that metal searches are valid under the Fourth Amendment's basic concern for reasonableness. For one thing, metal detectors are not surprise searches used to catch suspects red-handed. They are in place, in advance, and anyone who intends to enter the building is on notice that the detectors are there.

In fact, courts have allowed metal detector searches that led to criminal charges.[40] Similarly, at least one federal appellate court has allowed a metal detector search that was not announced in advance as part of school policy but hastily put together because of a report of a gun in school.[41] In these cases the courts have emphasized the allegedly unobtrusive nature of the search and characterized these searches as "administrative," even when they lead to individual criminal charges.[42] These decisions, however, appear to tip the balance more favorably to searches than a careful reading of the Supreme Court's opinion in *Earls* allows. The *Earls* balance begins with the lowered expectation of privacy all students have at school. That is not the entire equation, however. It also takes into account the intrusiveness of the search and the *consequences* of the search for the student.[43] Specifically in *Earls,* the possible consequences did not include criminal charges. The intrusiveness of the search, moreover, was affected by the announcement of a policy of drug testing; it was not a surprise.

37. *See, e.g.,* Justice v. Elrod, 832 F.2d 1048, 1050 (7th Cir. 1987).

38. United States v. Albarado, 495 F.2d 799 (2d Cir. 1974); *see also* McMorris v. Alioto, 567 F.2d 897, 900 (9th Cir. 1978) (finding metal detectors "a relatively inoffensive method of conducting a search . . . less intrusive than alternative methods").

39. *See, e.g.,* United States v. Cyzweski, 484 F.2d 509 (5th Cir. 1973), *cert. denied,* 415 U.S. 902, 94 S. Ct. 936, 39 L. Ed. 2d 459 (1974).

40. *See In re* F.B., 658 A.2d 1378 (Pa. Super. 1995); People v. Dukes, 151 Misc. 2d 295, 580 N.Y.S.2d 850 (1992).

41. Thompson v. Carthage School District, 87 F.3d 979 (8th Cir. 1996).

42. *See In re* F.B., 658 A.2d at 1381; *Dukes,* 580 N.Y.S.2d. at 852.

43. 122 S. Ct. at 2567.

On the other hand, the courts that have allowed generalized weapons searches with metal detectors probably are quite right in identifying one part of the equation: that the schools have a special need, related not to law enforcement but to public safety, to prevent weapons from entering school property. In other words, prevention of violence including possible killings is the reason for the search, not to gather evidence for a criminal investigation.

In any case, after *Earls* it seems likely that metal detectors in schools are permissible, as long as they are used pursuant to an announced policy rather than as an ad hoc investigative technique. The use of metal detectors would serve the special need of the school to provide a safe environment for students in light of the serious threat that weapons represent. In addition, if a teacher or administrator has a reasonable, individualized suspicion that searching a student would turn up a weapon, that teacher or administrator ought to be permitted to search that student, as long as the scope of that search is reasonably related to finding the suspected weapon, and as long as the search is not excessively intrusive.

5. Privacy Expectations

T.L.O. and *Earls* establish some general principles for school officials' searches or seizures of students, but both specifically address, broadly, only one type of search—the search of the students' persons. In *T.L.O.*, the assistant vice-principal searched the purse the student was carrying at that time. In *Earls,* the students' own bodies, in effect, were searched for the evidence of drug use. In each of those decisions, the Court began with the proposition that the students had legitimate privacy and personal security interests at stake, which had to be balanced against the schools' needs.

There are other sorts of searches, however, that might be acceptable because the students have no legitimate expectation of privacy. No one would suggest, for example, that if a student built a wooden box in shop class, he or she had a legitimate expectation that the shop teacher would not look inside it while examining it to give the student comments and advice. There is a real difference of opinion, however, about whether a student has a legitimate expectation of privacy in the contents of his or her locker. In *T.L.O.*, the Supreme Court explicitly refused to express an opinion on that topic, and it has not returned to the topic since.[44] Some courts

---

44. 469 U.S. at 741 n.5.

have ruled that where a school policy is promulgated that informs students that the school has joint control of lockers, and that the school reserves the right to examine their contents, the students have no legitimate expectation of privacy.[45] A few courts have held, to the contrary, that students do have an expectation of privacy in the contents of the lockers, a private space like a "home away from home."[46]

Even where the courts have found that students have an expectation of privacy in their lockers, however, that expectation would be no higher than the expectation one has in the privacy of one's own person. The same standards should apply for locker searches as apply to searches of a students' person or pocketbook. That is, when there is an individualized reasonable suspicion that a search will produce a weapon, the search would be justified as long as it is limited in scope to finding that weapon.

It is less clear, however, whether a school could conduct a general search of all lockers pursuant to the special need to provide a safe environment against dangerous weapons, if, as some courts have held, one assumes a student can claim an expectation of privacy in his or her locker. Especially in a school with a history of weapons and violence, and if the school announced in advance a policy of such searches, and if the school did not use the searches to obtain evidence for criminal proceedings, it is certainly plausible to suggest the Court's reasoning in *Earls* would apply to such locker searches, On the other hand, such a widespread practice could well be viewed as too intrusive and unreasonable. Any school engaging in it risks running afoul of the Fourth Amendment (assuming, again, that the court in question would even find that students have an expectation of privacy in their lockers).

6. Relative Unobtrusiveness

Finally, concentrating on whether a search is permissible at all should not obscure the equally important question of whether the manner of the search is permissible. In all three of its cases of school searches, the Supreme Court explained that a reasonable search cannot be one that is too intrusive. In *T.L.O.*, the Court emphasized that a reasonable search was not only based on a reasonable suspicion but also was "not excessively intru-

---

45. *See, e.g.,* Zamora v. Pomeroy, 639 F.2d 662 (10th Cir. 1981); Singleton v. Board of Educ. USD 500, 894 F. Supp. 386, 391 (D. Kan. 1995).
46. *See, e.g.,* State v. Engerund, 463 A.2d 934, 943 (N.J. 1983).

sive in light of the subject's age and sex."[47] In *Vernonia*, the Court only approved the drug-testing program for student athletes because it found three things: a "decreased expectation of privacy, the *relative unobtrusiveness* of the search, and the severity of the need met by the search. . . ." [48]

Most recently, the Court in *Earls* took pains to discuss why the urine test there was not too intrusive. For example, no one watched students urinate, but only listened for the "normal sounds of urination." Although that may seem intrusive at first, one must remember that this meant only that a student urinated in a closed stall in a school restroom while someone else was in that restroom, which is something most students do every day.[49] In *T.L.O.*, that meant that a search of the student's purse was acceptable, but it is doubtful that a "pat-down" search for cigarettes would have been. In *Earls,* the fact that students are not actually visually observed urinating may create some possible loophole for cheating, but it would be very risky to assume that this loophole would justify visual observation. For a concrete example of what counts as too intrusive, one could look to the decision in *Jenkins by Hall v. Talledega City Board of Education*, 95 F.3d 1063 (11th Cir. 1996). There, one second-grader told her teacher that $7 had been stolen from her; another student claimed to see two particular girls steal the money; and the two girls themselves did not deny the theft but tried to pin it on each other. Those facts give rise to much more than a reasonable suspicion that the girls stole the money and that searching them would locate the money. Still, the teacher violated the Fourth Amendment when she strip-searched the girls, causing them to disrobe down to their underwear. The court found this search was unreasonable, that the teacher could not claim qualified immunity for her decision, and that therefore she was exposed to liability under 42 U.S.C. Section 1983 for violating the girls' constitutional rights.

The teacher's search in *Jenkins* was grounded in individualized suspicion, yet it was too intrusive. Searches based on "special needs" where there is no individualized suspicion probably would be judged by an even stricter standard of intrusiveness. In other words, searching a girl's purse for cigarettes when there is a reasonable suspicion that she has been smoking in violation of school rules is not too intrusive, but a suspicionless

---

47. 469 U.S. 325, 342 (1985).
48. 515 U.S. at 664–65.
49. 122 S. Ct. at 2566.

search of all pocketbooks, purses, and backpacks looking for weapons might well be too intrusive. In other words, there is a difference between a metal detector and taking someone's closed bag away from him or her and looking through it. The latter is much more intrusive.

The distinction between a particularized search based on individual suspicion and a general search based on a special need unrelated to law enforcement is, as the hypothetical in the paragraph above suggests, in part that the former search can be more intrusive. Another difference is that the special-need search ought to be truly unrelated to investigations, and so ought to be part of an announced policy. For instance, where a school has reasonable grounds to believe that a student has a gun, searching that person's backpack might well be justified. The searchers would not want to notify the student in advance so he or she could hide the gun. On the other hand, where a school seeks to prevent guns coming onto the property, a metal detector search policy is quite successful if the students just do not bring their weapons with them.

D. CONCLUSION

Overall, the Fourth Amendment imposes a relatively light burden on school administrators searching students, especially when the problem being addressed affects student safety, be it illegal drugs or weapons. A reasonable suspicion that the student has a weapon, for instance, justifies a search of that particular student. Moreover, suspicionless searches of certain kinds appear to be possible as well. Metal detectors are almost surely acceptable, and many courts would allow locker searches (at least as long as the policy of such searches is announced). What remains most likely out of bounds are more intrusive searches and searches meant to discover evidence of particular violations of school rules undertaken without particularized and reasonable suspicion.

Zero-Tolerance Policies

4

David M. Pedersen

A. INTRODUCTION

In 2000, 700,000 students between the ages of 12 and 18 were victims of violent crime while at school.[1] This represents a 46 percent decline in violent crimes occurring in schools from 1992 to 2000.[2] Even though incidents of violent crime in schools are decreasing, more students feared being attacked at school than away from school in 2001.[3] The decrease in violent crime may be attributed to the increasing application of "Zero-Tolerance Policies" to serious student offenses. However, students' fear for their safety at school may indicate that zero-tolerance policies have not completely eliminated the threat of school violence.

. 1. Jill F. DeVoe et al., *Indicators of School Crime and Safety: 2002,* U.S. Departments of Education and Justice, NCES 2003-009/NCJ 196, Washington, D.C. (2002), *available at* http://nces.ed.gov.
2. *Id.*
3. *Id.*

Zero-tolerance policies provide predetermined consequences for specific offenses.[4] The consequences are typically harsh: expulsion and long-term suspension.[5] The offenses include possession of weapons or other dangerous objects; alcohol, drugs, or other controlled substances; threats of violence; assaults not involving weapons; and obscene, vulgar, or hate speech.[6]

Zero-tolerance policies were embraced as a solution to the public's perception of increasing school violence.[7] The public has become increasingly disturbed and outraged by American school violence, causing federal and state policymakers and school officials to abandon rehabilitative discipline models and employ rigid "get-tough" policies.[8] Congress responded with the Gun-Free School Act of 1994, which conditioned federal funding for public schools on each state adopting at least a one-year expulsion policy for any student in possession of a firearm at school.[9] However, the Act requires state law to allow the school administrator in charge of administering the zero-tolerance policy "to modify such expulsion requirement for a student on a case-by-case basis."[10]

By 1995, nearly all states had complied with the provisions of the Gun-Free School Act.[11] In 1998, nine out of 10 public schools employed zero-tolerance policies for the possession of firearms and weapons.[12] Additionally, 88 percent of schools enforced zero-tolerance policies for drugs, 87 percent for alcohol, and 79 percent for violence and tobacco.[13]

---

4. Alicia C. Insley, Comment, *Suspending and Expelling Children From Educational Opportunity: Time to Reevaluate Zero Tolerance Policies,* 50 Am. U.L. Rev. 1039, 1043 (2001).

5. Joan M. Wasser, Note, *Zeroing in on Zero Tolerance,* 15 J.L. & Pol. 747, 750 (1999).

6. *Id.*

7. Insley, *supra* note 4, at 1045.

8. *Id.*

9. 20 U.S.C. § 8921(b)(1) (2002).

10. *Id.*

11. Insley, *supra* note 4, at 1046.

12. *Id.*

13. *Id.* at 1048. Statistics taken from "Annual Report on School Safety, 1998," published by the U.S. Dept. of Education, 2001.

B. ZERO-TOLERANCE POLICIES TAKEN TO THE EXTREME

Overtones of absolutism and inflexibility accompany zero-tolerance policies, leading education and legal scholars to sharply criticize such policies.[14] Under zero-tolerance policies, educators are often unable to distinguish between threats to school safety and innocent mistakes by students.[15] The following are examples of rigid applications of zero-tolerance policies to seemingly innocuous behavior:

- A student at Blue Ridge Middle School in Loudon County, Virginia, was suspended for 16 weeks after he convinced a suicidal friend to give him the knife she intended to use to kill herself. The student put the knife in his locker and reported the incident to the principal. While the school praised the student for helping his friend, the school board determined that the student's actions violated the school's zero-tolerance policy with respect to possession of weapons and suspended the student.[16]
- At Taylor Elementary in Colorado Springs, Colorado, a 6-year-old was suspended for sharing his lemon drops with a classmate. School officials suspended the child for a half day and told his mother, "A child who brings candy to school is compared to a teenager who brings a gun to school."[17]
- In New Jersey, a group of kindergarten students were suspended for three days for playing "cops and robbers." The District Superintendent responded, "This is a no-tolerance policy. We're very firm on weapons and threats . . . given the climate of our society, we cannot take any of these statements in a light manner."[18]
- Waving a stapler on a school bus, pretending it was a gun, triggered the suspension of a 12-year-old Chesapeake, Virginia, student.[19]

---

14. James M. Peden, *Through a Glass Darkly: Educating with Zero Tolerance*, 10-SPG KAN. J.L. & PUB. POL'Y 369, 371 (2001).

15. *Id.* at 373.

16. Ratner v. Loudon County Public Schools, No 00-2157, 2001 WL 855606 (4th Dist. 2001).

17. Peden, *supra* note 14, at 373.

18. *Id.*

19. *Id.* at 374.

- After a friend gave 13-year-old Tyler Hagen a bag of marijuana, Tyler took it home and gave it to his parents, who turned the drug over to the Los Angeles Sheriff's Department. Law enforcement authorities contacted the school, who took action by giving Tyler the option to enroll in another school or attend a special class for kids in trouble. The assistant district superintendent commented, "If kids are in possession of drugs at school, our board has taken a 'zero-tolerance' stand. The principals are directed to bring forth a student for expulsion unless they find circumstances that make them think expulsion is not appropriate."[20]

These disproportionate punishments defy common sense and fuel the criticism of zero-tolerance discipline policies, raising important constitutional concerns. The inflexible application of these policies implies that students are inherently dangerous and may only be controlled by rigid policies that diminish the student's basic civil liberties.

C. CONSTITUTIONAL IMPLICATIONS OF ZERO-TOLERANCE POLICIES

1. Due Process Challenges

The Fifth and Fourteenth Amendments guarantee all people, including students, due process of law. The Fifth Amendment states that the federal government, its courts, and agencies shall not deprive persons of "life, liberty, or property, without due process of law."[21] The Fourteenth Amendment similarly prevents state governments, agencies, and courts from depriving "any person of life, liberty or property, without due process of law."[22] Due process consists of two components: procedural due process and substantive due process.

Substantive due process requires government action to be "genuinely fair and reasonable, and serve a legitimate governmental interest."[23] Students challenging zero-tolerance polices on substantive due process grounds

---

20. *Id.*
21. U.S. CONST. amend. V.
22. U.S. CONST. amend. XIV.
23. J. Kevin Jenkins & John Dayton, *Students, Weapons, and Due Process: An Analysis of Zero Tolerance Policies in Public Schools,* 171 ED. LAW REP. 13, 2 (2003).

typically argue that the "mandatory nature" of the policies is "excessive" and "lacks a rational connection to legitimate educational goals."[24] Substantive due process challenges are successful when zero-tolerance policies are an "extraordinary departure from established norms" and are "wholly arbitrary."[25] Therefore, a zero-tolerance policy will withstand judicial scrutiny if the school presents a reasonable justification for its policy.[26] Consequently, only two students have successfully challenged zero-tolerance policies on substantive due process grounds.[27]

In *James P. v Lemahieu*, a high school student was awarded preliminary injunctive relief to avert his expulsion.[28] The school attempted to suspend the student for attending a school luau after he had been drinking.[29] The student claimed that Hawaii's zero-tolerance policy[30] for possession of alcohol violated his substantive due process rights because the statute was "too vague to provide a person of ordinary intelligence sufficient notice of what conduct was forbidden under the statute."[31] The court agreed with the student, finding that the statute failed to adequately define "possession."[32] The court noted that the statute's ambiguity "would encourage arbitrary enforcement" in violation of substantive due process.[33]

The Sixth Circuit found a Tennessee high school student's substantive due process rights were violated by his school's zero-tolerance policy in *Seal v. Morgan*.[34] The policy mandated suspension or expulsion for a student in possession of a weapon, regardless of whether or not the student knowingly possessed the weapon.[35] The court found that the policy violated the student's substantive due process rights because "suspending or expelling a student for weapons possession, where the student did not

---

24. Insley, *supra* note 4, at 1056.

25. *Id.*

26. *Id.*

27. Jay M. Zitter, Annotation, *Validity, Construction, and Operation of School "Zero Tolerance" Policies Towards Drugs, Alcohol, or Violence*, 2002 A.L.R. 5th 5, 15 (2002).

28. James P. v. Lemahieu, 84 F. Supp. 2d 1113, 1123 (D. Haw. 2000).

29. *Id.* at 1116.

30. HAW. REV. STAT. § 302A-1134(a).

31. 84 F. Supp. 2d at 1120.

32. *Id.* at 1121.

33. *Id.*

34. Seal v. Morgan, 229 F.3d 567, 575–76 (6th Cir. 2000), *reh'g and suggestion for reh'g en banc denied* (Dec. 20, 2000).

35. *Id.* at 575–76.

knowingly possess any weapon, would not be rationally related to any legitimate state interest. No student can use a weapon to injure another person, to disrupt school operations, or for any other purpose if the student is totally unaware of its presence."[36]

Procedural due process ensures that students are given notice, representation, and a fair and impartial hearing before being deprived of life, liberty, or property.[37] A student may challenge a zero-tolerance policy on the grounds that the student's procedural due process rights have been violated if the school fails to provide the student with adequate notice, an impartial hearing, and the right to be heard before suspending or expelling the student under the zero-tolerance policy.[38]

Before procedural due process rights are implicated, a student must be deprived of life, liberty or property.[39] Zero-tolerance policies may implicate both property and liberty interests. Property interests are derived from state law.[40] Therefore, students residing in states that recognize the right to a free public education are deprived of a property interest when they are expelled from school.[41] The Supreme Court has also recognized that a student's liberty interest may be violated by school suspensions and expulsions.[42] Liberty interests arise "where a person's good name, reputation, honor, or integrity is at stake because of what the government is doing to him."[43] The court opined that suspensions and expulsions for misconduct could seriously damage a student's relationship with his or her peers and teachers and interfere with later opportunities for employment and education, thus invoking a liberty interest.[44]

Neither a property nor a liberty interest is implicated when a student is prevented from participating in interscholastic activities.[45] Additionally, an expelled student cannot claim he or she has been deprived of a property or liberty interest when the student's education continues through enroll-

---

36. *Id.* at 577.
37. Peden, *supra* note 14, at 375.
38. Insley, *supra* note 4, at 1056.
39. Goss v. Lopez, 419 U.S. 565, 572 (1975).
40. *Id.*
41. *Id.* at 573–74.
42. *Id.* at 574–75.
43. *Id.* at 574.
44. *Id.*
45. Jordan v. Edwards, 706 N.E.2d 137, 140–42 (1999).

ment in another school, an alternative education program, or being home-schooled.[46]

In *Goss v. Lopez*, the Supreme Court articulated the standard for procedural due process violations in relation to student suspensions and expulsions from school.[47] To avoid violating a student's procedural due process rights, a school must furnish the student "oral or written notice of the charges against him, and if he denies them, an explanation of the evidence that authorities have and an opportunity to present his side of the story" prior to suspension or expulsion.[48] At the very least, the Court requires "an informal give-and-take between the student and disciplinarian."[49] The Court limited its holding to short suspensions not exceeding 10 days, stating, "[L]onger suspensions or expulsions for the remainder of the school term, or permanently, may require more formal procedures."[50]

A sixth-grader's procedural due process rights were deemed violated by a zero-tolerance policy that "defer[red] to an unwritten blanket policy of expulsion according to the court in *Colvin v. Lowndes County*."[51] The student, who suffered from Attention Deficit Disorder and Attention Deficit Hyperactivity Disorder, was suspended for carrying a miniature Swiss-army-type knife.[52] The school board president acknowledged that the zero-tolerance policy under which the student was suspended was orally adopted by the board, but was not published in the student handbook.[53] The court was "offended by the manner in which [the school board] blindly meted out the student's punishment," stating that "employing a blanket policy of expulsion . . . precludes the use of independent consideration of relevant facts and circumstances."[54]

Typically, school policy satisfies the minimum procedural due process requirements of notice and opportunity to be heard.[55] As such, courts have rejected numerous procedural due process challenges. For example, in

---

46. Bundick v. Bay City Ind. Sch. Dist., 140 F. Supp. 2d 735, 739 (2001).
47. 419 U.S. 565 (1975).
48. *Id.* at 581.
49. *Id.* at 584.
50. *Id.*
51. Colvin v. Lowndes County, 114 F. Supp. 2d 504, 512 (N.D. Miss. 1999).
52. *Id.* at 506.
53. *Id.* at 512–13.
54. *Id.*
55. Insley, *supra* note 4, at 1056.

Hammock v. Keys,[56] the court determined that a student's procedural due process rights to a hearing were not violated, as she engaged in an "informal give-and-take" with the assistant principal to present her version of the facts. Additionally, the court in *J.M. v. Webster County Board of Education*[57] found that the presence of police and prosecutors at a school disciplinary hearing may be more intimidating for the student, but does not deny the student his opportunity to be heard.

Courts have been similarly unwilling to find procedural due process violations with respect to adequacy of notice. Students receive adequate notice of a school's zero-tolerance policy when the policy is published in the student handbook, according to the court in *In re Expulsion of Polonia*.[58] Additionally, a school is only required to give notice to one parent of a student facing a disciplinary hearing.[59]

Clearly, courts are unlikely to invalidate zero-tolerance policies for violation of due process unless the policies involve "blatant omissions of minimum procedures or extreme policies that present no rational connection."[60]

D. EQUAL PROTECTION CHALLENGES

The Equal Protection Clause of the Fourteenth Amendment prevents states from denying any person equal protection under the law.[61] To succeed on an equal protection claim, the plaintiff must show that "similarly situated persons were treated dissimilarly."[62] Courts have consistently rejected claims that school zero-tolerance policies violate equal protection because under school zero-tolerance policies all students are treated the same.[63] Equal protection claims have failed because students are unable to specify any identifiable group of which they are a member and which was subjected to purposeful discrimination by the school's zero-tolerance policy.[64]

---

56. Hammock v. Keys, 93 F. Supp. 2d 1222, 1228, 1230 (S.D. Ala. 2000).
57. J.M. v. Webster County Bd. of Educ., 534 S.E.2d 50, 57–58 (W. Va. 2000).
58. *In re* Expulsion of Polonia, 1996 WL 45169, *2 (1996).
59. *J.M.*, 534 S.E. at 58.
60. Insley, *supra* note 4, at 1057.
61. *Hammock*, 93 F. Supp. 2d at 1231.
62. *Id.*
63. *Id.*
64. *Bundick*, 140 F. Supp. 2d at 741.

1. First Amendment Challenges

The First Amendment protects students' free speech rights.[65] Zero-tolerance policies have also been unsuccessfully challenged on First Amendment grounds. In *Anderson v. Milbank School District 25-4,* a student challenged a school's zero-tolerance policy prohibiting the use of any profane or inappropriate language on school property, claiming that the policy violated the student's First Amendment rights.[66] The court upheld the student's suspension, stating, "School authorities can regulate indecent language because its circulation on school grounds undermines their responsibility to try to promote standards of decency and civility among school children."[67]

E. DEFERENCE TO LOCAL SCHOOL AUTHORITY'S DECISIONS

In rejecting students' constitutional challenges to zero-tolerance policies, courts have consistently emphasized that deference must be given to local school authorities' disciplinary decisions. The Supreme Court stated in *Wood v. Strickland,* "It is not the role of the federal courts to set aside decisions of school administrators that the court may view as lacking a basis in wisdom or compassion."[68] In conformity with this view, courts have recognized that local school officials are more appropriately suited to handle student discipline.[69] The Fourth Circuit has even declared, "The federal courts are not properly called upon to judge the wisdom of a zero-tolerance policy. . . ."[70] The widespread rejection of constitutional challenges to zero-tolerance policies may be attributed to the customary reluctance of courts to become involved in school disciplinary matters in an effort to "affirm the comprehensive authority of the States and of school officials."[71]

---

65. U.S. CONST. amend. 1.
66. Anderson v. Milbank School District 25-4, 197 F.R.D. 682, 684 (2000).
67. 197 F.R.D. at 688.
68. Wood v. Strickland, 420 U.S. 308, 326.
69. *Colvin,* 114 F. Supp. 2d at 513.
70. *Ratner,* 16 Fed. Appx. at 142.
71. Boucher v. School Board of the Sch. Dist. of Greenfield, 134 F.3d 821 (1998).

A Comprehensive State Response to School Violence: The New York Safe Schools Against Violence Act

5

Benjamin Ferrara

A. INTRODUCTION

In July 2000, Governor Pataki signed a comprehensive package of laws designed to make New York schools safer. The Project SAVE Act (Safe Schools Against Violence in Education Act), which contains 22 sections, addresses many different facets of the school safety issue.[1] Among other things, it authorizes teachers to remove disruptive students from the classroom, mandates new, more detailed codes of conduct, requires district-wide and building-level safety plans, and requires that instruction in civility and citizenship be added to each school's curriculum. In conjunction with the Project SAVE Act, the governor also signed a "School Employees Fingerprinting Bill," which requires all new school employees to be fingerprinted, ends the practice known as "silent resignations," and mandates the reporting of child abuse in the educational setting.

---

1. Laws of New York ch. 181 (2000).

New York's Project SAVE Act is one approach that has been effective in addressing school violence. This chapter will explain in detail the key provisions of the Project SAVE Act and the legal implications of each of these provisions. Understanding the legal implications of the New York solution will enable a school district to tailor a safety program that will effectively combat violence while protecting itself from lawsuits due to the change of school policy. School districts should be strongly encouraged to review all regulations with their school lawyers to ensure that they are taking all of the necessary and proper steps to comply with local and federal laws, rules, and regulations.

B. REMOVAL OF STUDENTS FROM THE CLASSROOM: MAINTAINING THE LEARNING ENVIRONMENT

Section two of the Project SAVE Act vests teachers with the authority to remove disruptive students from the classroom. Any such removal must be in accordance with the school district's code of conduct. This code must be developed according to the requirements enumerated in section three of the Act, discussed below. The ability to remove students from the classroom is intended to supplement teachers' traditional classroom management tools by giving them the power to impose an intermediate level of student discipline between detention and suspension. According to the authors of this legislation, this new tool enables teachers to stop focusing on the behavior issues of one or two problem students so they can teach the remaining students. Governor Pataki, in his state of the state address in 1996, commented:

> Just as teachers want to teach, most students want to learn. In order to create a safe and secure learning environment for teachers and students, I will propose giving real authority to teachers to remove disruptive students from the classroom. . . . We cannot allow those who refuse to learn to hold back those who want to learn.

Disruptive students are defined by the new law as elementary or secondary students, under age 21, who are substantially disruptive to the educational process or substantially interfere with the teacher's authority over the classroom. Such students may not return to class until either the principal makes a formal determination that the removal was not supported by substantial evidence or the period of removal expires, whichever occurs first.

Procedural requirements explained in the code of conduct must be followed when removing a student from the classroom. The teacher must first determine that a student is disruptive. The statutory definition of "disruptive," as enumerated above, is quite broad and leaves room for varying interpretation. As a result, school districts should consider developing guidelines listing the categories of behavior that fit within the definition of disruptive. Given the intent behind the statute, behavior should be of a sort that in a significant way prevents a teacher from teaching the students who want to learn.

If the student's conduct is disruptive, the teacher must notify the student of the reasons for the removal prior to the removal. The teacher must also allow the student an opportunity to explain his or her side of the story. There appears to be misleading language in the statute that may confuse some schoolteachers and administrators when performing this part of the removal procedure. The statute states that a school's code of conduct must include provisions for ". . . detention, suspension and removal from the classroom of students, consistent with [Section 3214 of the Education Law]." Section 3214 includes the procedural due process safeguards necessary when a student is suspended, such as the right to confront and cross-examine witnesses.[2] However, the State Education Department (SED) had indicated that removals from class are not treated as suspensions. Thus, it does not appear that teachers have to give students who are removed the same procedural due process safeguards. Further guidance on this issue from the SED will be needed to clarify this matter.

When a student's conduct poses a continuing danger to persons or property or an ongoing threat of disruption to the academic process, the teacher may immediately remove the student, without explaining the reasons for the removal. The teacher has 24 hours to notify the student of the reasons and allow a response. In all instances, the teacher must inform the principal of the basis for the removal. While there is no requirement under the law that this notification be in writing, it is recommended that districts develop forms for this purpose. This will assist the principal in the next phase of the process.

A number of procedural steps must be taken by the principal after a student has been removed from the classroom. First, the student's parent

---

2. Education Law, § 3214.

or guardian has a right to know the reasons for the removal within 24 hours. Next, if requested, the student and parent or guardian must be permitted the opportunity to discuss the reasons for the removal at an informal conference with the principal. If the student denies the charge, the student must be permitted to present his or her version of the events to the principal within 48 hours of the removal. Finally, the principal's decision as to whether the discipline will be upheld or set aside must be made by the close of the business day following the 48-hour period for the informal conference noted above. The principal may not set aside a student's removal unless the principal finds that (1) the charges are not supported by substantial evidence; (2) the conduct warrants suspension from school and a suspension will be imposed; or (3) the student's removal is in violation of law. The school district must provide continued educational programming to students who are removed from class. Principals may designate another school administrator to perform the functions required under the removal process.

Section two of the new law also permits principals to suspend students for up to five days without prior authorization of the Board of Education. Where the student does not pose a "continuing danger to persons or property" or an "ongoing threat of disruption to the academic process," the student or student's parent or guardian should be given an informal conference prior to the suspension to explain the student's version of the events leading to the removal. The student and parent(s) or guardian(s) should also be given the opportunity to question the complaining witness(es) at that time. Where the student is dangerous or disruptive of the academic process, the informal conference can take place after the suspension begins, but should be held as soon as is reasonably practicable.

C. CODES OF CONDUCT: LEGAL AUTHORITY TO REGULATE MORE THAN STUDENT CONDUCT

Section three of the Act requires school districts to develop and adopt a detailed code of conduct, addressing, through 13 separate topics, the maintenance of order on school property, including school functions. For the first time, a school district's code must govern the conduct, dress, and language of not only students, but teachers, other school personnel, and visitors as well. The Board must develop the code in collaboration with students, teachers, administrator and parent organizations, school safety personnel, and other school personnel.

The law presents strict requirements concerning distribution of the code. Generally, the Project SAVE regulations require the schools to make copies of the code of conduct available for review by students, persons in parental relation, teachers, and other community members. The code must be distributed to all students—kindergarten through twelfth grade—at a general assembly held at the beginning of each school year. Copies of the code must be made available to students and parents at the beginning of each school year. Districts must mail a plain-language summary of the code to parents before the beginning of each school year and make the summary available thereafter upon request. Districts are further required to take reasonable steps to ensure community awareness of the code provisions.

Several additional steps are required of school districts in developing and implementing the code of conduct. First, the code may not be adopted until the district holds at least one public hearing to permit participation from school personnel, parents and guardians, students, and other interested parties. Although not required, a legal notice should be published for the public hearing.

Second, the code must be reviewed on an annual basis, and updated if necessary. During the review and updating process, schools are directed to consider the effectiveness of code provisions and the fairness and consistency of its administration. If changes are made, districts may reapprove the updated code only after at least one public hearing is held. Finally, school districts must file a copy of the code of conduct and any future amendments with the Commissioner of Education no later than 30 days after adoption. Penalty provisions may apply to districts that are not in full compliance after that date.

1. Topics to Be Covered by the Code

The code of conduct is to include provisions regarding (1) conduct, dress, and language deemed appropriate and acceptable or inappropriate and unacceptable (for example, t-shirts depicting images of sex or drugs, gang-related dress, hats, and so on); (2) acceptable and respectful treatment of teachers, administrators, school personnel, students, and visitors (for example, no abusive language, cursing, excessive arguing with a teacher, and the like); (3) the appropriate range of disciplinary measures for violation of the code; and (4) the role of teachers, administrators, other school personnel, the school board, and parents and guardians. Standards and procedures used to ensure security and safety are to be included, along with provisions for the removal of disruptive students from the classroom and school property. Grounds for removal by teachers include such things as refusal to comply with teacher's direction, excessive arguing with a teacher, and consistent talking that interrupts instruction. Disciplinary measures to be taken for incidents involving use of illegal substances and weapons, physical force, vandalism, violation of another student's civil rights, and threats of violence must be covered by the code. Additionally, the code must include provisions regarding detention, suspension, and removal of students from the classroom; authority for districts to establish policies and procedures to ensure the provision of continued educational programming; and activities for students removed from the classroom, placed in detention, or suspended from school. The Project SAVE regulations indicate that these provisions must include alternative educational programs appropriate to individual student needs, but it is unclear what this entails.

The code of conduct must include procedures by which violations are reported and determined and discipline measures are imposed and carried out, along with provisions ensuring that the code is in compliance with laws relating to disabled students. Circumstances under which and procedures by which parents and guardians are notified of code violations by their children and procedures to inform local law enforcement of code violations that constitute a crime must be developed. Procedures for filing complaints in criminal court, juvenile delinquency, and petitions for assistance must be addressed, along with referral to the appropriate human services agency.

A minimum suspension period for students who repeatedly are substantially disruptive to the educational process or who substantially interfere with the teacher's authority in the classroom must be included. The district may reduce the suspension period on a case-by-case basis consistent with the law. The Project SAVE regulations define a student who "repeatedly is substantially disruptive of the educational process or substantially interferes with teacher's authority over the classroom" as one who is removed from the classroom by a teacher more than four times in a semester (three times in a trimester). Finally, a minimum suspension period for students who are deemed to be "violent pupils," as defined by Education Law Section 13214(2-a)(a), must be included. A violent pupil is an elementary or secondary student under age 21 who:

   (a)   commits an act of violence upon a teacher, administrator, or other school employee;

   (b)   commits, while on school district property, an act of violence upon another student or any other person lawfully upon said property;

   (c)   possesses, while on school district property, a gun, knife, explosive or incendiary bomb, or other dangerous instrument capable of causing physical injury or death;

   (d)   displays, while on school district property, what appears to be a gun, knife, explosive or incendiary bomb or other dangerous instrument capable of causing death or physical injury;

   (e)   threatens, while on school district property, to use any instrument that appears able to cause physical injury or death;

   (f)   knowingly and intentionally damages or destroys the personal property of a teacher, administrator, other school district employee or any person lawfully upon school district property; or

   (g)   knowingly and intentionally damages or destroys school district property.

In addition to the requirements set forth in the Project SAVE Act, the regulations include two other requirements that are a part of the existing commissioner's rules, which these regulations are intended to replace (8 N.Y.C.R.R. § 100.411). These regulations are (1) a "bill of rights and responsibilities of students," which focuses on "positive student behavior," which must be publicized and explained to "all students" on an annual basis; and (2) guidelines and programs for in-service programs for all school district staff to ensure effective implementation of the policy on conduct and discipline.

2. Other Concerns: How Much Latitude Is Afforded to Local School Districts?

When developing a code of conduct, school boards must bear in mind several legal issues. First, the Commissioner of Education has issued several rulings concerning what are and what are not appropriate dress codes for schools. There is some question about whether these decisions have been overruled with the passage of Project SAVE. There are also First Amendment concerns associated with such codes. In addition, the code will have to be enforced as written. Accordingly, school districts must strive to make their rule easy to consistently enforce. In the past, the Commissioner has held that a school board has the authority to regulate student dress only when it "threatens health and safety or otherwise disrupts the educational process." In other words, a dress code had to address a legitimate educational concern, such as teaching students socially appropriate behavior, the elimination of potential health/safety hazards, the integrity of the educational process, or the avoidance of school violence. A school board was not permitted to regulate a student's appearance where fashion or taste was the sole criterion.[3] Project SAVE requires codes of conduct to include provisions regarding dress "deemed appropriate and acceptable on school property and at school functions" in addition to what is considered to be inappropriate and unacceptable. Thus, it seems clear that schools will no longer be bound by the "health and safety or otherwise disrupts" standard regarding their dress codes. Whether a school district can now regulate a student's appearance where fashion or taste is the sole criterion is a question that will require further guidance from the Commissioner.

Another open question concerns school uniforms. The debate over public school uniforms has intensified in recent years. Various alternative public schools and charter schools in New York currently require students to wear a particular uniform. However, these schools all have voluntary enrollment. The Commissioner has never allowed school uniforms to be required where students had no option. Until there is guidance from the State Education Department to the contrary, dress codes promulgated under Project SAVE should not require students to wear a uniform.

When a school district enacts any policy, including a code of conduct, it may be subjected to a constitutional review by the courts. A school policy enacted by a school board is legally analogous to a law enacted by a state legislature or by the U.S. Congress. Just as state and federal laws may not infringe on the constitutional rights of individual citizens, a code of conduct must not infringe on the constitutional rights of students. In *Olesen v. Board of Education of School District No. 228,* the court upheld a school board policy that prohibited male students from wearing earrings as part of an effort to curb the presence and influence of gangs in the school.[4] The district provided evidence to the court of gang presence, ac-

---

3. *Appeal of Parsons,* 33 Educ. Dep't Rep. 672 (1993); *Appeal of Pintka,* 33 Educ. Dep't Rep. 228 (1993).
4. Olesen v. Board of Educ. of Sch. Dist. No. 228, 676 F. Supp. 820 (N.D. Ill. 1987).

tivity, and violence in the schools. A student who was disciplined for wearing an earring challenged the policy, claiming that it violated his First Amendment rights. The court concluded that the board's concern for the safety and well-being of its students and the curtailment of gang activities was rational and did not violate the First Amendment. However, in *Stephenson v. Davenport Community School District*, the Court of Appeals for the Eighth Circuit ruled that a school regulation aimed at preventing gang activity in school was unconstitutional because it was vague.[5] The regulation stated, without further clarification, that "[g]ang-related activities such as display of colors, symbols, signals, signs, etc., will not be tolerated on school grounds." Students who violated the regulation would be suspended from school and/or recommended to the school board for expulsion. An honor student who had a small tattoo of a cross between her thumb and index finger was ordered by the district to remove or alter the tattoo or face expulsion from school. The student had no record of disciplinary problems and there was no evidence that the student was involved in gang activity. She sued the school district, claiming the regulation violated her constitutional rights. The court concluded that the "regulation violates the central purpose of the vagueness doctrine because it fails to provide adequate notice regarding unacceptable conduct and fails to offer clear guidance for those who apply it."

Likewise, in *Chalifoux v. New Cancy Independent School District*, the court found it unconstitutional for a school district to prohibit students from wearing rosary beads.[6] The district's dress code prohibited the wearing of gang-related apparel. The list of gang-related apparel found in the student handbook did not contain rosaries. The court determined that the wearing of rosaries by non-gang members was symbolic speech protected under the First Amendment as religious expression. The court further found that there was insufficient evidence of actual disruption or anticipated disruption to infringe upon the student's religiously motivated speech. The court found that the district's policy on gang-related activity was void for vagueness in that it failed to provide adequate notice to students regarding prohibited conduct and that it would not be overly burdensome for the district to provide a definite list of prohibited items and updated that list as needed. The court determined that the students had a sincere religious belief subject to First Amendment protection and that the prohibition on

---

5. Stephenson v. Davenport Cmty. Sch. Dist., 110 F.3d 1303 (8th Cir. 1997).
6. Chalifoux v. New Cancy Indep. Sch. Dist., 976 F. Supp. 659 (S.D. Tex. 1997).

rosaries placed an undue burden on the students who were not trying to identify themselves as gang members, but who were sincerely expressing their religious beliefs.

Finally, codes of conduct must be drafted in such a way that they are easy to enforce. For example, districts should avoid establishing procedural requirements that are not mandated by the state constitution or other applicable laws and should avoid excessively high standards. When a board of education policy sets a higher standard of due process than the Education Law requires, the board must follow its own policy. In *Appeal of Pronti,* the district adopted a policy of providing students an opportunity to present witnesses in suspensions of five days or less even though Education Law Section 3214 only requires an opportunity to question complaining witnesses.[7]

Again, in *Appeal of Nuttall,* an athletic discipline policy provided that "all accused athletes will receive a hearing with the head coach of the sport in which the athlete was participating and the Director of Athletics and Executive Principal" and that "the parent or guardian of the athlete may be present at this hearing if they desire." The commissioner held that these procedures were not followed on this case and that the athletic suspension of the student should be overturned.[8]

Prohibited student conduct should be easy to prove. Excessively high standards, overly vague, and overly specific prohibitions should be avoided. In *Appeal of Brenner,* the school district had a policy of permitting student publications "so long as they do not physically interfere with the orderly and efficient operation of the schools, nor the health or safety of the students and staff."[9] The Commissioner held that a district was free to establish its own policy granting students broader free speech protections than those required to be given under a certain line of U.S. Supreme Court cases. Since the student's material was not obscene or libelous or disruptive of the educational process, the Commissioner ruled that the material should not have been censored.

D. SCHOOL SAFETY PLANS

According to section four of the Act, boards of education must adopt a comprehensive district-wide school safety plan and building-level school

---

7. Appeal of Pronti, 31 Ed. Dep't Rep. 259 (1992).
8. Appeal of Nuttall, 30 Ed. Dep't Rep. 351 (1991).
9. Appeal of Brenner, 28 Ed. Dep't Rep. 402 (1989).

safety plans regarding crisis intervention, emergency response, and management. As with the code of conduct, districts must develop these detailed plans in collaboration with various interest groups.

The district-wide team is appointed by the board of education and must include representatives of the school board, students, teachers, administrator and parent organizations, school safety personnel, and other school personnel. The building-level team is appointed by the building principal and must include representatives of teacher, administrator, and parent organizations; school safety personnel and other school personnel; community members; local law enforcement officials; local ambulance or emergency response agencies; and any other persons deemed appropriate by the board of education.

The Project SAVE Act mandates that the Commissioner of the State Education Department provide school districts and Boards of Cooperative Educational Services (BOCES) with a form or template for creating such plans. In addition, schools will be able to include much of their existing school emergency management plans, which were required under the Commissioner's existing regulations (8 N.Y.C.R.R. Section 155.17), in their new plans.

Before adoption, the plans must be made available by the board for public comment at least 30 days prior to their adoption. Only summaries of the building-level plans should be made available. The law recognizes that building-level plans are confidential and are not subject to disclosure, even under New York's Freedom of Information Law (FOIL). Boards may adopt the plans after holding a public hearing allowing for participation by school personnel, parents and guardians, students, and other interested parties.

A copy of the building-level plan must be filed with the state police and appropriate local law enforcement agencies within 30 days of adoption. The district-wide plan must be filed with the Commissioner within 30 days of its adoption. Public money may be withheld from any district by the Commissioner for failing to file in accordance with the new law. There are generally no exceptions to the filing requirements. However, the Commissioner may grant a waiver for up to two years for districts that filed plans that were in "substantial compliance" with the law (that is, "school emergency management plans" under 8 N.Y.C.R.R. Section 155.17, discussed above).

1. District-Wide Safety Plan

Several topics must be covered under the district-wide plan. Minimum requirements include policies for responding to threats or acts of violence by students, teachers, other school personnel, and visitors, including consideration of a zero-tolerance policy for school violence; prevention/intervention strategies; policies and procedures for contacting law enforcement officials and parents and guardians in the event of a violent incident; school building security; the dissemination of informative materials regarding early detection of potentially violent behaviors; and annual school safety training for students and staff. Additionally, the plan must address protocols for responding to bomb threats, hostage situations, intrusions, and kidnapping; strategies to improve communication among students and between students and staff regarding the reporting of violent incidents; and the description of duties for hall monitors, training required for all school safety personnel, and the hiring and screening process for all school employees.

The Project SAVE regulations provide more details with regard to the contents of the district-wide safety plan. Specifically, the regulations would require the following, in addition to the provisions listed above:

(a) the identification of sites of potential emergency;

(b) a description of plans for taking the following actions in response to an emergency where appropriate: school cancellation, early dismissal, evacuation, and sheltering;

(c) appropriate prevention/intervention strategies, such as collaborative arrangements with state and local law enforcement officials designed to ensure that school safety officers and other security personnel are adequately trained—including being trained to de-escalate potentially violent situations—and are effectively and fairly recruited; nonviolent conflict-resolution training programs; peer mediation programs and youth courts; and extended-day and other school safety programs;

(d) a description of the arrangements for obtaining assistance during emergencies from emergency services organizations and local governmental agencies;

(e) the procedures for obtaining advice and assistance from local government officials, including the county or city officials responsible for implementation of article 2-B of the Executive Law (State and Local Natural and Man-Made Disaster Preparedness Law);

(f) the identification of district resources that may be available for use during an emergency;

(g) a description of procedures to coordinate the use of school district resources and manpower during emergencies, including identification of the officials authorized to make decisions and of the staff member assigned to provide assistance during emergencies;

(h) policies and procedures for contacting parents, guardians, or persons in parental relation to the students of the district in the event of a violent incident or an early dismissal;

(i) policies and procedures relating to school building security including, where appropriate, the use of school safety officers and/or security devices or procedures;

(j) strategies for improving communication among students and between students and staff and reporting of potentially violent incidents, such as the establishment of youth-run programs, peer mediation, conflict resolution, creating a forum or designating a mentor for students concerned with bullying or violence, and establishing anonymous reporting mechanisms for school violence;

(k) in the case of a school district, a system for informing all educational agencies within such school district of an emergency; and

(l) in the case of a school district, certain information about each educational agency located in the school district, including information on school population, number of staff transportation needs, and the business and home telephone numbers of key officials of each such agency.

2. Building-Level School Safety Plan

The building-level school safety plan is defined as a building-specific "school emergency response plan" that addresses crisis intervention, emergency response, and management at the building level. The school emergency response plan must be developed by the building-level school safety team. This plan must include a school emergency response plan developed by the building-level school safety team to be appointed by the building principal in accordance with regulations or guidelines of the school board. It must also include safe evacuation policies and procedures to be utilized in the event of a "serious violent incident" or other emergency. The phrase "serious violent incident" is to be defined in the Commissioner's Regulations. According to the Project SAVE regulations, a serious violent incident means an incident of violent criminal conduct that is or appears to be life-threatening and warrants the evacuation of students and staff because of an imminent threat to their safety or health, including, but not limited to, the use or threatened use of a firearm, explosive, bomb, incendiary device, chemical or biological weapon, knife, or other dangerous instrument capable of causing death or serious injury; riot; hostage-taking; or kidnapping.

The school safety team must be composed of school personnel, local law enforcement officials, and representatives from emergency response agencies. A post-incident response team, consisting of appropriate school and medical personnel and mental health counselors, should also be established. Procedures to ensure that crisis response and law enforcement officials have access to floor plans, blueprints, and other maps of school property; establishment of internal/external communication systems in emergencies; and definition of the chain of command in a manner consistent with the National Interagency Incident Management System (NIMS)/Incident Command System (ICS) must be included in the school emergency response plan. Additionally, the school safety plan must be coordinated with the statewide plan to ensure that the school has access to federal, state, and local mental health resources in the event of a violent incident, and policies and procedures to restrict access to the crime scene in order to preserve evidence in cases of violent crimes on school property.

Finally, procedures for the conduct of drills to test components of the emergency response plan are also required. The Project SAVE regulations require that these tests include "tabletop exercises, in coordination with local and county emergency responders and preparedness officials."[10] Generally speaking, a tabletop exercise is an activity in which officials and key staff with emergency management responsibilities are gathered together informally to discuss actions to be taken during an emergency based upon the emergency management plan. It is a verbal walk-through of a response to an emergency situation. The tabletop exercise is designed to elicit constructive discussion by the participants, without time constraints, as they examine and resolve problems based on the plan. The purpose of a tabletop exercise is to have participants practice problem solving and resolve questions of coordination and assignment of responsibilities in a nonthreatening format under minimum stress.

---

10. 8 N.Y.C.R.R. § 155.17.

E. THE UNIFORM VIOLENT INCIDENT REPORTING SYSTEM

Section 5 of the Act creates "The Uniform Violent Incident Reporting System," which requires school districts to report annually, on a particular form and by a particular date, certain information concerning violent and disruptive incidents that occurred in the prior school year. A summary of such information must also be included in the school district report cards. The Commissioner of Education is required to establish regulations in conjunction with the Commissioner of the Department of Criminal Justice Services defining violent or disruptive incidents. They must also promulgate regulations with respect to uniform reporting of types of incidents/ responses and the confidentiality of all personally identifiable information contained in such reports.

F. SELECTED ADDITIONAL PROVISIONS OF PROJECT SAVE—YOUTHFUL OFFENDER

Section 14 of the Act creates a new section of the Criminal Procedure Law (Section 380.90) to provide that a court sentencing a student under age 19 for a crime must provide notification to the district's designated educational official in the school in which the student is enrolled. The notification will not become part of the student's permanent school record, and any documentation regarding the same must be destroyed when the student is no longer enrolled in the district. The law seems to prohibit one school district from forwarding such notification to a new school district should the student transfer.

Criminal Procedure Law Section 720.35, entitled "Youthful Offender Adjudication," is amended by Section 15 of the Act to provide that official records and papers with regard to a student adjudicated a youthful offender shall not be deemed confidential as they relate to dissemination to the designated educational official. However, designated educational officials are only permitted to have notice of the adjudication; they may not have access to any other official records and papers. It does not appear that the district will receive notice of the underlying crime resulting in the youthful offender adjudication.

Section 16 of the Act provides that any court adjudicating a student as a youthful offender will provide notice to the school district in which the student is enrolled. The same requirements dealing with confidentiality and purging of the student's records apply. The Family Court Act is also amended to require the designated educational official to be advised by the Family Court whenever a student is adjudicated a juvenile delinquent and has been placed with the Office of Children and Family Services.

G. LABOR RELATIONS IMPLICATIONS

As previously noted, it is likely that a school district would have to bargain with both instructional and non-instructional unions (upon request of such unions) over the impact of the Project SAVE Act on the terms and conditions of their members' employment. Districts must be prepared to respond to demands for bargaining on topics such as additional pay for time spent serving on safety teams or committees outside of regular work hours, safety-related issues associated with assigned roles during school emergencies, additional time involved in meetings resulting from student removal, and notice or other procedures regarding reports about the employee to police or other agencies (such as child abuse in the educational setting, discussed below). While unions may have legitimate concerns arising from Project SAVE legislation, districts must be careful to avoid limiting their ability to function properly in carrying out their obligations for safety in schools.

H. SCHOOL EMPLOYEE FINGERPRINTING LAW

For a number of years, New York's Vehicle and Traffic Law has required all school bus drivers and attendants to undergo fingerprinting and criminal background checks. Under a new law signed by the governor on July 24, 2000, all prospective school employees and contractors with direct student contact must undergo a similar process. This new law substantially changes the hiring process for school districts and the Board of Cooperative Educational Services (BOCES), a New York Education department program designed to help public schools control costs by sharing services. It requires the Commissioner of Education to develop regulations and forms necessary for implementing the program, which should address most of these concerns.

1. School's Responsibilities Under the Fingerprinting Law

Prior to initiating the fingerprinting process, the school must do two things: First, it must provide prospective employees with written notice on a form to be created by the Commissioner concerning the fingerprinting requirement and their right to obtain, review, and seek correction of their criminal history reports. Second, it must obtain a signed, informed consent from each prospective employee to perform the criminal history check—also on a form to be created by the Commissioner. The term "employee" includes any individual (1) who may have direct student contact and receives compensation for work from a school district; (2) is an employee of a contracted service provider; or (3) is placed within the school under a public-assistance employment program pursuant to Title 9-B of Article 5 of the Social Services Law.

As a general rule, once the prospective employee has received the required notice and consented to the background check, schools must fingerprint the prospective employee and forward the fingerprints to the State Education Department (SED). The fingerprints must be collected on a form created by the Commissioner in conjunction with Department of Criminal Justice Services (DCJS). However, the law does exempt several individuals from the fingerprinting requirement. These people include current employees, any prospective employee who was fingerprinted in order to receive a teaching certificate and whose fingerprints remain on file with the DCJS, any prospective employee fingerprinted pursuant to Vehicle and Traffic Law Section 509-cc or 1229-d (that is, bus drivers, school bus attendants, and traffic guards), and any prospective employee previously fingerprinted and cleared by SED for employment. If a current employee who has not been fingerprinted leaves a job with one district and seeks employment with another district, the employee must be fingerprinted by the second district. Schools are also required to notify the Commissioner every time they hire someone or an employee leaves their district through discharge or resignation. This notification must include the name of the employee and the position the employee holds currently or held prior to leaving the district.

2. SED's Requirements Under the Fingerprinting Law

Once SED receives the fingerprints, it will submit them to the New York State Department of Criminal Justice Services and the Federal Bureau of Investigation for a criminal background check (on a state and nationwide level). As noted above, it requires the Commissioner to develop three forms: (1) one for school districts obtaining and submitting fingerprints; (2) another to inform prospective employees about the fingerprinting requirement and the right to obtain, review, and seek correction of the criminal history report; and (3) another for schools to obtain a signed, informed consent from a prospective employee to perform the criminal history check. Obtaining the criminal history check consent form indicates that the person has been informed about the fingerprinting requirement and the right to obtain, review, and seek to correct the information in the criminal history report; consented to such request for a criminal history report; supplied the prospective employer with a current mailing or home address; been informed of the right to withdraw the application for employment, without prejudice, at any time before employment is offered or declined; been informed that the fingerprints will be destroyed 12 months after the individual is no longer employed with any district; and been informed of the manner in which the prospective employee may submit additional information to the Commissioner relevant to the clearance determination, including information pertaining to good conduct and rehabilitation. The SED is then required to clear prospective employees for hiring by the schools, applying the criteria set forth in the Executive Law and the Correction Law.

The Office of Professional Discipline will have to consider the criminal history records pursuant to Article 23-A of the Correction Law. Article 23-A prohibits denying a license or employment to a convicted offender or from finding that an applicant lacks good moral character when the finding is based upon a criminal conviction, unless there is a direct relationship between one or more of the previous criminal offenses and the specific license or employment sought, or granting the license or employment would involve an unreasonable risk to property or to the safety or welfare of specific individuals or the general public. The Correction Law requires that the following factors be considered when making such a determination:

(1) the public policy of New York state, which is to encourage the licensure and employment of persons previously convicted of one or more criminal offenses;
(2) the specific duties and responsibilities necessarily related to the license or employment sought;
(3) the bearing, if any, the prior criminal offense(s) will have on the applicant's fitness or ability to perform one or more such duties or responsibilities;
(4) the time that has elapsed since the occurrence of the criminal offense(s);
(5) the applicant's age at the time the prior criminal offense(s) occurred;

(6)   the seriousness of the offense(s);

(7)   any information produced by the applicant, or produced on the applicant's behalf, regarding the applicant's rehabilitation and good conduct;

(8)   the legitimate interest of the licensing entity or employer in protecting property, and the safety and welfare of specific individuals or the general public; and

(9)   the existence of a certificate of relief from disabilities or a certificate of good conduct issued to the applicant. The certificate creates a presumption of rehabilitation regarding the offense(s) specified in the certificate.

In addition, provision of the criminal history record to the Commissioner by the DCJS is subject to Executive Law Section 296 (16). That law prohibits discrimination in licensing or employment based upon any arrest or criminal accusation not then pending against an individual that was followed by a termination of that criminal action in favor of the individual. Once a determination is made, the Commissioner is required to "promptly" notify the school district whether the employee is "cleared for employment." For those prospective employees who are denied clearance, the Commissioner must grant them the right to a due process hearing in accordance with the regulations of the Commissioner.

The Commissioner is also required to establish regulations for fingerprinting and performing criminal background checks on applicants for teaching certificates. The procedures for granting or denying certificates parallel the procedures, described above, for clearing an applicant for employment. Those whose applications are denied are also given the right to a due process hearing.

3. Fees Under the Fingerprinting Law

Both DCJS and the FBI impose a processing fee on the prospective employees and applicants for teaching certificates. In addition, the entity that actually takes the fingerprints may impose a fee. Not all prospective employees are required to pay the fees associated with performing a criminal background check. The bill exempts employees participating in a public assistance program or receiving employment services through the federal Temporary Assistance for Needy Families block grant. In addition, a local school board may waive payment of the fee by any prospective employee if the board determines that payment of the fee would impose an unreasonable financial hardship on the applicant or his or her family. If the board decides to waive payment of the fee by a prospective employee, the board becomes responsible for paying the fee on the prospective employee's behalf.

4. Silent Resignations

School administrators are not permitted to agree to withhold information from law enforcement officials, school superintendents, or the Commissioner about allegations of child abuse in an educational setting against an employee or volunteer in exchange for that individual's resignation or voluntary suspension. A violation of this provision is considered a class E felony and carries a civil penalty of up to $20,000.

5. Practical Questions About the Fingerprinting Law

There are a number of questions and concerns raised by the new law. It is assumed that most of them will be answered by the Commissioner's Regulations, which have yet to be written. For example, the new law applies to all employees of a district as well as any "employee of a contracted service provider whereby such services performed by such person involve direct student contact." There is no definition of the phrase "direct student contact" in the law. It is possible that certain employees may be exempt from the fingerprinting and criminal history check requirements because they do not have such direct contact (for example, janitorial staff, district administrative staff members, groundskeeper, and so on). However, districts should include as many prospective employees as possible

The new law also fails to define "contracted service providers." These might include food service workers; school physicians, nurses, and other health care providers; and school lawyers (if they are involved in student disciplinary hearings, for example). Additionally, the law does not expressly address the issue of whether an applicant can be hired contingent upon clearance by SED. It does provide that prospective employees must be notified that they have a right to withdraw their applications prior to offers of employment being extended. Thus, it would seem that the criminal history check would have to take place before an offer was extended. If this is true, it will create administrative problems. While it is uncertain how long it will take SED to clear prospective employees for employment, there will likely be a significant lag time. The lag time for bus driver clearance is currently between one and two months. Thus, a school may be delayed substantially in its attempt to fill a job vacancy.

Another concern is whether schools will have to fingerprint all applicants, including the ones they do not intend to interview. Under the existing bus driver clearance process, schools may hire bus drivers contingent on a favorable criminal background check. Schools submit a bus driver's fingerprints to the Department of Motor Vehicles (DMV) and receive an interim qualification letter within three to four weeks. This simply indicates that the DMV has received the fingerprints. The final qualification letter is received between one and two months after the fingerprints are submitted. It is understood that many schools permit the drivers to work until they are disqualified. It seems likely that there will be a similar provision in the Commissioner's regulations.

Finally, the regulations leave open the question of whether teachers who go through the process to obtain certification are permanently cleared. The new law provides that once a teacher has been fingerprinted for purposes of obtaining a teaching certificate, subsequent school employers are not required to retake and resubmit the teacher's fingerprints. This does not mean, however, that these teachers are permanently cleared. According to one SED official, the DCJS will keep the fingerprints on file and notify the Commissioner of any arrests following the initial clearance. The FBI, however, will not provide this ongoing notification. Thus, we assume that SED, and not the school district, will resubmit the fingerprints to the FBI each time it receives notification that a teacher has been hired.

I. CHILD ABUSE IN AN EDUCATIONAL SETTING

The new law also requires school employees to report all allegations of "child abuse in an educational setting" to appropriate authorities. Child abuse is defined as intentionally or recklessly inflicting physical injury,[11] serious physical injury, or death; intentionally or recklessly engaging in conduct that creates a substantial risk of such physical injury, serious physical injury, or death; any child sexual abuse, including offenses contained in Articles 130 (misdemeanor sexual misconduct offenses to felony rape) and 263 (sexual performances by a child) of the Penal Law; or the commission or attempted commission against a child of the crime of dissemi-

---

11. "Physical injury" is defined in the Penal Code as "impairment of physical condition or substantial pain."

nating indecent materials to minors pursuant to Article 235 of the Penal Law—committed by an employee or volunteer of the district. An educational setting is defined as the building and grounds of a public school district; the vehicles provided by the school district for the transportation of students to and from school buildings, field trips, and cocurricular and extracurricular activities both on and off school district grounds; all cocurricular and extracurricular activity sites; and any other location where direct contact between an employee or volunteer and a child has allegedly occurred.

When certificated employees, such as teachers, administrators, or guidance counselors, receive an oral or written report of child abuse in an educational setting, the employee must promptly complete a written report of such allegation on a form that will be developed by the Commissioner of Education. The written report should include the full name of the child alleged to be abused; the name of the child's parent(s) or guardian(s); the identity of the person making the allegation and their relationship to the alleged child victim; the name of the employee or volunteer against whom the allegation was made; and a listing of the specific allegations of child abuse in the educational setting. The employee must promptly personally deliver a copy of the written report to the principal of the school in which the child abuse allegedly occurred. The principal or superintendent must then determine whether there is reasonable suspicion to believe that an act of child abuse has occurred. The term "reasonable suspicion" is not defined in the law, nor are there any instructions with regard to how a principal or superintendent is to arrive at this determination. However, the Commissioner is empowered to develop regulations for training necessary for the implementation of the new law. It is assumed that this matter will be clarified in those training materials.

When the allegation is made by the child or someone other than the parent, assuming that there is reasonable suspicion, the principal or the superintendent must promptly notify the child's parent or guardian that an allegation of child abuse has been made. The principal or superintendent must provide the parent or guardian with a written statement prepared on the form developed by the commissioner setting forth parental rights, responsibilities, and procedures under this law and attempt to ascertain from the person making the report the source and basis for such allegation (if the person making the report is someone other than the child or parent). Where a school administrator receives a written report, the administrator must promptly provide a copy of such report to the superintendent and promptly forward the report to appropriate law enforcement authorities. Reporting to law enforcement authorities cannot be delayed because of an inability to contact the superintendent. A superintendent or principal who has forwarded a written report of child abuse to law enforcement authorities must also forward it to the Commissioner.

Any report of child abuse in an educational setting that does not, after investigation, result in a criminal conviction must be expunged from any record that may be kept by a school or school district after a period of five years from the date of the making of the report or at an earlier time set by the school or school district. Where a criminal investigation of an allegation of child abuse by an employee or volunteer is undertaken as a result of a written report, and where law enforcement authorities have provided the report to the district attorney and have requested assistance, the district attorney must notify the superintendent of an indictment or the filing of an accusatory instrument against the employee or volunteer. The district attorney must also notify the superintendent of the disposition of the criminal case against such employee or volunteer or the suspension or termination of the criminal investigation.

If the employee or volunteer is convicted of child abuse, the district attorney will notify the Commissioner and the superintendent. The Commissioner must then determine (pursuant to his or her regulations) whether the individual possesses good moral character. Employees or volunteers who have adverse actions taken against them because of any report made against them under this law are entitled to receive a copy of such report and respond to the allegations. Any employee or volunteer is also entitled to seek disclosure of such report pursuant to Article 6 of the Public Officers Law (Freedom of Information Law).

1. Immunity for Reporting

Any employee or volunteer who reasonably and in good faith makes a report of allegations of child abuse in an educational setting to a person and in the manner described above will have immunity from civil liability that might otherwise result by reason of such actions. Likewise, any school administrator or superintendent who reasonably and in good faith makes a report of allegations of child abuse in an educational setting or reasonably and in good faith transmits such a report to a person or agency as required by the law will also have immunity from civil liability.

2. Penalties for Failing to Report

A willful failure of an employee to prepare and submit a written report of an allegation of child abuse (as required in the law) will be considered a class A misdemeanor. A willful failure of a principal or superintendent to submit a written report of child abuse to the appropriate law enforcement authority is also a class A misdemeanor. Any failure, willful or otherwise, to submit a written report of child abuse to the appropriate law enforcement authority will also result in a fine of up to $5,000 upon an administrative determination by the Commissioner.

Workplace Violence: School Liability 6

Mark A. Lies II

A. INTRODUCTION

As the pace and emotional pressures of everyday life impact employees at home and in the workplace, a distressing and tragic trend is occurring: Employees are unable to control their emotions at work, and violence erupts toward co-employees, customers, or third parties. The unfortunate statistics show that homicide is the number-one cause of death for women in the workplace and that assaults and violent acts, which include homicides, are the third overall cause for men and women.[1] The workplace for many employees in our society is a school building, which for much of the day is filled with children or young adults engaged in learning. Obviously, a school building is not an environment that can tolerate workplace violence or even the threat of such activity. Yet, because of the issues brought to the school workplace by the employees who come to work each day, violence can erupt

---

1. Bureau of Labor Statistics, Census of Fatal Occupational Injuries (2002).

81

or unsafe circumstances are created not by the students, but by the employees who may be charged with the responsibility for teaching children or providing for their care.

Certainly, no employer wants such incidents to occur. Ironically, however, as employers, including public and private school employers, struggle to avoid potential legal liabilities through creation and enforcement of stringent employment policies, they are met with a host of federal and state laws that may protect certain employee conduct. More important, since an employer has no objective litmus test for predicting which employee may become violent under particular triggering circumstances, there is no foolproof way to effectively eliminate the hazard. The risk of violence in the school workplace is of heightened concern, since the effects of any violence in a school setting can have serious long-term consequences to a vulnerable and impressionable population. This chapter will discuss certain factors that must be considered to anticipate, avoid, and respond to the threat of violence and/or disruption that is brought to the school setting by employees.

B. CAUSES OF VIOLENCE IN THE WORKPLACE

While many incidents of workplace violence appear to be random and unpredictable, most commentators agree that such incidents are predictable and result from the interaction of two dynamics in an employee's life:

- Personal factors—Numerous factors occurring in the employee's personal life outside of the school environment (including marital problems, prior history of physical or mental impairments, drug or alcohol abuse, or the same circumstances occurring to a member of the employee's immediate family).
- Workplace factors—Interacting with real or perceived factors occurring in the school environment that simultaneously impact the employee (potential layoffs or reductions in force; lack of career opportunity; unequal or unfair opportunities for training, benefits, or overtime; or harassment by co-employees).

Fortunately for our society and the workplace, most employees are able to control their emotions when these two dynamics collide and somehow deal with their day-to-day side effects. However, since no employee will typically announce to the employer that he or she is no longer able to maintain a sometimes delicate and tenuous emotional balance when dealing with these dynamics, and that a sudden and potentially violent physical or emotional outburst is going to occur, the employer cannot conveniently schedule a police, medical, security, or other intervention to preempt such event. In order to have any reasonable chance of predicting and avoiding workplace violence, the employer (through its supervisors) must become more sophisticated in observing, identifying, and understanding the signs and symptoms that frequently telegraph that these underlying dynamics are at work and may be about to overwhelm the employee's ability to cope in a rational manner. Once these signs and symptoms are identified, the employer must take prompt action, which may include a "fitness for duty" (FFD) evaluation.

C. CONFLICTING EMPLOYER DUTIES

1. Employer Obligations

Every employer has a legal duty to prevent violence and the underlying behavior that may generate it, based upon several different areas of federal and state law. Perhaps the most well-known duty arises out of Title VII of the Civil Rights Act of 1964, 42 U.S.C. Section 2000e *et seq.,* which requires an employer to protect its employees against all forms of workplace harassment (such as of sexual, racial, religious, or national origin) that may create a hostile or offensive workplace environment. Frequently, employee violence is triggered as a response to such harassing behavior, which causes the victim (or the victim's spouse or relative) to react to the harasser (and sometimes to innocent co-employees or students) with a reflexive anger in the form of verbal outbursts or even physical acts. The same anti-harassment rules have been applied under the Age Discrimination in Employment Act, 29 U.S.C. Sections 621 *et seq.* and the Americans with Disabilities Act, 42 U.S.C. Sections 12101 *et seq.*

Under the federal Occupational Safety and Health Act, 29 U.S.C. Sections 650 *et seq.,* an employer is also required to protect employees against "recognized" workplace safety and health hazards that are likely to cause serious injury or death. OSHA has identified workplace violence as such a hazard, particularly in the health care, retail, and taxicab industries. The agency has issued citations with monetary penalties alleging that employers have failed to develop and enforce appropriate workplace violence policies. OSHA has also issued guidelines and recommendations that can be useful in developing such programs, and that can be found at its Web site, www.osha.gov.

In addition to the federal laws, most states have developed liability doctrines under common law (based upon a negligence theory), where an employer may be held liable for the violent acts of an employee if the employer:

- negligently hired the employee (for example, failure to investigate the employee's work history to determine if there is prior violent conduct);
- negligently supervised the employee (failure to warn or discipline an employee who engaged in threatening conduct);
- negligently trained the employee (failure to provide training regarding prohibited conduct that may give rise to violence and the consequences of engaging in such conduct); or
- negligently retained the employee (failure to terminate an employee who has engaged in acts or threats of violence).

Though not limited to the school context, another potential source of liability to which schools and school districts may be exposed to liability results from the recommendations that a school district administrator makes for employees who have left or are looking to separate from a school district.

2. Public School Immunity to Claims of Negligent Retention and Hiring

While the spectre of liability for torts (such as negligent hiring, retention, and supervision) exists, the school district may consider a challenge to such a claim on the grounds of municipal immunity under state law. Because most state tort immunity acts do not explicitly shield municipalities from negligence liability, the issue becomes whether the discretionary function immunity of the state's municipal tort act applies.[2] The crux of the defense is whether the school's decision to employ, retain, and supervise the potentially violent employee was a discretionary function. The reported decisions are divergent on this issue.

---

2. Adding to the confusion, some state tort acts apparently explicitly exempt school districts from negligence liability because they are state agencies. *See* Gonzales v. Brown, 768 F. Supp. 581 (S.D. Tex. 1991) (Texas governmental immunity law immunizes school district from suits grounded in negligence unless waived by Tort Claims Act).

In *Doe v. Cedar Rapids Community School District,* 2002 Iowa Sup. LEXIS 164, 652 N.W.2d 439 (Iowa 2002), the Iowa Supreme Court concluded that the decisions of the school to hire and retain a teacher accused of physical and sexual violence against students were not directly related to the exercise of governmental policy judgments. The court first looked to whether the challenged conduct was a matter of choice for the school district, and then whether the district's judgment was of the type intended to be shielded from liability. Here, the court found the school had made a professional judgment when it hired the teacher, when it retained the teacher after the initial allegations of misconduct, and when it supervised the teacher, so the first prong of the defense was met. However, the court found there were no underlying policy determinations behind the decision to hire, retain, and supervise the teacher, since it did not involve any economic, social, or political policy concerns. Thus, liability was found against the district. Cases cited within supporting this proposition include: *Doe v. Estes,* 926 F. Supp. 979 (D. Nev. 1996); *Willis v. Dade County School Board,* 411 So. 2d 245 (Fla. Dist. Ct. App. 1982), *pet. denied,* 418 So. 2d 1278 (Fla. 1982).

A body of cases went the other way to find in favor of discretionary function immunity. See, for example, *Davis v. DeKalb County School District,* 996 F. Supp. 1478 (N.D. Ga. 1998); *Does 1, 2, 3, and 4 v. Covington County School Board,* 969 F. Supp. 1264 (M.D. Ala. 1997); *C.B. v. Bobo,* 659 So. 2d 98 (Ala. 1995); *Willoughby v. Lehrbass,* 150 Mich. App. 319, 388 N.W.2d 688 (Mich. App. 1986); *Doe v. Park Center High School,* 592 N.W.2d 131 (Minn. App. 1999); *Oslin v. State,* 543 N.W.2d 408 (Minn. App. 1996). While a number of these decisions did not involve a school setting, they generally hold that the hiring, retention, training, and supervision of public employees involve discretionary, policy-related decisions. In the school context, *Gordon v. Ottumwa County School District,* 115 F. Supp. 2d 1077 (S. D. Iowa 2000), found that a school district was immune from a negligent hiring claim regarding a volunteer coordinator who sexually abused students under the discretionary function exception to the state municipal tort act. This federal court decision must be contrasted with the Iowa Supreme Court decision in *Doe,* discussed above.

A school district may lose its potential immunity by failing to perform a background check required by statute. In *Mueller v. Community Consolidated School District 54,* 287 Ill. App. 3d 337, 678 N.E.2d 660 (Ill. Ct.

App. 1997), without deciding whether the district enjoyed immunity for negligent hiring and negligent supervision under the Local Governmental and Governmental Tort Immunity Act, the court found that a state statute requiring criminal background investigation of school employees, 105 ILCS 5/34-18.5(d), vitiated any potential immunity because the school had failed to engage in any type of background check of a coach who allegedly sexually assaulted a student.

3. Public School Liability Based on Claim of Negligent Referral

Though not limited to the school context, another potential source of liability of which schools and school districts should be aware is negligent referral of a current or former employee who has a history of violent or threatening behavior, thus creating the potential for violence at another school district.

In *Randi W. v. Muroc Joint Unified School District,* 14 Cal. 4th 1066, 929 P.2d 582 (Cal. 1997), the court found that liability could be imposed on the school district based upon the failure to use reasonable care in the recommendations of a former administrator. The court deemed the glowing letters of recommendation, which failed to disclose information about disciplinary action taken against the administrator resulting from sexual harassment and his resignation under pressure due to sexual misconduct charges, constituted an "affirmative representation." The court also found that the prospective employer, another school district, relied upon the letters of recommendation in its decision to hire. Subsequently, the former administrator sexually assaulted a student at the new school district. In examining the issue of recommendations, the court determined that a party that gives a letter of recommendation owes a duty to third persons not to misrepresent the qualifications of the subject employee if the misrepresentations present a substantial, foreseeable risk of physical injury to the third persons.

Thus, the court opined, when the school district elected to provide some information about the administrator, it was obligated to disclose all other material facts, including the negative information about prior sexual misconduct issues.

4. Nondisclosure Agreements as Shield for Potential Violence

A potential impediment to the full disclosure of negative information about a prior teacher could be the confidentiality provisions in a nondisclosure agreement in a separation or settlement. The case law appears to support the principle of disclosure of potentially violent conduct of a former teacher, despite the clear language of such agreement. For example, a state court of appeals concluded that a nondisclosure agreement between a teacher and a school board, which prohibited the disclosure of the teacher's molestation of female students, was void and unenforceable as a matter of public policy.[3] After a large number of children reported molestation by the teacher to the school board, and an investigation revealed numerous instances of inappropriate contact between the teacher and students, the parties entered into a settlement agreement whereby the teacher agreed to resign and the board agreed not to disclose the incidents except subject to a court order. Thereafter, a board member learned that the teacher was working for another school district. He contacted the district and informed them why the teacher was fired. The former teacher filed suit based upon a breach of the nondisclosure agreement. Analyzing the agreement, the court found the nondisclosure clause illegal per se because it purported to suppress information regarding the commission of felonies, and void and unenforceable on public policy grounds because it was designed to shield information about the teacher's pedophilia while the teacher remained in the profession. It appears that a school district could make a successful argument that student safety outweighs the teacher's right to confidentiality.

5. Potential Liability to School Stemming from Its Special Relationship to Its Students

The duty to prevent violence can also be premised on the school's "special relationship" with the student. Some courts have concluded that public schools have an affirmative duty to prevent harm to students based upon a special relationship with the students. The government, being in charge of the students and their surroundings at school, must exercise "the same

---

3. Bowman v. Parma Bd. of Educ., 44 Ohio App. 3d 169, 542 N.E.2d 663 (Ohio Ct. App. 1988).

care toward them as a parent of ordinary prudence would observe in comparable circumstances."[4]

In those cases where school districts have been charged with negligent hiring, supervision, and retention claims, the liability analysis has hinged on whether the district knew, or should have known, of the employee's propensity toward violent or other unlawful behavior. The crucial factual inquiry has focused on the chronology of the underlying events and the manner in which the school district became aware and reacted to them.

In *Knicrumah v. Albany City School District,* 241 F. Supp. 2d 199 (N.D.N.Y. 2003), a student filed suit claiming, among other allegations, that he was subjected to corporal punishment by a teacher as a result of a violation of Section 1983 based on the school's failure to properly train the teacher or through the school's policy of deliberate indifference to student needs.[5] The student also claimed that the defendants breached a duty of care to protect him at school through negligent hiring and retention, negligent training, negligent failure to implement and follow proper procedures regarding aggressive behavior at school, and negligent failure to react to incidents of teacher-student violence.

Analyzing the negligence claims, the court noted that there was no evidence presented that the school had taken prior discipline against the teacher, or that there were indicators showing the teacher's propensity toward violence. The court opined, "[I]t is well settled that defendants cannot be held liable for their alleged negligent hiring, training, supervision, or retention of [an employee accused of wrongful conduct] unless they had notice [of said employee's] propensity for the type of behavior causing plaintiff's harm." (Citations omitted and emphasis added.) Therefore, the court dismissed the negligent hiring, retention, supervision, and training claims.

The case of *Peck v. Siau,* 65 Wash. App. 285, 827 P.2d 1108 (Wash. Ct. App. 1992), involved a librarian who was forced to resign after pleading guilty in criminal court for having oral sex with a minor student. The minor and his parents sued the school district, claiming that it knew of the propensities of the librarian because a teacher gained knowledge of the librarian's contact with the minor. The alleged victim's brother had told a teacher, who was a former teacher of his, about the librarian's sexual advances on his

---

4. Doe v. Cedar Rapids Cmty. Sch. Dist., 2002 Iowa Sup. LEXIS 164, 652 N.W.2d 439 (Iowa 2002) (citing City of Cedar Falls v. Cedar Falls Cmty. Sch. Dist., 617 N.W.2d 11, 18 (Iowa 2000)).

5. The Section 1983 claim will be analyzed further later in this chapter.

brother. The teacher, however, did not notify any employees or officials of the school district about the conversation. In granting summary judgment to the defendants on the plaintiffs' negligent hiring, retention, and supervision claims, the court concluded that the teacher's knowledge could not be imputed to the school district because the teacher who failed to report the complaint did not have any hiring or supervisory powers over the librarian, and thus the school district could not be considered to have been on notice of his behavior.

The decision in *Hart v. Paint Valley Local School District,* 2002 U.S. Dist. LEXIS 25720 (S.D. Ohio Nov. 15, 2002) illustrates the dilemma that a school district faces as to what extent it must take disciplinary action against a teacher to protect the students when the underlying information about the teacher is inconclusive. A teacher allegedly fondled a fourth-grade male student. After his parents learned of the incident, they contacted the sheriff, who in turn contacted the school board. The school district then employed a permanent teacher's aide to remain in the classroom with the teacher so that he would not be alone with any of the students. Though the sheriff and the county department of children's services investigated the incident, the school board did not launch an independent investigation.

Evidence at trial showed that there were prior complaints against the teacher that were related to the school and school board. One prior allegation resulted in the principal asking the teacher to leave the classroom door open at all times but did not result in any criminal action. The second complaint resulted in a sheriff's investigation, which concluded there was no substantiating evidence to back up the claim of abuse. The defendants argued that these earlier accusations did not inform them that the teacher had a propensity toward criminal, tortious, or otherwise dangerous conduct because they were unsubstantiated. Though the court agreed that the school district knew of the prior complaints, that did not compel a finding that the school district knew of sufficient criminal, tortious, or otherwise dangerous conduct that would have justified firing the teacher. Further, the court reasoned, the teacher was subject to a collective bargaining agreement that required just cause for termination, and thus the school district was not obligated to terminate the teacher's employment based on the earlier complaints.

Frequently, a school district's failure to follow its own policies that recognize this "special relationship" has resulted in liability for sexual assaults on students. In *Shedivy v. Independent School Dist. 279,* 2000 Minn. App. LEXIS 916 (Minn. Ct. App. Aug. 29, 2000) (unpub.), a high school student alleged that the school district negligently implemented its policies, which resulted in her relationship with an administrative assistant, which led to his inducement of her to perform oral sex. The school had adopted a policy that assigned specific students to administrative assistants by last name and also prohibited the assistants from fraternizing with students. Further, the school had a policy for determining if a student was spending an impermissible amount of time with a staff member. The court affirmed the denial of summary judgment to the school district, finding that there were fact questions as to whether the school failed to follow its own policies that were intended to implement the special relationship with the students.

6. Potential Liability of Public School Districts Under Section 1983

School districts can also face liability for violence under 42 U.S.C. Section 1983. Though not a school law case, the Supreme Court's findings in *DeShaney v. Winnebago County Department of Social Services,* 489 U.S. 189 (1989), form the rationale for imposing liability under Section 1983 in school violence settings.

DeShaney concerned whether the public employer, through a social worker, knew or should have known that a minor in its custody would be seriously injured by his father by being returned to the father's custody. The Court rejected the plaintiff's argument that a "special relationship" was created between the state and the minor by virtue of social welfare services provided by the state. The Court found that "a State's failure to protect an individual against private violence simply does not constitute a violation of the Due Process Clause."

Section 1983 can impose municipal liability at a policy-making level, but not through the traditional doctrine of respondeat superior. Thus, a plaintiff must show that there was a municipal policy, custom, or practice that allegedly deprived him or her of a federal or constitutional right.[6] A plaintiff can allege a policy is facially unconstitutional,[7] or unconstitutional as applied due to the defendant's "deliberate indifference" to the rights of the plaintiff.

In conducting the liability analysis, most courts assume, without discussing, that the public school employee is acting under color of state law

---

6. Monell v. Dep't of Social Services, 436 U.S. 658 (1978).
7. City of Canton v. Harris, 489 U.S. 378 (1989).

when engaged in abuse of a student. While many challenged municipal policies are not actual written policies, in order to establish the second prong of liability, many plaintiffs will claim that an unwritten custom or practice is what caused the constitutional violation. The following cases demonstrate the interaction of these elements.

In *K.L. v. Southeast Delco School District,* 828 F. Supp. 1192 (E.D. Pa. 1993), the court held that while states do not have an affirmative duty to protect students in public schools from abusive conduct by their teachers, school districts and school officials do have such a duty because these entities have direct supervisory authority over the teachers. However, the court explicitly stated that this ruling did not extend to other school workers, such as janitors or cafeteria workers. Thus the court held that the school district was not entitled to qualified immunity for the allegations of abuse of a student by a teacher that took place in school.

A student's claim of violation of Section 1983, in *Banks v. Board of Education of the City of Chicago,* 1999 U.S. Dist. LEXIS 19164 (N.D. Ill. Dec. 2, 1999), was unsuccessful when the court found that a single assault by a teacher did not prove a "policy or custom" sufficient to impart liability under Section 1983. In this case, the complaint alleged that a teacher threw a 12-year-old student into a chalkboard and hit him on the nose.

In *Knicrumah v. Albany City School District,* 241 F. Supp. 2d 199 (N.D.N.Y. 2003) (discussed above on other grounds), a student filed suit claiming, among other allegations, that he was subjected to corporal punishment by a teacher as a result of a violation of Section 1983 based on the school's failure to properly train the teacher or through the school's policy of deliberate indifference to student needs. The court focused on the fact that there was no proof of a causal link between the defendant's alleged failure to train and the student's injuries. The court opined that for the plaintiff to show failure to supervise or failure to discipline amounting to deliberate indifference (and thus a policy violation), evidence must show that the municipality persistently fails to investigate complaints or discipline the alleged perpetrators. Though the plaintiff here had claimed that there were numerous complaints of use of excessive force by teachers against students, the court found no evidence of the complaints in the record.

The plaintiff in *Sherman v. Helms,* 80 F. Supp. 2d 1365 (M.D. Ga. 2000), was unable to establish a policy to support the Section 1983 claim. A female student was allegedly sexually assaulted by a school janitor. In her Section 1983 claim, she alleged that the school's decision to limit surveillance cameras to cover only the interior of the main building, and not the on-campus building where the alleged assault occurred, amounted to a policy of deliberate indifference because it "emboldened" the janitor. The court disagreed, finding that there was no basis for finding the school's decision to utilize limited resources on a security system could amount to an unlawful policy, and that it was not shown to have been the moving force behind the janitor's actions.

In *P.H. v. The School District of Kansas City,* 265 F.3d 653 (8th Cir. 2001), the student unsuccessfully attempted to establish a policy violation for failure to investigate. The student, who had engaged in a two-year sexual relationship with a teacher, claimed that the district was liable because it failed to act on claims of abuse. The court found that the district did not have notice until the plaintiff's mother complained, at which point the district removed the teacher and commenced a criminal investigation. Though the plaintiff argued that the district should have known that he was spending excessive time with the teacher, which led to tardiness, falling grades, and absences, the court found that the principal did confront the teacher and student about this, but that the failure to do anything more amounted to negligence at most and not a violation of a policy. Finally, though there was a prior allegation of sexual abuse regarding the teacher more 20 years before the facts of this case, the court found that this one complaint could not have provided a pattern of abuse sufficient to put the school district on notice of the teacher's proclivities. Thus the court affirmed summary judgment for the school district.

In *Hackett v. Fulton County School District,* 238 F. Supp. 2d 1330 (N.D. Ga. 2002), the court found no policy violation regarding background checks. The student, who was allegedly sexually molested by a teacher, claimed that it was the custom of the school district to fail to conduct proper background checks of prospective teachers and that it was a widespread practice of the district to ignore complaints about teacher misconduct toward students. Though the teacher had a long history of allegations of abuse, the court noted he did not completely fill out his employment application, omitting schools from which he had been terminated or asked to resign. Further, no school district, except for Fulton County, had reported the allegations of abuse to the police. Thus the school district's failure to detect the teacher's lies regarding his employment history did not constitute a custom or policy under Section 1983.

7. Compliance with Policy Necessary

In many cases, despite injury to a student, the school district can avoid liability by establishing that it followed its policy.

In *Tilson v. School District of Philadelphia,* 1990 U.S. Dist. LEXIS 8964 (E.D. Pa. July 12, 1990), *aff'd,* 932 F.2d 961 (3d Cir. 1991), the plaintiff claimed that the school and school district's failure to create effective policies regarding employment of personnel, investigation of suspected child abuse, and prevention of child abuse violated the plaintiff's constitutional rights.

The plaintiff was a 4-year-old student who was allegedly molested by a substitute teacher in the lavatory while he was escorting the plaintiff there. The substitute was subsequently convicted of several counts of child rape and child sexual assault and sent to prison. The court opined that to find the defendants liable for an omission, the omission must amount to official indifference to the constitutional rights involved. A background check the school ran when the substitute was hired revealed an arrest for a drug offense, but not a conviction. State law and school board policies in effect at the time prohibited the school district from using the arrest as a basis not to hire the substitute. Because of these laws, and the fact that the arrest did not establish that the substitute lacked a good moral character, the court held that the plaintiff could not prove the Section 1983 claim based on the hiring of the substitute. Regarding the absence of policies dictating who can take children into washrooms, the court noted that the school board had a policy that detailed the reporting and investigation of suspected child abuse. This policy was followed here, the court noted, as the substitute was immediately suspended once the allegations of abuse came forward. Specifically regarding taking children to washrooms, the court found no reason for the school to implement a "same-sex" policy, as allegations of abuse with the school system had involved alleged offenders of both genders. Thus the plaintiffs could not satisfy the "deliberate indifference" standard.

This decision also is of interest because it discusses whether a "special relationship" exists between a school and students, requiring schools to investigate and take reasonable steps to protect students from sexual abuse by teachers. While there is dicta in *DeShaney,* discussed above, that suggests that children put into a foster home might be considered similar to an incarcerated person, which some courts have read to indicate that children subject to compulsory school attendance are in the same situation, here, the court noted that since *preschool* attendance was not compulsory, no special relationship existed. *But see Doe v. Hillsboro Independent School District,* 113 F.3d 1412 (5th Cir. 1997), where the Fifth Circuit refused to find that compulsory attendance laws create a special relationship between a school and its students.

In *Doe v. Estes,* 926 F. Supp. 979 (D. Nev. 1996), the court found the school district's failure to have a policy and follow it to be fatal. A student was allegedly sexually molested by a teacher. The school district filed a motion for summary judgment, claiming that there was no special relationship between the public school and students that would subject it to Section 1983 liability. The court disagreed, stating that the basis for responsibility was the school district's authority to control and supervise the teacher's behavior, and a finding of a special relationship was not required. Thus, the issue was whether the school district maintained a policy or custom that reflected a deliberate indifference to the plaintiff's constitutional rights. Analyzing what other circuit court decisions have required to prove this standard, the court found that prior to the arrest of the accused teacher, the school district did not have any policy regarding the reporting of suspected incidents of sexual abuse of students, had not trained its employees in recognizing signs of abuse, and had not given its staff guidelines for dealing with suspicions of abuse. Because the danger of students being sexually abused at school was so obvious, the court ruled that the absence of such a policy precluded the grant of summary judgment for the school district.

The school district in *Thrasher v. General Casualty Co. of Wisconsin,* 732 F. Supp. 966 (W.D. Wis. 1990), maintained a "physical force" policy that stated any physical force should be limited to using hands to direct a student toward a location or removing the student from class; should be used without malice or revenge; and should be explained to parents. The student claimed that a teacher threw him against the blackboard when the teacher asked him to remain after class to discuss discipline problems. In denying the claim, the court found the physical force policy was not the "moving force" behind the alleged constitutional violation and because the policy on its face did not condone random violence or violence intended to harm students.[8]

---

8. This case provides a detailed anaysis of case law regarding the elements necessary to establish a policy of deliberate indifference in the sexual abuse area.

Eight students alleged that they were subjected to verbal and physical abuse by an elementary school teacher in *Gonzales v. Brown,* 768 F. Supp. 581 (S.D. Tex. 1991). They claimed that the district was liable under Section 1983 because the district had a policy or custom of retaining teachers who used abusive disciplinary techniques by transferring them within the district instead of firing them, and by discouraging reports of such abuse from teachers. In denying the Section 1983 claim, the court looked to the actual policies proffered by the school district, which showed that termination of employees was in fact approved for physical violence and that only certain types of discipline of students by teachers was allowed. Further, the court found no evidence of a custom of retaining abusive teachers, noting that the transfer of the teacher at issue did not reflect a widespread practice.

The policy established by the school district in *P.H. v. The School District of Kansas City,* 265 F.3d 653 (8th Cir. 2001), was sufficient to avoid liability in a case where a student who had engaged in a two-year sexual relationship with a teacher alleged liability for the school district under Section 1983 for failure to adequately train its employees to report and prevent sexual abuse of students, claiming the policies in place prohibited only unwelcome sexual contact. Analyzing the policy, the court disagreed, finding that the policy defined sexual harassment broadly, encompassing both wanted and unwanted contact, and thus the school district met its obligation to address potential reporting and response to such complaints.

8. Employee Rights

When employers attempt to aggressively enforce a workplace violence policy, they are frequently confronted by federal and state laws that protect employees against discrimination involving mental or emotional conditions that may constitute legally protected disabilities. Under the Americans with Disabilities Act (ADA), 42 U.S.C. Section 12101 *et seq.,* an employer is limited in its ability to screen and reject a potential employee on the suspicion that the individual may become violent because of a mental or emotional impairment. Further, after the employment relationship exists, an employer may have to accommodate a disruptive employee with a mental or emotional disability until such employee engages in conduct that renders him or her "unqualified" to continue to perform the job or that poses a "direct threat" to the safety or health of the employee himself or to other employees. In addition, many state right-to-privacy laws may severely restrict an employer's ability to obtain information about an employee's mental or emotional status and relevant activities outside of the workplace that might be essential in determining whether an employee poses such a risk. For example, many states have laws that prevent employers from taking adverse job actions against employees for engaging in lawful off-duty conduct or using lawful products (smoking, for example), or for engaging in off-premises recreational activities outside of working hours.

D. PREVENTIVE ACTION: WORKPLACE VIOLENCE POLICY

Against this potential liability minefield, an employer must develop an effective written workplace violence policy that must be communicated to all employees if it hopes to have any defense against these potential claims. At a minimum, the written workplace violence prevention policy should include the following elements:

- A stated school administration and board commitment to protecting employees and students against the hazards of workplace violence, including both physical acts and verbal threats;
- A statement that the school district has a "zero-tolerance" policy toward threats or acts of violence and will take appropriate disciplinary action against employees who engage in such conduct;
- Means and methods for employees and students to notify the school district of perceived threats of violent acts in a confidential manner;
- A means to promptly investigate all such threats or violent acts;
- Consistent, firm discipline for violations of the policy;
- Training for administrators, teachers, and employees to identify signs and symptoms of employee behavior that may be predictive of potential violence (erratic behavior toward co-employees and students; employee comments regarding homicide or suicide; provocative communications; disobedience of policies and procedures; presence of alcohol, drugs, or weapons on the worksite; physical evidence of employee abuse of alcohol or drug use, which should be reported to the employer;
- A team of qualified individuals (such as in human resources, risk management. legal, medical, and security areas), either within the

school district or readily available third parties, to respond to a potential or actual incident; and

* An Employee Assistance Plan (EAP) to provide assistance to employees who may be experiencing mental or emotional stress.

E. THREAT ASSESSMENT

In the typical situation, a co-employee or supervisor either observes or learns of questionable, threatening, or outright bizarre employee verbal or physical behavior either on or off the workplace that creates a concern, and sometimes a palpable fear, that the employee is about to engage in some type of activity that may result in injury to the employee him- or herself (suicide) or to other employers (threats, hostile acts). The frightened or concerned co-employee or supervisor brings this information to the employer and asks management to address such problems.

It is hoped the employer has a written workplace violence policy and that managers have been trained to be receptive to receiving and responding to this disturbing information from employees. At this stage, the employer must begin an expedited process to focus on this information and commence the preliminary process of assessing whether there may be a threat, and if so, what response, if any, is necessary or appropriate. This response may include a Fitness for Duty (FFD) evaluation, which is discussed below.

1. Caution

A word of caution is in order before proceeding with this process. Because of the heightened sensitivity in the media to spectacular and tragic workplace violence incidents, many employers feel compelled to engage in a lightning strike, knee-jerk reaction by immediately terminating or imposing significant discipline upon the questionable employee. Such vigilante-like justice may eventually be found to have no foundation when the subsequent management investigation reveals that the conduct or comments were ambiguous or misquoted, or, worse, that the complaints made against the employee were fabricated by other employees for an ulterior purpose. If so, the potential for employment-related litigation is substantial.

2. Fitness for Duty Evaluation Options

Once the employer has received information that an employee has engaged or threatened to engage in physical or verbal conduct that has the
potential to cause physical or emotional harm to co-employees or third
parties, the employer must make a determination as to what action should
be taken. Obviously, if the conduct is sufficiently egregious, there is no
need to consider an FFD evaluation, and termination or other severe discipline will be warranted.

The need for an FFD evaluation typically arises where the employee's
conduct raises the following issues:

- Is the employee mentally and emotionally qualified to continue to
  perform the job?
- Does the employee pose a direct threat to the safety of the employee, a co-employee or a third party, including a student?

The employer confronted with these questions has several potential
options to obtain an FFD evaluation, within limitations, under the following laws:

- Americans with Disabilities Act
- Family and Medical Leave Act
- Federal and State Worker's Compensation Acts

The application, scope, and limitations of these laws are in many aspects both complementary and conflicting, which requires careful analysis
before seeking an FFD evaluation.

F. CONCLUSION

The hazard of workplace violence involves numerous potential liability
issues under federal and state law. If the school district follows the recommendations set out above, it can substantially reduce such liability if an
incident were to occur.

Due Process for Students 7

Edgar H. Bittle
James C. Hanks
Ronald L. Peeler
Andrew J. Bracken

A. INTRODUCTION

The due process clause protects the liberty and property interests of public school students who are disciplined for misconduct.[1] These same due process principles may also be applied

---

1. Goss v. Lopez, 419 U.S. 565, 573–74 (1975). *See also* Paredes v. Curtis, 864 F.2d 426 (6th Cir. 1988); Wise v. Pea Ridge Sch. Dist., 855 F.2d 560 (8th Cir. 1988); Gorman v. University of R.I., 837 F.2d 7 (1st Cir. 1988); Giangrasso v. Kittatinny Regional High Sch. Bd. of Educ., 865 F. Supp. 1133 (D. N.J. 1994); Mifflin County Sch. Dist. v. Stewart, 503 A.2d 1012 (Pa. Cmwlth. 1986).

The protections of the due process clause may also be implicated when a student is excluded from school for reasons other than misconduct. *See, e.g.*, Horton v. Marshall Public Schools, 769 F.2d 1323, 1333 (8th Cir. 1985) (holding that students excluded from school on the basis of ineligibility under state law must be given due process protection); Engele v. Independent Sch. Dist. No. 91 (D. Minn. 1994) (holding that a student could not be removed from school for his own protection following threats from other students without "being afforded some minimum due process protection").

in private institutions.[2] The U.S. Supreme Court also held that a public employee who is entitled under state law to continued employment has a property interest in the employment, which cannot be terminated without due process unless there is just cause for dismissal.[3]

Public school officials must be sensitive to the rights of their employees and students. Administrators have been reprimanded before licensing agencies and professional practice commissions for ignoring these rights.[4] Public school officials have also incurred financial liability for depriving employees and students of their rights guaranteed by the Constitution or by statute.[5] Because the courts and agencies have imposed these sanctions, school officials must use care to conduct administrative proceedings that satisfy the due process requirements of the Constitution.

The procedures that due process may require depend upon the action contemplated as well as the nature of the protected interest. There is no rigid standard of due process. The U.S. Supreme Court has stated that

---

2. It is important to note the general rule, however, that a student in a private school has no constitutional right to due process because no state action is involved. A student's rights in the private school context are based on a contractual relationship with the school. Thus, a student undergoing a discipline procedure at a private school is entitled only to the procedural safeguards the school provides. *See* Warren v. Drake Univ., 886 F.2d 200, 202 (8th Cir. 1989); Corso v. Creighton Univ., 731 F.2d 529, 533 (8th Cir. 1984); Boehn v. University of Pa. Sch. of Veterinary Med., 573 A.2d 575, 579 (Pa. Super. Ct. 1990). The majority rule is that a private school must substantially comply with the procedures it has established prior to the suspension or expulsion of a student. Some courts, however, have granted judicial review of rules established by private schools and require that those rules comport with basic rules of due process and fundamental fairness. Boehm v. University of Pa. Sch. of Veterinary Med., 573 A.2d at 580 (citing Clayron v. Trustees of Princeton Univ., 608 F. Supp. 413 (D. N.J. 1985) (holding that a student subjected to a disciplinary hearing for cheating has a judicially protectable interest in undergoing fundamentally fair proceedings)).

3. *See* Cleveland Bd. of Educ. v. Loudermill, 470 U.S. 532, 533 (1985). *See also* Wallace v. Tilley, 41 F.3d 296 (7th Cir. 1994); Winegar v. Des Moines Indep. Cmty. Sch. Dist., 20 F.3d 895 (8th Cir. 1994), *cert. denied*, 115 S. Ct. 426 (1994); Brown v. Georgia Dep't of Revenue, 881 F.2d 1018 (11th Cir. 1989).

4. Kempe v. Raisch & Rockwell, Iowa Professional Teaching Practices Comm'n, Hearing Dec. No. 79-5 (July 1979).

5. Hafer v. Melo, 502 U.S. 21 (1991); State of Maine v. Thiboutot, 448 U.S. 1 (1980); Owen v. City of Independence, 445 U.S. 622 (1980), *reh'g denied*, 446 U.S. 993 (1980); Monell v. Department of Social Servs., 436 U.S. 658 (1978); Carey v. Piphus, 435 U.S. 247 (1978); Wood v. Strickland, 420 U.S. 308 (1975); Blessum v. Howard County Bd. of Supervisors, 295 N.W.2d 836 (Iowa 1980).

unlike some legal rules, due process "is not a technical concept[] with a fixed content unrelated to time, place, and circumstances."[6] The clear rule is that "[t]he minimum procedural requirements necessary to satisfy due process depend upon the circumstances and the interests of the parties involved."[7] Clearly, *Goss v. Lopez*, the seminal case on student due process, suggests this flexible standard.[8]

The courts have used a balancing test to determine whether a trial procedure must be used or a more informal procedure may be followed. The courts have balanced the party's need for procedural protection against the burden on the government in providing a hearing.[9]

In *Goss v. Lopez*, the U.S. Supreme Court ruled that due process did not require confrontation and cross-examination for suspending a student for up to 10 days; however, minimal due process—notice and an opportunity to be heard—was required.[10] The Court noted that sanctions imposed on a student in addition to a 10-day suspension may in some instances necessitate a higher level of procedural protections.[11] In *Donovan v. Ritchie*,[12] the First Circuit held that a school's ban on participation in inter-

---

6. Cafeteria & Restaurant Workers Union, Local 473 v. AFL-CIO, 367 U.S. at 895 (citing Joint Anti-Fascist Refugee Committee v. McGrath, 341 U.S. 123, 162-63 (1951) (Frankfurter, J., concurring).

7. Cafeteria & Restaurant Workers Union Local 473, AFL-CIO v. McElroy, 367 U.S. 886, 895 (1961); Cliff v. Board of Sch. Comm'rs, 42 F.3d 403 (7th Cir. 1994); Winegar v. Des Moines Indep. Cmty. Sch. Dist., 20 F.3d 895 (8th Cir. 1994), *cert. denied*, 115 S. Ct. 426 (1994); Vukadinovich v. Board of Sch. Trustees of Mich. City Area Sch., 978 F.2d 403 (6th Cir. 1992), *cert. denied*, 114 S. Ct. 133 (1993); Allen v. Denver Pub. Sch. Bd., 928 F.2d 978 (10th Cir. 1991); Smith v. Town of Eaton, 910 F.2d 1469 (7th Cir. 1990), *cert. denied*, 499 U.S. 962 (1991); Ferguson v. Thomas, 430 F.2d 852, 856 (5th Cir. 1970); Dixon v. Alabama State Bd. of Educ. 294 F.2d 150, 155 (5th Cir. 1961); Engele v. Independent Sch. Dist. No. 91, 846 F. Supp. 760 (D. Minn. 1994); Booher v. Hogans, 468 F. Supp. 28, 32, *aff'd without opinion*, 588 F.2d 830 (6th Cir. 1978); Graham v. Knutzen, 351 F. Supp 642, 664 (D. Neb. 1972); *In re Monica Schnoor,* 1 D.P.I. App. Dec. 136 (Iowa 1977).

8. Goss v. Lopez, 419 U.S. 568, 578 (1975).

9. *See* Mathews v. Eldridge, 424 U.S. 319, 355 (1976). The balancing test stated in *Mathews* considers three factors: the private interest that will be affected by the official action, the risk of erroneous deprivation of the private interest through the procedures used and the value of additional safeguards, and the fiscal and administrative burdens on the governmental unit that additional procedures would involve. *Id.*

10. Goss v. Lopez, 419 U.S. 565, 581 (1975).

11. *See id.* at 584.

12. Donovan v. Ritchie, 68 F.3d 14 (1st Cir. 1995).

scholastic athletics and other school activities in addition to a 10-day suspension did not require additional procedures or formalities.[13] In the case of suspensions longer than 10 days, more stringent procedural protections may be required.[14] In *Ingraham v. Wright*, a corporal punishment case, the Court concluded that the cost of providing a full evidentiary hearing outweighed the benefit, noting that common law protects against the abuse of the privilege of corporal punishment.[15] It appears that discipline or dismissal for academic reasons may require even less procedural protection than that mandated for disciplinary problems by *Goss v. Lopez*. In *Board of Curators v. Horowitz*,[16] a medical student sued after being dismissed from the university's program, alleging the school denied her due process.[17] The Court emphasized the need for flexibility regarding due process procedures, stating that there is a "significant difference between the failure of a student to meet academic standards and the violation by a student of valid rules of conduct. This difference calls for far less stringent procedural requirements in the case of an academic dismissal."[18] The Court found that more formal trial-like procedures were not necessary.[19]

With regard to the procedures necessary to satisfy due process, Davis and Pierce, in the *Administrative Law Treatise*, state:

> The [Supreme] Court would do well to apply the principles and reasoning of *Goss* to agency adjudications on a near universal basis. Agencies rarely take actions whose adverse effects on an indi-

---

13. *Id.* at 18. "The mere fact that other sanctions are added to a short suspension does not trigger a requirement for a more formal set of procedures." *Id.* (citing Goss v. Lopez, 419 U.S. at 569 n.4); *see also* Palmer v. Merluzzi, 868 F.2d 90, 95–96 (3d Cir. 1989) (holding that a 60-day athletic suspension in addition to a 10-day academic suspension did not necessitate further procedural protections).

14. *See, e.g.*, Dixon v. Alabama State Bd. of Educ., 294 F.2d 150, 158–59 (5th Cir.), *cert. denied*, 368 U.S. 930 (1961) (holding that due process required notice and "the rudiments of an adversary proceeding" prior to expulsion).

15. Ingraham v. Wright, 430 U.S. 651, 674–75 (1977). *See also* Wise v. Pea Ridge Sch. Dist., 855 F.2d 560–64, (8th Cir. 1988) (holding that a student's substantive due process rights were not violated by the infliction of corporal punishment).

16. Board of Curators of the Univ. of Mo. v. Horowitz, 435 U.S. 78 (1978).

17. *Id.* at 80–81.

18. *Id.* at 86. The Court recognized that the dismissal in this case was far more serious than the 10-day suspension in Goss. *Id.* n.3. However, the Court concluded that the severity of the deprivation, when balanced with the historically supported interest of schools in preserving academic standards, did not necessitate further procedural protections. *Id.*

19. *Id.* at 85.

vidual are so trivial that the action should be taken without notice and an opportunity for an informal hearing. The few minutes required to provide the kind of hearing described in *Goss* imposes little burden on an agency relative to its benefits in the form of enhanced fairness and accuracy. . . .

Conversely, agencies rarely take actions whose effects on an individual are so devastating that the agency should be compelled to incur the extreme costs of a trial-type hearing. . . .

The Court [should] focus its attention on the nature of the informal hearing appropriate to varying decision-making contexts.[20]

B. PROTECTED INTERESTS

The liberty interests protected by due process include preserving one's good name, reputation, honor, or integrity.[21] Constitutionally protected property interests extend beyond tangible property and include government entitlements,[22] the right to a public education,[23] and, under certain circumstances, the right to continued employment.[24]

---

20. 2 KENNETH C. DAVIS & RICHARD J. PIERCE, JR., ADMINISTRATIVE LAW TREATISE § 9.3, at 17 (3d ed.1994).

21. *See* Board of Regents v. Roth, 408 U.S. 564, 573 (1972); Wallace v. Tilley, 41 F.3d 296 (7th Cir. 1994); Winegar v. Des Moines Ind. Cmty. Sch. Dist., 20 F.3d 895 (8th Cir. 1994), *cert. denied*, 115 S. Ct. 426 (1994); Warrent v. National Ass'n of Secondary Sch. Principals, 375 F. Supp. 1043, 1048 (N.D. Tex. 1974).

22. *E.g.,* Goldberg v. Kelly, 397 U.S. 254, 262 n.8 (1970).

23. Goss v. Lopez, 419 U.S. 565, 574 (1975). *See* C.B. v. Driscoll, 82 F.3d 383, 387 (11th Cir. 1996); Gorman v. University of R.I., 837 F.2d 7–12 (1st Cir. 1988); Engele v. Independent Sch. Dist. No. 91, 846 F. Supp. 760–65 (D. Minn. 1994). *But see* Dillingham v. University of Colo., Bd. of Regents, 790 P.2d 851, 854 (Colo. App. 1989) (finding the determination to dismiss a student was for academic reasons not well-suited for judicial or administrative decision making, so the due process clause did not require a formal hearing).

24. Cleveland Bd. of Educ. v. Loudermill, 470 U.S. 532, 533 (1985). *See generally* Covert & Chidester, *Procedural Due Process for School Administrators and School Board Members*, 1 NSBA SCH. L. IN REV., 88–113 (1985); Cliff v. Board of Sch. Comm'rs of City of Indianapolis, 42 F.3d 403 (7th Cir. 1994); Williams v. Texas Tech. Univ. Health Sciences Ctr., 6 F.3d 290 (5th Cir. 1993), *cert. denied*, 114 S. Ct. 1301 (1994); Allen v. Denver Public Sch. Bd., 928 F.2d 978 (10th Cir. 1991); Brown v. Georgia Dep't of Revenue, 881 F.2d 1018 (11th Cir. 1989); Tolson v. Chariton Sch. Dist., 703 F. Supp. 766 (E.D. Ark. 1988); Borschel v. City of Perry, 512 N.W.2d 565 (Iowa 1994). *But see* Mitchell v. Glover, 996 F.2d 164 (7th Cir. 1993) (holding that an at-will government employee had no property interest in employment).

The courts have also defined "property" to include a student's right to a public education. In *Goss v. Lopez*, the Court held that a student has a property right to a public education when state law provides for free education and compulsory attendance.[25] This property interest was discussed in *C.B. v. Driscoll*,[26] in which a student alleged that her suspension from school following an altercation with another student constituted a violation of her substantive due process rights.[27] The Eleventh Circuit found this argument to be without merit. The Court noted that the right to attend a public school is a state-created right, not a fundamental right for the purposes of substantive due process.[28] Because the right to attend school is only a state-created right, that right can be abridged as long as school officials follow proper procedural protections in doing so.[29] Furthermore, the Court held that a student's liberty interests were involved when a student was excluded from school because the exclusion could harm the student's reputation and cause adverse consequences after graduation.[30] Because of the student's property interest in education and liberty interest in reputation, a student may not be excluded from school, by suspension or expulsion, without due process of law.[31]

Courts differ on whether a student has a property interest in participation in extracurricular activities, such as athletics. Many courts refuse to characterize such participation as a property interest, instead labeling it a privilege.[32] Other courts, however, have recognized that exclusion from

25. Goss v. Lopez, 419 U.S. 565, 572–74 (1975).

26. C.B. v. Driscoll, 82 F.3d 383 (11th Cir. 1996).

27. *Id.* at 387.

28. *Id.* (citing Plyler v. Doe, 457 U.S. 202, 221 (1982) (noting that although societally important, "[p]ublic education is not a 'right' granted to individuals by the Constitution")).

29. *Id.*

30. *Id.* at 574–75.

31. *Id. See* Honig v. Doe, 484 U.S. 305 (1988); Palmer v. Merluzzi, 868 F.2d 90 (3d Cir. 1989); Paredes v. Curtis, 864 F.2d 426 (6th Cir. 1988); Gorman v. University of R.I., 837 F.2d 7 (1st Cir. 1988); Engele v. Independent Sch. Dist. No. 91, 846 F. Supp. 760 (D. Minn. 1994). *Cf.* Killion v. Burl, 860 F.2d 306 (8th Cir. 1988) (finding no liberty or property interest in promotion from first to second grade); Mifflin County Sch. Dist. v. Stewart, 503 A.2d (Pa. Cmwlth. 1986) (finding no property interest in attendance at graduation ceremonies).

32. *See* Herbert v. Ventetuola, 638 F.2d 5, 6 (1st Cir. 1981) (exclusion from participation in hockey); Pegram v. Nelson, 469 F. Supp. 1134, 1139 (M.D.N.C. 1979) (exclusion from track); Fowler v. Williamson, 448 F. Supp. 497, 502 (W.D.N.C. 1978) (exclusion from graduation ceremony). *See, e.g.,* Albach v. Odle, 531 F.2d 983, 984–

the activities, which are an integral part of the education process, can be a sufficient deprivation to implicate due process.[33] Courts similarly have split on whether the exclusion would impinge upon the student's liberty interests.[34] Due to the uncertainty of the law in this area, prudent school officials should follow some measure of due process procedure in excluding a student from extracurricular activities.

C. NECESSITY FOR POLICIES, RULES, AND REGULATIONS

Due process clearly requires that a person be given notice and an opportunity to be heard before being deprived of liberty or property. Another important element of due process is the existence of preannounced rules. Through preannounced rules, students are put on notice that their actions may be the basis for disciplinary action.

Preannounced rules should be the first step in any procedural due process system. The rules must be sufficiently definite to provide prior notice to students, employees, and others that certain standards of conduct, behavior, and performance are expected, and failure to comply with those standards may result in sanctions, discipline, or discharge. No discipline can be imposed except on the basis of substantial evidence of violation of one or more specific rules or policies.[35]

---

85 (10th Cir. 1976); Dallam v. Cumberland Valley Sch. Dist., 391 F. Supp. 358, 361 (M.D. Pa. 1975); Bradstreet v. Sobol, 630 N.Y.S.2d 486 (Supp. 1995); Caso v. New York State Pub. High Sch. Athletic Ass'n, 434 N.Y.S.2d 60 (App. Div. 1980); Menke v. Ohio High Sch. Athletic Ass'n, 441 N.E.2d 620, 624 (Ohio Ct. App. 1981); Whipple v. Oregon Sch. Activities Ass'n, 629 P.2d 384 (Or. Ct. App. 1981); Adamek v. Pennsylvania Interscholastic Athletic Ass'n, 426 A.2d 1206, 1207–08 (Pa. Commw. Ct. 1981); Eanes Indep. Sch. Dist. v. Logue, 712 S.W.2d 741 (Tex. 1986); Spring Branch Ind. Sch. Dist. v. Stamos, 695 S.W.2d 556, 561 (Tex. 1985), *appeal dismissed*, 475 U.S. 1001 (1986).

33. *See* Palmer v. Merluzzi, 868 F.2d 90, 95–96 (3d Cir. 1989); Davis v. Central Dauphin Sch. Dist., 466 F. Supp. 1259, 1265 (M.D. Pa. 1979); Regents of the Univ. of Minn. v. NCAA, 422 F. Supp. 1158, 1161 (D. Minn. 1976), *rev'd on other grounds*, 560 F.2d 352 (8th Cir. 1977).

34. *Compare* Fowler v. Williamson, 448 F. Supp. 497, 501-02 (W.D.N.C. 1978) (no liberty interest) *with* Warren v. National Ass'n of Secondary Sch. Principals, 375 F. Supp. 1043, 1048 (N.D. Tex. 1974) (upholding liberty interest).

35. Pesce v. J. Sterling Morton High Sch., 830 F.2d 789 (7th Cir. 1987); Sullivan v. Houston Ind. Sch. Dist., 307 F. Supp. 1328, 1346 (S.D. Tex. 1969), *cert. denied*, 414 U.S. 1032 (1973); Texarkana Indep. Sch. Dist. v. Lewis, 470 S.W.2d 727, 737-38 (Tex. 1971).

In reviewing school disciplinary actions, courts have generally declined to review the substance of rules. The U.S. Supreme Court, in *Wood v. Strickland*, said:

> It is not the role of the federal courts to set aside decisions of school administrators which the court may view as lacking a basis in wisdom or compassion. . . . [The Civil Rights Statute] does not extend the right to relitigate in federal court evidentiary questions arising in school disciplinary proceedings *or the proper construction of school regulations.*[36]

Courts generally look at the substance of rules only to determine if the district had authority to promulgate the rule and to examine the reasonableness of the rule. For example, in *Caldwell v. Cannady,*[37] the court upheld the validity of a rule that any student found to possess drugs would automatically be expelled from school. Students who were expelled challenged the rule, which the court upheld, saying:

> It is obvious to this court that the possession, or certainly the use, of drugs by a student could have an adverse effect on the quality of the educational environment in a school at any level, but particularly so when children high school age or younger are involved. The court therefore holds that the enactment of a policy which prohibits student possession of dangerous drugs . . . is a reasonable exercise of the power vested in this local school board.[38]

Courts generally place the burden of proving the unreasonableness of a rule upon the person challenging the rule. School regulations and rules are presumed to be valid unless proved otherwise. For a court to find a rule unreasonable, the challenger must show that the rule does not sufficiently relate to the governance of the school or is arbitrary, unreasonable, discriminatory, or constitutionally invalid.

36. Wood v. Strickland, 420 U.S. 308, 326 (1975) (emphasis added), *reh'g denied,* 421 U.S. 921 (1975).
37. Caldwell v. Cannady, 340 F. Supp. 835 (N.D. Tex. 1972).
38. *Id.* at 838.
39. Rose v. Locke, 423 U.S. 48 (1975).

Rules must be drafted so individuals can clearly understand what conduct is prohibited so they can conform their conduct to the rules. In *Rose v. Locke,*[39] the U.S. Supreme Court reviewed the concept of voiding a statute because it was vague and therefore unconstitutional. While the case dealt with a challenge to a criminal statute, the language is pertinent to school regulations. The Court said:

> It is settled that the fair-warning requirement embodied in the Due Process Clause prohibits the States from holding an individual "criminally responsible for conduct which he could not reasonably understand to be proscribed." But this prohibition against excessive vagueness does not invalidate every statute which a reviewing court believes could have been drafted with greater precision. Many statutes will have some inherent vagueness, for "[i]n most English words and phrases there lurk uncertainties." Even trained lawyers may find it necessary to consult legal dictionaries, treatises, and judicial opinions before they may say with any certainty what some statutes may compel or forbid. . . . All the Due Process Clause requires is that the law give sufficient warning that men may conduct themselves so as to avoid that which is forbidden.[40]

Several student discipline cases have involved the question of whether the "void for vagueness" doctrine applies to student disciplinary regulations. Courts have generally held that while student disciplinary regulations must be sufficiently specific, they need not be as specific as criminal statutes.

The Court considered the "void for vagueness" doctrine as applied to student disciplinary regulations in *Bethel School District v. Fraser.*[41] In *Bethel*, the Court held that a student's First Amendment right to freedom of speech does not prevent school officials from suspending a student for delivering an offensively lewd and indecent speech to the student body.[42] Fraser, the student, also challenged his suspension because the disciplinary rule under which he was punished was unconstitutionally vague and overbroad. The rule provided that a student could be disciplined for disruptive conduct, which included "the use of obscene, profane language or

---

40. *Id.* at 49–50.
41. Bethel Sch. Dist. v. Fraser, 478 U.S. 675 (1986).
42. *Id.* at 686.

gestures."[43] The Supreme Court held Fraser's argument to be without merit. The Court, in holding that the rule gave Fraser adequate warning, stated:

> We have recognized that "maintaining security and order in the schools requires a certain degree of flexibility in school discipline procedures, and we have respected the value of preserving the informality of the student-teacher relationship." (citation omitted) *Given the school's need to be able to impose disciplinary sanctions for a wide range of unanticipated conduct disruptive of the educational process, the school rules need not be as detailed as a criminal code which imposes criminal sanctions.*[44]

In the case of *Alex v. Allen,*[45] a federal district court held the terms "flagrant disregard of teachers," "loitering," and "rowdy behavior" were not so vague as to violate constitutional standards. The court noted that while these terms might not meet the constitutional requirements of criminal statutes, "a looser standard of constitutional review of high school regulations is appropriate because of the greater flexibility possessed by the state to regulate the conduct of children as opposed to adults."[46]

In the case of *Sullivan v. Houston Independent School District,*[47] the court also held the "void for vagueness" doctrine applicable in some measure to school regulations but not to the extent it would apply to criminal statutes. The court said:

---

43. *Id.* at 693 (Stevens, J., dissenting).

44. *Id.* at 686 (emphasis added).

45. Alex v. Allen, 409 F. Supp. 379 (W.D. Pa. 1976).

46. *Id.* at 384. *See* Borger v. Bisciglia, 888 F. Supp. 97 (E.D. Wis. 1995). In *Berger*, the court considered the school board's use of the rating system of the Motion Picture Association of America in determining what films would be allowed as part of the school curriculum. *Id.* at 98. Under the policy, films with an MPAA rating of R, N17, or X were not to be shown to students. *Id.* The plaintiffs argued that the use of the MPAA rating system to determine use of a film violated the First Amendment. *Id.* at 100. The court noted that while such a rating system could not be used to determine whether a film receives constitutional protection, the school board could utilize the rating system as a "filter of films." *Id.* Because schools and classrooms are nonpublic forums, "school boards have more discretion to censor within that environment." *Id.* The school board established that relying on the rating system was a reasonable way of determining what movies were appropriate. *Id.* at 100–01.

47. Sullivan v. Houston Indep. Sch. Dist., 307 F. Supp. 1328 (S.D. Tex. 1969), *cert. denied*, 414 U.S. 1032 (1973).

[I]n this court's judgment, these fundamental concepts of constitutional law must be applied "in some measure" even to high schools. The "measure" should reach only to rules the violation of which could result in expulsion or suspension for a substantial period of time. When faced with such drastic consequences, a high school student has no less a right to a clear, specific normative statement which does not infringe on free expression than does a university student or possibly even the accused in a criminal case. If the punishment could be this severe, there is no question but that a high school student as well as university student might well suffer more injury than one convicted of a criminal offense. *School rules probably do not need to be as narrow as criminal statutes, but if school officials contemplate severe punishment they must do so on the basis of a rule which is drawn so as to reasonably inform the student what specific conduct is proscribed.* Basic notions of justice and fair play require that no person shall be made to suffer for a breach unless standards of behavior have first been announced. . . .[48]

The "void for vagueness" doctrine as it relates to a rule should not be confused with the required specificity in giving reasons for the suspension or expulsion of a student.

The courts have carefully scrutinized school districts' regulations that touch upon First Amendment rights to free speech and association. Regulations that impermissibly limit protected speech are said to be "overbroad." To avoid a challenge based upon overbreadth, policies and regulations addressing the distribution of written material and with restrictions of speech must be clearly drawn and related to some legitimate educational interest.

The U.S. Supreme Court, in *Hazelwood School District v. Kuhlmeier*,[49] determined that school authorities may regulate student expression, even though students in public schools do not shed their First Amendment rights at the schoolhouse door. In *Hazelwood*, the principal decided to remove two pages from the student newspaper because the articles violated the privacy rights of pregnant students.

The Court that found the school newspaper published by journalism students could not be characterized as a "public forum." As a result, school

---

48. *Id*. at 1344–45 (emphasis added).
49. Hazelwood Sch. Dist. v. Kuhlmeier, 484 U.S. 260 (1988).

officials retained the right to impose reasonable restrictions on speech that went into the newspaper, where students publishing the newspaper received grades and academic credit for the performance, and the journalism teacher retained final authority over almost every aspect of production and publication. Because the newspaper was a school-sponsored publication, the school had authority to censor it as long as the officials' actions were reasonably related to legitimate educational concerns.[50]

Since the Court's *Hazelwood* decision, few real restrictions exist on a school official's right to censor student expression that occurs during the course of a school-sponsored activity, because the school official will almost always be able to show that the censorship was reasonably related to some legitimate educational concern.[51] Consequently, educators are entitled to exercise greater control over school-sponsored expression than over students' personal speech to ensure that the students learn whatever lessons the activity is designed to teach.[52]

D. INVESTIGATION

The first step in any due process hearing is determining whether misconduct or activity has occurred that warrants action by the governmental body. To accomplish this, a thorough investigation of the facts is mandated.

Often misconduct will be observed by the complaining school employee or individual. In this circumstance, interviews of the witnesses to the incident should be sufficient. However, a situation may arise during the investigation in which a school official desires to conduct a search of the individual, his locker or other possessions. For example, an official may want to search a student to confirm a reliable report that the student is in possession of contraband items, such as tobacco, drugs, or weapons. In conducting this search, the official must take care not to violate the

---

50. *Id.* Some states, however, have enacted statutes to limit the broad authority given to school officials in the *Hazelwood* case. *E.g.*, Iowa Code § 280.22 (1995).

51. *See, e.g.*, Borger v. Bisciglia, 888 F. Supp. 97 (E.D. Wis. 1995). In *Borger*, the court upheld the school district's policy of refusing to show "R" rated movies as part of the curriculum. *Id.* at 101. According to the court, the district's refusal to show an award-winning historical film that was "R" rated was reasonably related to legitimate pedagogical concerns of not subjecting students to too much violence, nudity or "hard" language. *Id.* at 100.

52. *Id.*

individual's Fourth Amendment right to freedom from unreasonable search and seizure.

The Fourth Amendment, applicable to the states through the Fourteenth Amendment, protects the privacy of individuals from invasion by unreasonable government searches of the person and those places and things in which the person has a reasonable expectation of privacy.[53] These amendments do not prohibit all investigatory searches—only those that are unreasonable. Whether the individual has a reasonable expectation of privacy and whether the intrusion is reasonable are determined by balancing the interests of the government against the privacy interests of the individual.[54]

In determining the reasonableness of a search, courts have balanced the following factors: the intrusiveness of the search;[55] the public interest in conducting the search (for example, the threat to public and employee safety);[56] and the individual's interest in being free from unreasonable search and seizure.[57] Random or blanket searches of all employees are generally held to be unreasonable unless such searches are necessary for safety or

---

53. Terry v. Ohio, 392 U.S. 1, 9 (1969); *see also* Minnesota v. Olson, 495 U.S. 91 (1990) (upholding a subjective expectation of privacy under the Fourth Amendment if society is prepared to recognize it as "reasonable"); Horton v. California, 496 U.S. 128 (1990) (finding all searches conducted outside the judicial process per se unreasonable, subject to established exceptions).

54. United States v. Martinez-Fuerte, 428 U.S. 543, 555 (1976).

55. *Compare* Tucker v. Dickey, 613 F. Supp. 1124 (W.D. Wis. 1985) (finding urinalysis is as intrusive as a body cavity search) *with* Fraternal Order of Police v. City of Newark, No. L-095001-85 (Essex. County Sup. Ct. March 20, 1986) (holding the bodily intrusion of urinalysis minimal when balanced against the public interest in the proper enforcement of narcotics statutes) *and* Skinner v. Railway Labor Executives Ass'n, 489 U.S. 602 (1989) (finding breath, blood, and urine testing not so intrusive as to be unreasonable in railroad industry).

56. *See* Division 241, Amalgamated Transit Union v. Suscy, 538 F.2d 1264 (7th Cir. 1976) (determining public interest in safety of mass transit riders outweighs the interest of a driver who is reasonably suspected of intoxication or drug use); Allen v. City of Marietta, 601 F. Supp. 482 (N.D. Ga. 1985) (upholding policy of requiring urinalysis of electrical employees reasonably suspected of drug use); Turner v. Fraternal Order of Police, 500 A.2d 1005 (D.C. 1985) (supporting drug testing of police officers suspected of drug use because of interest in public safety).

57. *See* McDonell v. Hunter, 809 F.2d 1302 (8th Cir. 1987) (conducting drug test as a part of routine physical does not violate employee's Fourth Amendment rights); Seelig v. McMickens, No. 14285/86 (N.Y. Sup. Ct. July 29, 1986) (finding drug tests could be performed as part of required periodic physical).

another important governmental interest.[58] Rather, a search should be based upon a reasonable suspicion that the employee has violated a school rule or law, and that the search will yield evidence of this violation.[59]

The U.S. Supreme Court addressed the student search issue in the landmark decision of *New Jersey v. T.L.O.*,[60] in which the Court held that the Fourth Amendment protections applied to searches conducted by school officials.[61] The Court further held that a school official could conduct a warrantless[62] search of a student as long as the search was reasonable.[63] The Court set forth a twofold analysis for determining the reasonableness of the search.

---

58. *Compare* Skinner v. Railway Labor Executives' Ass'n, 489 U.S. 602 (1989) (finding individualized suspicion to conduct drug tests not required because of governmental interest involved and pervasive request of industry) *and* National Treasury Employees Union v. Von Raab, 489 U.S. 656 (1989) (upholding U.S. Custom Services' suspicionless drug testing of employees applying for promotion to positions involving interdiction of illegal drugs or requiring them to carry firearms) *with* Capua v. City of Plainfield, 643 F. Supp. 1507 (D. N.J. 1986) (holding firefighters cannot be forced to submit to urine tests without reasonable individualized suspicion of drug use) *and* Patchague-Medford Congress of Teachers v. Board of Educ., 505 N.Y.S.2d 888 (N.Y. App. Div. 1986), *aff'd*, 510 N.E. 2d 325 (N.Y. 1987) (administering drug tests can only be done on reasonable suspicion that individual tested has used drugs).

59. *See supra* note 7.

60. New Jersey v. T.L.O., 469 U.S. 325 (1985).

61. *Id.* at 335–37. Prior to the Court's decision in *T.L.O.*, some courts had "concluded that school officials [were] exempt from the dictates of the Fourth Amendment." *Id.* at 336. This exemption was based on the "special nature" of school officials' authority over schoolchildren. *See, e.g.*, RCM v. State, 660 S.W.2d 552 (Tex. App. 1983). According to the court in *R.C.M.*, teachers and school administrators act in loco parentis in their association with students; thus, their authority is that of parents, not the state, and therefore should not be subject to Fourth Amendment strictures. *Id.* The Court noted in *T.L.O.* that other constitutional protections had been applied to the actions of school officials in their capacity as state actors and saw no reason for distinguishing the Fourth Amendment. New Jersey v. T.L.O., 469 U.S. at 336 (citing Tinker v. Des Moines Indep. Cmty. Sch. Dist., 393 U.S. 503 (1969) (First Amendment); Goss v. Lopez, 419 U.S. 565 (1975) (Due Process Clause of the Fourteenth Amendment)).

62. New Jersey v. T.L.O., 469 U.S. 325, 340 (1985). The Court noted that "[t]he warrant requirement . . . is unsuited to the school environment: requiring a teacher to obtain a warrant . . . would unduly interfere with the maintenance of the swift and informal disciplinary procedures needed in the schools." *Id.*

63. The Court noted that most searches require "probable cause" that a violation of the law has occurred in order to justify the search. *Id.* However, the Court also noted that a reasonableness standard is proper when "a careful balancing of governmental and private interests suggests that the public interest is best served" by such a standard.

First, the search must be justified at its inception;[64] it cannot be legitimized by what is found. A search of a student is justified at its inception "when there are reasonable grounds for suspecting that the search will turn up evidence that the student has violated or is violating either the law or the rules of the school."[65] The factors that should be taken into account in determining whether a search is justified at its inception are: the probative value and reliability of the information used as justification for the search; the child's age, history, and school record; the prevalence and seriousness of the problem in the school to which the search is directed; and the exigency of the situation requiring the search without delay.[66]

Second, the search as actually conducted must be reasonably related in scope to the circumstances that justified the search in the first place.[67] A search is permissible in its scope when the techniques used are "reasonably related to the objectives of the search" and are "not excessively intrusive in light of the age and sex of the student and the nature of the infraction."[68] Thus, if a school official suspects that a student has a knife in his or her possession, the requirements for a reasonable search may be less stringent than if the student is suspected of possessing a stolen item.

Since the Supreme Court's decision in *New Jersey v. T.L.O.*, the circuit courts have had many occasions in which to interpret and apply the test established by the Court. In *Cornfield v. Consolidated High School District No. 230*,[69] the Seventh Circuit found that a strip search of a male high school student who was suspected of having drugs in the crotch of his pants did not violate the student's rights. In applying the first prong of the *T.L.O.* test, the Court noted that an administrator does not have the "right to search a student who merely acts in a way that creates reasonable suspicion that the student has violated *some* regulation or law."[70] A search is

---

Id. at 341. The Court balanced the privacy interests of students against the need for school officials to maintain order, and concluded that the Fourth Amendment did not mandate strict adherence with the probable cause requirement under such circumstances. *Id.*

64. *Id.* (citing Terry v. Ohio, 392 U.S. 1, 20 (1967)).

65. *Id.* at 342.

66. *See* JOHN H. DISE, ET AL., SEARCHES OF STUDENTS, LOCKERS AND AUTOMOBILES § 1.1, at 11 (1994).

67. *Id.* at 341 (citing Terry v. Ohio, 392 U.S. at 20).

68. *Id.* at 342.

69. Cornfield v. Consolidated High Sch. Dist. No. 230, 991 F.2d 1316 (7th Cir. 1993).

70. *Id.* at 1320.

authorized "only if the student's conduct creates a reasonable suspicion that a *particular* regulation or law has been violated."[71] The court found that the administrators did have sufficient cause to believe a particular law or regulations had been broken by the plaintiff. As to the second prong of the test, the court concluded that the strip search was reasonable under the circumstances. While noting that the impact of a strip search on a 16-year-old boy could be substantial, the court thought it to be the least intrusive way, when compared to a pat-down search, to confirm or deny their suspicions.[72] The two administrators present during the search were both male, the search was conducted in the boys' locker room, and the boy was never physically touched. The fact that no drugs or other contraband were found, according to the court, did not render the search unreasonable.[73]

The test set forth in *New Jersey v. T.L.O.* is similar to the "reasonable suspicion" standard that previously had been applied by many courts.[74] Lower court decisions have suggested that searches based on a generalized suspicion, and not on a suspicion particularized for each search, are not constitutionally permissible.[75] In contrast, the Supreme Court recently

---

71. *Id.* (emphasis added)

72. *Id.* at 1323.

73. *Id.*

74. *See, e.g.,* Tarter v. Raybuck, 742 F.2d 977 (6th Cir. 1984), *cert. denied,* 470 U.S. 1051 (1985); Bilbrey v. Brown, 738 F.2d 1462 (9th Cir. 1984); Horton v. Goose Creek Indep. Sch. Dist., 690 F.2d 470 (5th Cir. 1982), *cert. denied,* 463 U.S. 1207 (1983); Bellnier v. Lund, 438 F. Supp. 47 (N.D.N.Y. 1977); M. v. Board of Educ. Ball-Chatham Cmty. Unit Sch. Dist., 429 F. Supp. 288 (S.D. Ill. 1977); *In re W.,* 105 Cal. Rptr. 775 (Ct. App. 1973); State v. Baccino, 282 A.2d 869 (Del. Super. Ct. 1971); State v. D.T.W., 425 So. 2d 1383 (Fla. Dist. Ct. App. 1983); State v. Young, 216 S.E.2d 586 (Ga. 1975); *In re J.A.,* 406 N.E.2d 958 (Ill. App. Ct. 1980); People v. Ward, 233 N.W.2d 180 (Mich. Ct. App. 1975); Doe v. State, 540 P.2d 827 (N.M. Ct. App. 1975); People v. D., 315 N.E.2d 466 (N.Y. 1974); State v. McKinnon, 558 P.2d 781 (Wash. 1977); *In re L.L.,* 280 N.W.2d 343 (Wis. Ct. App. 1979).

75. *See* Edwards v. Rees, 883 F.2d 882 (10th Cir. 1989); Cason v. Cook, 810 F.2d 188 (8th Cir. 1987), *cert. denied,* 482 U.S. 930 (1987); Bellnier v. Lund, 438 F. Supp. 47, 54 (N.D.N.Y. 1977); Kuehn v. Renton Sch. Dist., 694 P.2d 1078, 1081 (Wash. 1985). The Court in *New Jersey v. T.L.O.* did not decide whether individualized suspicion is an essential element of the reasonableness standard. *New Jersey v. T.L.O.,* 469 U.S. at 342 n.8. The Court noted that in contexts other than a school situation, it has held that although "some quantum of individualized suspicion is usually a prerequisite to a constitutional search or seizure, . . . the Fourth Amendment imposes no irreducible requirement of such suspicion." *Id.* (citing United States v. Martinez-Fuerte, 428 U.S. 543, 560–61 (1976). The Court went on to state that exceptions to the individualized suspicion requirement are permissible only when the privacy interests implicated are

authorized both blanket and random searches in the form of drug tests of student athletes.[76] Some states, however, have passed student search statutes that require individualized suspicion.[77]

The Seventh Circuit Court of Appeals determined that a public school teacher or administrator who seizes a student while attempting to maintain discipline violates the Fourth Amendment only if the restriction of liberty is unreasonable under the circumstances then apparent.[78] In *Wallace*, a high school teacher grabbed Wallace's wrist and elbow to speed her departure from the classroom. Wallace and another student had been arguing and the other student had "taken a swing" at Wallace. Neither party disputed that the teacher ordered Wallace out of the classroom and grabbed her to prevent a fight and restore order and discipline. The court explained:

> The reasonableness of a Fourth Amendment seizure of a public school student by a teacher must be evaluated in the context of the school environment, where restricting the liberty of students is a *sine qua non* of the educational process. Deprivations of liberty in schools serve the end of compulsory education and do not inherently pose constitutional problems.
>
> . . . [g]iven the wide range of methods that teachers and administrators exercise in legitimately restricting students' liberty during the educational process, any rule designed to protect students' limited liberty rights must identify a recognizable level at which such restrictions become unreasonable in light of the Fourth Amendment.
>
> We thus hold that, in the context of a public school, a teacher or administrator who seizes a student does so in violation of the Fourth Amendment only when the restriction of liberty is unreasonable under the circumstances then existing and apparent. Therefore, in seeking to maintain order and discipline, a teacher or administrator is simply constrained to taking reasonable action to achieve those goals. Depending on the circumstances, reasonable

minimal and when "other safeguards" are available to protect the individual's rights. *Id.* (citing Delaware v. Prouse, 440 U.S. 648, 654–55 (1979)).

76. Vernonia Sch. Dist. 47J v. Acton, 115 S. Ct. 2386 (1995). *See infra* note 77 and accompanying text.

77. *See, e.g.*, IOWA CODE § 808A (1995).

78. Wallace v. Batavia Sch. Dist. 101, 68 F.3d 1010 (7th Cir. 1995).

action may certainly include the seizure of a student in the face of provocative or disruptive behavior.

This test should afford teachers and administrators an acceptable range of action for dealing with disruptive students while still protecting students against the potentially excessive use of state power.[79]

The court concluded, "[t]he only thing unreasonable in this scenario is that Wallace has made a federal case out of a routine disciplinary matter."[80]

The performance of a drug test constitutes a search and seizure and, consequently, is regulated by the above-stated principles.

The U.S. Supreme Court, however, recently pronounced that a school district may randomly drug-test its student-athletes in *Vernonia School District 47J v. Acton*.[81] The Court found that the school district had an immediate legitimate concern in preventing student-athletes from using drugs and that student-athletes have a lesser legitimate privacy expectation than other public school students. Therefore, the school district was not required to find the "least intrusive" method with which to search the student-athlete.

E. NOTICE OF THE CHARGES

A fundamental concept of due process is that the "accused" must be aware of the charges. Once an investigation has yielded evidence of misconduct, the next requirement of due process is to advise the offender of the charge and the identity of the accuser, and to grant the offender an opportunity to confront the accuser.[82]

---

79. *Id.* at 1013–14.
80. *Id.* at 1015.
81. Vernonia Sch. Dist. 47J. v. Acton, 115 S. Ct. 2386 (1995); *see also* Schaill v. Tippecanoe County Sch. Corp., 864 F.2d 1309 (7th Cir. 1988) (finding probable cause and warrant requirements of the Fourth Amendment did not apply to school district's random urine testing program for interscholastic athletes and cheerleaders).
82. *See* Goss v. Lopez, 419 U.S. 565, 579 (1975); Boner v. Eminence R-1 Sch. Dist., 55 F.3d 1339 (8th Cir. 1995); Wallace v. Tilley, 41 F.3d 296 (7th Cir. 1994); Winegar v. Des Moines Indep. Com. Sch. Dist., 20 F.3d 895 (8th Cir. 1994), *cert. denied*, 115 S. Ct. 426 (1994); Smith v. Town of Eaton, Ind., 910 F.2d 1469 (7th Cir. 1990); Brown v. Georgia Dep't of Revenue, 881 F.2d 1018 (11th Cir. 1989); Palmer v. Merluzzi, 868 F.2d 90 (3d Cir. 1989); Paredes v. Curtis, 864 F.2d 426 (6th Cir. 1988); Newsome v. Batavia Local Sch. Dist., 842 F.2d 920 (6th Cir. 1988); Gorman v. University of R.I., 837 F.2d 7 (1st Cir. 1988); Kendall v. Board of Educ. of Memphis City, 627 F.2d (6th Cir. 1980); Brouillette v. Board of Dirs. of Merged Area IX, 519 F.2d 126,

In *Texarkana Independent School District v. Lewis*,[83] the Texas Court of Civil Appeals noted:

> The Trial Court was correct in holding that procedural due process was violated in the giving of written notice of the charges against the students. Since there are no pleadings in such hearings, it is necessary that the student be apprised with some particularity of the offense with which he is charged. It need not be drawn with the precision of a criminal indictment, but it should contain "a statement of the specific charges and grounds which, if proven, would justify 'discipline.'" [citation omitted] "A student cannot be punished on the basis of some ground other than that stated in the written charge."[84]

In that case, the court found that the school did not notify the student with sufficient particularity of the specific violation with which he was charged to avoid a violation of due process. The court also went on to say:

> The student should also be advised of the name of at least the principal witnesses against him and the nature of their testimony [citation omitted], and it must be done in some adequate manner.[85]

In *Newsom v. Batavia School District*,[86] however, the court determined that a district did not have to release the identities of the witnesses against a student accused of drug possession and distribution. The court found that to do so would place the witnesses in risk of ostracism or reprisals. The court found that in this specific circumstance, the principal's opportunity to interview and determine the credibility of the witnesses was sufficient.

---

128 (8th Cir. 1975); Gonzales v. McEuen, 435 F. Supp. 460, 467 (C.D. Cal. 1977); Weyenberg v. Town of Menasha, 401 F. Supp. 801, 803 (E.D. Wis. 1975); Graham v. Knutzen, 351 F. Supp. 642, 665 (D. Neb. 1972); Stratton v. Wenona Com. Unit Dist. No. 1, 551 N.E.2d 640 (Ill. 1990).

83. Texarkana Indep. Sch. Dist. v. Lewis, 470 S.W.2d 727 (Tex. Civ. App. 1971).

84. *Id.* at 734 (quoting *The Constitution on the Campus*, 22 Vand. L. Rev. 1027, 1072 (1969)). *See also* Hammond v. South Carolina State College, 272 F. Supp. 947, 950 (D.S.C. 1967); Woody v. Burns, 188 So. 2d 56, 57 (Fla. Dist. Ct. App. 1966); Schank v. Hegele, 521 N.E.2d 9 (Ohio Com. Pl. 1987).

85. *Id.* at 734–35. *But see* Paredes v. Curtis, 864 F.2d 426 (6th Cir. 1988) (finding student was not entitled to know identity of school informant on charge of look-alike drug possession).

86. Newsome v. Batavia Local Sch. Dist., 842 F.2d 920 (6th Cir. 1988).

Labrosse v. St. Bernard Parish School Board[87] further illustrates this point. This case involved a student who was expelled for smoking marijuana in a trailer across the street from school property during his lunch hour. A Louisiana statute provided for the expulsion of a student who uses a controlled substance "in school buildings, on school grounds, or on school buses." In its notice to the student, the stated reason for his expulsion was "possession of marijuana."

The *Labrosse* court struck down the expulsion because the student was not guilty of possessing or using a controlled substance on school property. The Louisiana statute also allowed expulsion for a student's participation in immoral or vicious practices, for leaving school grounds without permission, and for committing any other serious offense—grounds that arguably would have supported the expulsion of Labrosse. The court, however, refused to consider these other provisions. To do so, in the court's opinion, would violate the student's rights to due notice of the nature and cause of the charges against him.[88]

The Supreme Court in *Goss v. Lopez*[89] also discussed the requirement of notice before imposing disciplinary sanctions on students. The Court noted that either oral or written notice of the charges could be given, and that there need not be a delay between the notice and the hearing.[90] *Goss*, however, involved a short-term suspension of a student for one to 10 days. If the suspension is for a longer time, courts might require that the notice be in writing and substantially precede the hearing.

Additionally, the notice must be delivered to the student or his parents or guardians. The school must make a good-faith effort to deliver the notice to the student. However, the student will lose the right to be heard if he or she fails to attend the hearing at the appointed time or if it is impossible, despite diligent efforts, to give notice of the hearing.[91]

---

87. Labrosse v. St. Bernard Parish Sch. Bd., 483 So. 2d 1253 (La. Ct. App. 1986).

88. *Id.* at 1258.

89. Goss v. Lopez, 419 U.S. 565 (1975).

90. *Id.* at 581; Brown v. Georgia Dep't of Revenue, 881 F.2d 1018 (11th Cir. 1989); Stratton v. Wenona Com. Unit Dist. No. 1, 551 N.E.2d 640 (Ill. 1990).

91. *See* Wright v. Texas S. Univ., 392 F.2d 728 (5th Cir. 1968); Gonzales v. McEuen, 435 F. Supp. 460 (C.D. Cal. 1977); Smith v. Miller, 514 P.2d 377 (Kan. 1973); Texarkana Indep. Sch. Dist. v. Lewis, 470 S.W.2d 727 (Tex. Civ. App. 1971). *See infra* Appendix A. *Cf.* Rosa R. v. Connelly, 889 F.2d 435 (2d Cir. 1989) (determining student's due process rights were not violated when board failed to give student notice he would be denied credit for "time served" during pendency of expulsion hearing when student requested postponement of hearing).

In a teacher termination case known as *Brouillette v. Board of Directors of Merged Area IX*,[92] the Eighth Circuit said: "Although some of the charges could have been more precise, nevertheless, they were, in view of their nature, specific enough to allow plaintiff to present rebuttal evidence and he did so with the aid of his attorney."[93]

The court determined that the teacher

> knew the names of those persons who had placed the charges against him and, although at the public hearing [teacher's] counsel objected to the vagueness of the charges, at no time did he seek to examine either [of them] or have them specify the factual basis for the charges nor did he challenge their credibility.[94]

Additionally, the Eighth Circuit noted that prior to the public hearing there had been a faculty meeting where the charges had been specified in the presence of the teacher.[95]

In the case of handicapped students, the regulations under the Individuals with Disabilities in Education Act (IDEA) specifically set forth the contents of the notice to be given.[96] Under that section, the notice requires a full explanation of the procedural safeguards available to parents or guardians, a description of the action proposed or refused by the agency, an explanation of why the agency proposes or refuses to take the action, the description of any options the agency considered, and the reasons why those options were rejected.[97] Evaluation procedures must be described, as well as tests, records, or reports used as the basis for the proposal or refusal.[98] Further, a description of any other factors relevant to the proposal or refusal must be given.[99] The notice must be given in language that the general public understands and provided in the native lan-

---

92. Brouillette v. Board of Directors of Merged Area IX, 519 F.2d 126 (8th Cir. 1975).

93. *Id.*

94. *Id. See* Cliff v. Board of Sch. Comm'rs, 42 F.3d 403 (7th Cir. 1994).

95. Brouillette v. Board of Directors of Merged Area IX, 519 F.2d at 129. *See* Smith v. Town of Eaton, 910 F.2d 1469 (7th Cir. 1990), *cert. denied*, 499 U.S. 962 (1991).

96. 34 C.F.R. § 300.505 (1996).

97. *Id.* § 300.505(a)(1), (2).

98. *Id.* § 300.505(a)(3).

99. *Id.* § 300.505(a)(4).

guage of the parent or guardian, or other mode of communication used by the parent or guardian, unless it is not feasible to do so.[100] A party may prohibit the introduction of any evidence at a hearing that has not been disclosed to the other party at least five days before the hearing.[101]

F. PROCEDURAL REQUIREMENTS OF HEARING

1. Right to Hear and Present Evidence, to Present a Defense, and to Cross-Examine

In *Dixon v. Alabama State Board of Education,*[102] the Fifth Circuit considered whether due process required an opportunity for hearing before students could be expelled for misconduct. The court concluded that a hearing should be provided so the board could hear in considerable detail the facts presented by both sides. The court said:

> This is not to imply that a full-dress judicial hearing, with the right to cross-examine witnesses, is required. Such a hearing, with the attending publicity and disturbance of college activities, might be detrimental to the college's educational atmosphere and impractical to carry out. Nevertheless, the rudiments of an adversary proceeding may be preserved without encroaching upon the interests of the college. In the instant case, the student should be given the names of the witnesses against him and an oral or written report on the facts to which each witness testifies. He should also be given the opportunity to present to the Board, or at least to an administrative official of the college, his own defense against the charges and to produce either oral testimony or written affidavits of witnesses in his behalf. If the hearing is not before the Board directly, the results and findings of the hearing should be presented in a report open to the student's inspection. If these rudimentary elements of fair play are followed in a case of misconduct of this particular type, we feel that the requirements of due process of law will have been fulfilled.[103]

---

100. *Id.* § 300.505(b)(1), (2).

101. *Id.* § 300.508(a)(3).

102. Dixon v. Alabama State Bd. of Educ., 294 F.2d 150 (5th Cir. 1961), *cert. denied,* 368 U.S. 930 (1961).

103. *Id.* at 159. *See also* Fielder v. Board of Educ., 346 F. Supp. 722 (D. Neb. 1972)

The nature of the hearing and the need to preserve the right of confrontation and cross-examination will depend upon the nature of the hearing and the nature of the sanction to be imposed. *Goss v. Lopez* makes it clear that in the case of a suspension of a student for fewer than 10 days, a student must be given some kind of notice and hearing.[104]

After school administrators have completed their investigation, they must meet with the student informally and state the nature of the charges. If the student denies the charges, the administrator must explain the evidence and give the student a chance to explain his or her position. This must occur before the student is suspended absent unusual situations. Where a student's continuing presence "poses a continuing danger to persons or property or an ongoing threat of disrupting the academic process," the student may be immediately removed from school, and the notice and informal hearing should follow as soon as practicable.[105]

In *Board of Curators of the University of Missouri v. Horowitz*, the U.S. Supreme Court considered dismissal for failure to meet academic standards of a medical student. In commenting upon the requirements set out in *Goss v. Lopez*, the Court noted:

> In *Goss v. Lopez*, [citation omitted], we held that due process requires, in connection with the suspension of a student from public school for disciplinary reasons, "that the student be given oral or written notice of the charges against him and, if he denies them, an explanation of the evidence the authorities have and an opportunity to present his side of the story.". . . The Court of Appeals apparently read *Goss* as requiring some type of formal hearing at

---

(finding the procedures followed by a high school in expelling students were unconstitutionally impermissible where a hearing was offered 30 days after the expulsion and the [reporting teachers] did not attend hearing and were unavailable for cross-examination).

104. Goss v. Lopez, 419 U.S. 565, 579 (1975). *See also* Wise v. Pea Ridge Sch. Dist., 855 F.2d 560 (8th Cir. 1988) (finding no violation of due process when notice and opportunity to be heard were not given to student for three-day in-school suspension); Stratton v. Wenona Com. Unit Dist. No. 1, 551 N.E.2d 640 (Ill. 1990) (giving notice to parents two days before expulsion proceeding did not deny due process).

105. *Id.* at 582. *See* Engele v. Independent Sch. Dist. No. 91, 846 F. Supp. 760 (D. Minn. 1994) (student excluded from last 10 days of school for his own personal safety was not denied procedural due process after he requested that he finish the school year at home and school officials acquiesced).

which respondent could defend her academic ability and performance. All that *Goss* required was an "informal give-and-take" between the student and the administrative body dismissing him that would, at least, give the student "the opportunity to characterize his conduct and put it in what he deems the proper context." But we have frequently emphasized that "(t)he very nature of due process negates any concept of inflexible procedures universally applicable to every imaginable situation." *Cafeteria Workers v. McElroy*, 367 U.S. 886, 895.

. . . .

Even in the context of a school disciplinary proceeding, however, the Court stopped short of requiring a formal hearing since "further formalizing the suspension process and escalating its formality and adversary nature may not only make it too costly as a regular disciplinary tool but also destroy its effectiveness as a part of the teaching process."[106]

In the *Horowitz* case, the U.S Supreme Court clearly held that the hearing required by *Goss* is not a formal one and the procedures necessary for longer suspensions or criminal trials are not necessary. This suggests that the student's right to cross-examination, to call witnesses, or to have a representative present are not necessary when *short* suspensions of up to 10 days are imposed, as long as the student is given notice, an explanation of the evidence against the student, and a chance to rebut it.

A federal district court in Virginia held that the *Goss* standard applied to a short-term suspension of only three days.[107] *Goss* involved a 10-day suspension. so *Goss* clearly applies to shorter suspensions. Districts should follow the *Goss* procedures whether they apply to a one-day or 10-day suspension. If a suspension extends beyond 10 days, generally stricter procedures should be followed.

---

106. Board of Curators of the University of Mo. v. Horowitz, 435 U.S. 78, 85–89 (1978). *See also* Gorman v. Univ. of R.I., 837 F.2d 7 (1st Cir. 1988) (finding proper inquiry is whether the individuals had an opportunity to answer, explain, and defend); *see supra* notes 8–14 and accompanying text.

107. Hillman v. Elliott, 436 F. Supp. 812 (W.D. Va. 1977) (student suspended for using abusive language toward another student had been afforded sufficient procedural due process in the way of notice and an opportunity to present his version of the evidence).

2. Procedural Requirements for Long-Term Suspensions and Expulsions

If a student is suspended for an extended time, more formal procedures than those required for short-term suspensions must be followed. School districts should allow the student to confront adverse witnesses and to call witnesses on his or her own behalf. Districts may also want to allow a more formal hearing before the board of directors, rather than just before the principal or superintendent, where the student could have a representative present.

These procedures for lengthy suspensions may be mandated implicitly by *Goss v. Lopez*.[108] In discussing short-term suspensions, the Court said school officials need not allow the students to have representatives present or to confront and cross-examine adverse witnesses. The Court may feel, however, that a greater deprivation of the right to education exists under longer suspension, and, therefore, the due process clause of the U.S. Constitution requires a greater degree of protection. The Court noted:

> We stop short of construing the Due Process Clause to require, countrywide, that hearings in connection with *short suspensions* must afford the student the opportunity to secure counsel, to confront and cross-examine witnesses supporting the charge, or to call his own witnesses to verify his version of the incident. Brief disciplinary suspensions are almost countless. To impose in each such case even truncated trial-type procedures might well overwhelm administrative facilities in many places and, by diverting resources, cost more than it would save in educational effectiveness.
>
> . . . .
>
> We should also make it clear that we have addressed ourselves solely to the short suspension, not exceeding 10 days. Longer suspensions or expulsions for the remainder of the school term, or permanently, may require more formal procedures. Nor do we put aside the possibility that in unusual situations, although involving only a short suspension, something more than the rudimentary procedures will be required.[109]

---

108. Goss v. Lopez, 419 U.S. 565 (1975).
109. *Id.* at 583–84 (emphasis added).

It is unclear from case law precisely how many days of suspension will call the greater due process rights into play. *Goss* dealt with suspensions of up to 10 days. The *Goss* Court also noted that suspensions for the remainder of a school term, if lengthy, could require greater protections. The Court, however, did not set a day limit for suspensions before the protections would come into play; so it is unknown if a 15- or 20-day suspension would require more formal proceedings than a 10-day suspension. Districts should resolve this open-ended question by allowing more formal procedures for any suspension exceeding 10 days. The more formal procedures required for longer suspensions have not been set out by the Court.[110]

In the case of *Graham v. Knutzen*,[111] a federal district court in Nebraska discussed the nature and requirements for confrontation in the context of a discipline proceeding. The court recognized but declined to impose the requirements of confrontation and cross-examination of student witnesses or accusers as a necessary element of an on-the-premises hearing prior to suspension. The court found that due process was followed when an investigative action was taken by the principal on an oral statement of the charges, and an opportunity to answer the charges was presented to the student to be suspended. The court held due process satisfied where the principal conducted his own investigation, confronted the student, and gave the student an opportunity to explain his side or to challenge the facts.[112]

The court acknowledged that "due process is an elusive concept" and the "exact boundaries are undefinable," and "its content varies according to specific factual context." The court cited *Hannah v. Larche*,[113] which stated: "Whether the Constitution requires that a particular right obtained in a specific proceeding depends upon a complexity of factors. The nature of the alleged right involved, the nature of the proceeding, *and the possible burden on that proceeding*, are all considerations which must be taken into account."[114]

---

110. *See also* Alex v. Allen, 409 F. Supp. 379 (W.D. Pa. 1976) (requiring more stringent standards where a student was suspended for 30 days). *See, e.g.,* DeJesus v. Penberthy, 344 F. Supp. 70 (D. Conn. 1972) (requiring more stringent standards where a student was expelled from school).

111. Graham v. Knutzen, 351 F. Supp. 642 (D. Neb. 1972).

112. *Id.* at 665. *See* Parades v. Curtis, 864 F.2d 426 (6th Cir. 1988); Newsome v. Batavia Local Sch. Dist., 842 F.2d 920 (6th Cir. 1988); Stratton v. Wenona Community Unit Dist. No. 1, 551 N.E.2d 640 (Ill. 1990).

113. Hannah v. Larche, 363 U.S. 420 (1960).

114. Graham v. Knutzen, 351 F. Supp. at 666 (emphasis added). *See supra* notes 8–10, 105 and accompanying text.

In *Gonzales v. McEuen*,[115] the court refused to consider hearsay statements because the accused student was deprived of the constitutional right to confront and cross-examine his accuser. The court found: "Although strict adherence to common law rules of evidence is not required in school disciplinary proceedings, where a student is faced with severe sanctions of expulsion, due process does not permit ex parte evidence given by witnesses not under oath, and not subject to an examination by the accused student."

The court ruled that admission of hearsay statements without opportunity to cross-examine the declarant deprived the student of his rights to confrontation.[116]

In another case, the court ruled that the right to cross-examination and confrontation was not mandatory but that it is desirable in those circumstances involving the credibility of witnesses.[117] If a witness will be placed at risk of danger if made to testify, then hearsay statements may be allowed.

3. Right to Be Represented by Counsel

In the *Texarkana Independent School District v. Lewis*[118] case, the court said:

> No doubt, justice would be more effectively and efficiently administered if counsel for the student were present, but the presence of counsel is not mandatory where counsel for the school is not present. *Madera v. Board of Education*, 386 F.2d 778 (2nd Cir. 1967). However, the student's right to counsel, should the matter appear to him to be of sufficient gravity to make legal assistance desirable, should receive ungrudging recognition. If, however, the Board of Trustees proceeds through counsel, as it did in this case, at the hearing before the Board, then the student has the right to be represented by counsel of his own choice at his own expense, and in this instance the Board of Trustees shall notify the student in writing that he has a right to be represented by counsel.

---

115. Gonzales v. McEuen, 435 F. Supp. 460 (C.D. Cal. 1977).

116. *Id. But see supra* note 92 and accompanying text.

117. Texarkana Indep. Sch. Dist. v. Lewis, 470 S.W.2d 727, 736 (Tex. Civ. App. 1971).

118. *See supra* note 116.

This shall be true in all preliminary hearings where the school district proceeds through counsel, and particularly when the school intends to expel the student. It is not necessary to notify the student of his right to counsel in preliminary hearings before the superintendent, principal or administrative committee when the school district does not elect to proceed through counsel and does not intend to expel the student.[119]

The better practice is to advise a student or an employee of the right to counsel or representation and to accommodate that right where serious sanctions are imposed.

Under the IDEA regulations, a party to a hearing involving a handicapped student has the right to be accompanied and advised by counsel and by individuals with special knowledge or training with respect to the problems of handicapped children.[120]

4.   Burden of Proof and Sufficiency of Evidence

The burden of proof in an administrative hearing is initially upon the school. Generally, the school must establish, by substantial evidence, facts that justify its desired actions. The quantum of evidence may vary by statute or core decisions in various states. On appeal from an adverse decision of the board, however, the burden of proof shifts to the teacher or student to show that the evidence presented to the board did not support the decision, or that the board failed to follow proper procedure.

In *Conley v. Board of Education of City of New Britain*,[121] the court upheld the dismissal of a teacher. The court said:

> The decision of the board must be based upon the evidence directed to this specific charge (gross inefficiency) and upon no other. Such evidence must carry the burden of proving by a preponderance, to the satisfaction of the majority of the board, that the plaintiff was grossly inefficient . . . . Because of the requirement of the tenure act that the decision of the board shall be based upon the evidence supporting the specific charge or charges, and upon no

119.   Texarkana Indep. Sch. Dist. v. Lewis, 470 S.W.2d 727, 735 (Tex. Civ. App. 1971).

120.   34 C.F.R. § 300.508.

121.   Conley v. Board of Educ. of New Britain, 123 A.2d 747 (Conn. 1956).

other evidence, proof of gross inefficiency must be made by evidence adduced at the hearings and may not, as in other cases before administrative agencies, include what the members may properly have learned by personal observation.[122]

In *Conley*, the teacher asserted that the court erred in placing the burden upon the teacher to show that the board's action was arbitrary, unreasonable, and an abuse of its discretion. The court noted that the teacher's employment could be terminated only if the charge of "gross inefficiency" was "supported by a preponderance of the evidence." The statute provided: "If the board shall find by a majority vote that the charges are supported by a preponderance of the evidence, such teacher may be dismissed, provided that the burden of proof shall be on the board."

Although the burden of proof was initially on the board to show by a preponderance of the evidence that the teacher could be dismissed, on appeal of the board determination, the burden shifted to the teacher to show there was not a preponderance of the evidence and the record before the board did not support its action.[123]

Other courts reviewing a decision of a school board will uphold the decision if it is based upon substantial evidence. This will generally be the standard that is applied absent statutory provisions that require a preponderance of the evidence. Evidence is substantial when a reasonable mind would accept it as adequate to reach a conclusion.[124] The Iowa Supreme Court said: "While the substantiality of evidence must take into account whatever in the record fairly detracts from its weight . . . the possibility of drawing two inconsistent conclusions from the evidence does not prevent an administrative agency's finding from being supported by substantial evidence."[125]

---

122. *Id*. at 751.

123. *Id*. at 752. *See* Board of Educ. of Ft. Madison Community Sch. Dist. v. Youel, 282 N.W.2d 677 (Iowa 1979) (on appeal from school board decision to terminate, nonprobationary teacher/coach had burden of demonstrating error); Wilson v. Des Moines Indep. Cmty. Sch. Dist., 389 N.W.2d 681 (Iowa Ct. App. 1986) (nonprobationary teacher had burden of proving that the school board committed an error in adopting a recommendation for her termination).

124. Briggs v. Board of Dirs. of Hinton Cmty. Sch. Dist., 282 N.W.2d 740, 743 (Iowa 1979) (school board's termination of principal was supported by substantial evidence showing continued deficiencies).

125. *Id*.

In *McConnell v. Alamo Heights Independent School District*,[126] the court discussed the substantial evidence rule in Texas:

> In a trial under the substantial evidence rule, on appeal to the district court from an order of an administrative agency, the proceeding is not a trial de novo. The plaintiff has the burden of proving the absence of substantial evidence, that is, the burden of proving that the action of the . . . board was illegal, arbitrary, capricious, unreasonable or discriminatory. It is the evidence adduced in the trial court, not in the hearing, if any, conducted by the administrative agency, which is determinative of the issue of substantial evidence. The issue of substantial evidence is one of law to be answered by the court—not a question of fact to be answered by the jury. Under the substantial evidence rule, the administrative order in question will be upheld if, considering the entire record in the trial court, that order finds reasonable support in the evidence.[127]

5. Findings and Conclusions

In *State ex rel. Newton v. Board of School Trustees of the Metropolitan School District of Wabash County*,[128] the court commented on administrative findings and noted:

> [t]he existence of such findings is essential to preserve the limited scope of a reviewing court's inquiry. "The absence of findings invites a reweighing of the evidence on review, thereby paving the way for judicial intrusion into matters committed to administrative decision. . . ." An administrative body has the duty to make a finding of the pertinent facts on which its decision is based in order to facilitate judicial review.[129]

---

126. McConnell v. Alamo Heights Indep. Sch. Dist., 576 S.W.2d 470 (Tex. 1979).

127. *Id.* at 475 (quoting Rock Island Indep. School Dist. No. 907 v. County Bd. of Sch. Trustees, 423 S.W.2d 665 (Tex. Civ. App. 1968)). *See, e.g.,* Smith v. Miller, 514 P.2d 377 (Kan. 1973).

128. State *ex rel.* Newton v. Board of Sch. Trustees, 404 N.E.2d 47 (Ind. Ct. App. 1980).

129. *Id.* at 48–49.

In *Erb v. Iowa State Board of Public Instruction*,[130] the Iowa Supreme Court noted the requirement to make findings of fact in an adjudicatory proceeding. The court said:

> Boards are required, even without statutory mandate, to make findings of fact on issues presented in any adjudicatory proceeding. Such findings must be sufficiently certain to enable a reviewing court to ascertain with reasonable certainty the factual basis and legal principle upon which the administrative body acted. *Cedar Rapids Steel Transportation, Inc. v. Iowa State Commerce Commission*, 160 N.W.2d 825, 837 (Iowa 1968), *cert. denied*, 394 U.S. 918.[131]

In the case of a hearing involving a disabled student, the regulations under the IDEA require written findings of fact and decisions.[132]

6. Court Reporter or Recording of the Proceedings

While not specifically required by due process principles, the board or hearing officer is well-advised to electronically record the proceedings or to have a court reporter record the proceedings. A recorded record will support whatever written findings of fact and conclusions are made and can make the difference between success or failure on appeal.

In the case of a hearing for a disabled student, the regulations mandate a written or electronic verbatim record of the hearing.[133]

7. Issue and Claim Preclusion

After a student has been given a hearing in a state forum that complies with due process requirements, the student may be precluded from bringing a Section 1983 action in federal district court because of issue or claim preclusion.[134]

---

130. Erb v. Iowa State Bd. of Pub. Instruction, 216 N.W.2d 339 (Iowa 1974).

131. *Id.* at 342. *See also* State *ex rel.* Newton v. Board of Sch. Trustees, 404 N.E.2d 47 (Ind. Ct. App. 1980); Fairfield Community School District v. Justmann, 476 N.W.2d 335 (Iowa 1991) (although board decision was sparse, it was sufficient to give inference of the board's findings on issues of credibility).

132. 34 C.F.R. § 300.508.

133. *Id.*

134. *See, e.g.,* Migra v. Warren County Sch. Dist., 465 U.S. 75, 83–87 (1984) (holding an administrator who failed to bring a section 1983 claim in state court was precluded from bringing a section 1983 claim in federal district court after the state law

In a recent Eighth Circuit Court of Appeals case,[135] the court determined that issue and claim preclusion barred a Section 1983 claim.[136] Plough was a student in defendant school district who admitted he had been in possession of LSD on school grounds in violation of the school's substance abuse policy. Following a hearing before the school district's board of directors, the board retired for private consideration of the case. During the discussion, two school board members claimed personal knowledge of the case and spoke out against Plough. The board subsequently voted to expel Plough from school. Plough did not have an opportunity to question the school board members or refute their allegations because he was unaware of the statements until after the board's decision. Plough appealed to the Iowa State Board of Education, claiming a due process violation by the board's consideration of the members' personal opinions. The State Board held an evidentiary hearing and affirmed the school board's disposition of the case. Instead of appealing the State Board's decision to the Iowa district court, as was his right under Iowa law, Plough filed a Section 1983 action in federal district court. The district court determined that Plough's Section 1983 claim was barred because Plough litigated his due process claim in a state forum.[137] The Eighth Circuit affirmed, finding Plough's claim barred by both issue[138] and claim[139] preclusion.

---

claims were litigated in state court); West v. Wessels, 534 N.W.2d 396 (Iowa 1995) (determining a schoolteacher was precluded from bringing a claim for money damages that were dependent on the teacher's contract termination or measured by the loss of the contract after the teacher's termination was upheld by both the Iowa District Court and the Iowa Court of Appeals); Kahrs v. Board of Trustees for Platt County Sch. Dist. No. 1, 901 P.2d 404 (Wyo. 1995) (finding terminated teacher was barred from bringing suit in federal district court because teacher failed to appeal original decision in state forum).

135. Plough v. West Des Moines Community Sch. Dist., 70 F.3d 512 (8th Cir. 1995).

136. *Id.* at 516–17.

137. *Id.* at 517.

138. *Id.* at 516. "Issue preclusion or collateral estoppel provides that 'once a court has decided an issue of fact or law necessary to its judgment, that decision may preclude relitigation of the issue in a suit on a different cause of action involving a party to the first case.'" *Id.* at 515 (quoting Allen v. McCurry, 449 U.S. 90, 94 (1980) (citations omitted)).

139. *Id.* at 517. "Claim preclusion, or res judicata, provides that 'a final judgment on the merits of an action precludes the parties or their privies from relitigating issues that were or could have been raised in that action.'" *Id.* at 515 (quoting Allen v. McCurry, 449 U.S. at 94 (citations omitted)).

The court gave the agency's factual findings preclusive effect, using the *Elliott*[140] "eligibility" factors.[141] Although Plough argued that the factual issues presented to the State Board and the federal district court were not identical because the relief requested was not the same, the Eighth Circuit determined that the requested remedies need not be the same for a prior determination to be given issue-preclusive effect.[142]

Plough's claim was also barred by claim preclusion.[143] The court found Plough originally chose to litigate his due process claim in a state forum and the State Board's adverse decision became final when Plough chose not to appeal it to the Iowa district court.[144] Consequently, Plough was barred from relitigating the same claim in federal court.[145]

Although the court labeled the testimony of the two school board members "improper" and "unfortunate," it determined that any error caused by the testimony was harmless.[146] Plough had a full and fair opportunity to litigate his claims before the Iowa State Board of Education.

G. HEARING BEFORE AN IMPARTIAL DECISION MAKER

The board or hearing officer must be an impartial decision maker. The board or the hearing officer must not be involved in the investigation, recommendation, or prosecution of the case, and no member of the board or hearing panel can be biased or have a personal interest in the action to be taken.[147]

---

140. University of Tenn. v. Elliott, 478 U.S. 788, 799 (1986) (quoting United States v. Utah Constr. & Mining Co., 384 U.S. 394, 422 (1966)). The *Elliott* eligibility factors are as follows: (1) whether the state agency was acting in a judicial capacity; (2) in resolving disputed issues of fact properly before it; (3) that the parties had an adequate opportunity to litigate. *Id.*

141. Plough v. West Des Moines Cmty. Sch. Dist., 70 F.3d at 515.

142. *Id.* at 516 (citing United States v. Utah Constr. & Mining Co., 384 U.S. at 418 (holding that an agency's factual findings were preclusive in a later suit even though the request for damages was not the same in the two proceedings)).

143. *Id.* at 516–17.

144. *Id.* at 517.

145. *Id.* (citing Clarke v. Redeker, 406 F.2d 883, 885 (8th Cir. 1969) (precluding a section 1983 claim for damages based on an earlier action seeking injunctive relief on essentially the same facts), *cert. denied*, 396 U.S. 862 (1969)).

146. *Id.*

147. *See, e.g.*, Brouillette v. Board of Directors of Merged Area IX, 519 F.2d 126, 128 (8th Cir. 1975); Gonzales v. McEuen, 435 F. Supp. 460, 465 (C.D. Cal. 1977); Schank v. Hegele, 521 N.E.2d 9 (Ohio Com. Pl. 1987); Keith v. Community Sch. Dist. of Wilton, 262 N.W.2d 249, 258–61 (Iowa 1978).

In *Brouillette v. Board of Directors of Merged Area IX,*[148] the court, in dealing with procedural due process requirements in a teacher termination proceeding, held that one of the minimal requirements of due process is a hearing before an impartial board or tribunal.[149]

Mere familiarity with the facts of a case gained by the school board in the performance of its statutory role will not necessarily disqualify it as a decision maker. In *Withrow v. Larkin,*[150] a case dealing with suspension of a physician's license by the Wisconsin Medical Examining Board, the Supreme Court said:

> The mere exposure to evidence presented in nonadversary investigative procedures is insufficient in itself to impugn the fairness of the Board members at a later adversary hearing. Without a showing to the contrary, state administrators "are assumed to be men of conscience and intellectual discipline, capable of judging a particular controversy fairly on the basis of its own circumstances." *United States v. Morgan*, 313 U.S. 409, 421, 61 S. Ct. 999, 1004, 85 L. Ed. 1429 (1941). The risk of bias or prejudgment in this sequence of functions has not been considered to be intolerably high or to raise a sufficiently great possibility that the adjudicators would be so psychologically wedded to their complaints that they would consciously or unconsciously avoid the appearance of having erred or changed position. The initial charge or determination of probable cause and the ultimate adjudication have different bases and purposes. The fact that the same agency makes them in tandem and that they relate to the same issues does not result in a procedural due process violation. Clearly, if the initial view of the facts based on the evidence derived from nonadversarial processes as a practical or legal matter foreclosed fair and effective consideration at a subsequent adversary hearing leading to ultimate decision, a substantial due process question would be raised. But in our view, that is not this case. That the combination of investigative and adjudicative functions does not, without more, constitute a due process violation does not, of course, preclude a court from

148. *Id.* at 128.
149. Brouillette v. Board of Directors of Merged Area IX, 519 F.2d 126 (8th Cir. 1975).
150. Withrow v. Larkin, 421 U.S. 35 (1975).

determining from the special facts and circumstances present in the case before it that the risk of unfairness is intolerably high.[151]

In *Hortonville Joint School District No. 1 v. Hortonville Education Association,*[152] the Supreme Court reviewed a decision in which the Wisconsin Supreme Court had ruled that teachers who were dismissed because of an illegal strike were denied due process of law. The finding of a denial of due process was based upon the conclusion that the hearings were not considered and their discharges were ordered by an impartial decision maker. The Wisconsin Supreme Court decision noted that the requirement of an impartial decision maker is an essential component of procedural due process; and on the facts of this case, where the board was engaged in collective bargaining with the teachers' representative, the board was not an impartial decision maker or hearing officer as constitutionally contemplated.[153]

On appeal, the U.S. Supreme Court disagreed and ruled that under those circumstances the board could, indeed, be an impartial decision maker. The Court found that the board members did not have a personal or financial interest, and nothing in the record supported charges of personal animosity. The Court also found the mere fact that the school board was involved in negotiations that preceded and precipitated the striking teachers' discharge did not disqualify the board from exercising its statutory duty. The Court stated:

> Mere familiarity with facts of a case gained by an agency in the performance of its statutory role does not, however, disqualify a decision maker. . . . Nor is a decision maker disqualified simply because he has taken a position, even in public, on a policy issue related to the dispute, in the absence of a showing that he is not "capable of judging a particular controversy fairly on the basis of its own circumstances."[154]

---

151. *Id.* at 55–58.

152. Hortonville Joint Sch. Dist. No. 1 v. Hortonville Educ. Ass'n, 426 U.S. 482 (1976).

153. *Id.* at 426.

154. *Id.* at 493. *See also* Rucker v. Colonial Sch. Dist., 517 A.2d 703 (Del. Super. Ct. 1986) (finding no due process violation where hearing officer was an employee of the school district); Kizer v. Dorchester County Vocational Educ. Bd. of Trustees, 340 S.E.2d 144 (S.C. 1986) (presuming board members to act fairly and impartially; to overcome the presumption, actual bias rather than potential bias must be shown).

The consideration of evidence that violates an expungement statute may not result in an impartial hearing. In *Ambus v. Granite Board of Education*,[155] the court determined that because the school board improperly considered a teacher's criminal records, which were ordered sealed and expunged, due process was implicated.[156]

Ambus was a teacher who was arrested for agreeing to distribute marijuana. The school board suspended Ambus. The charges against Ambus were dropped because he became an informant for the police. Afterwards, the school board terminated Ambus's employment. Ambus then requested a hearing, and the hearing officer "strongly recommended" that the termination be revised and Ambus reinstated.[157] The board then held its own hearing and voted to reject the recommendation, using testimony from participants in the criminal activity but not the expunged records. Two board members admitted that unless "forced by judicial decree to reemploy Ambus, they would not do so, and the board members '[didn't] care if the records were expunged or not.'"[158]

The court determined that the board was impartial because one of the challenged board members did not sit at the second hearing, and the other member's comment "did not show bias but rather was based on the evidence before him at the time."

1. Overfamiliarity of the Board

In *Bishop v. Keystone Area Education Agency No. 1*,[159] the court did not require complete lack of knowledge by a board member. In that case, the court said a board member is not disqualified unless the board member feels that personal knowledge would prevent him or her from reaching a fair decision. Only if a board member harbors prejudice or predilection would the court require a board member to excuse him- or herself.

The South Dakota Supreme Court, in *Schneider v. McLaughlin Independent School District No. 21*,[160] held there was no actual bias on the part of the board nor did circumstances exist that would establish unacceptable

---

155. Ambus v. Granite Bd. of Educ., 975 F.2d 1555 (10th Cir. 1992).
156. *Id.*
157. *Id.* at 1568–69.
158. *Id.* at 1558.
159. Bishop v. Keystone Area Educ. Agency No. 1, 275 N.W.2d 744 (Iowa 1979).
160. Schneider v. McLaughlin Indep. Sch. Dist. No. 21, 241 N.W.2d 574 (S.D. 1976).

risk of actual bias or prejudgment. In that case, the teachers in the principal's building petitioned the board, criticizing the principal. The board reviewed the petition and the contents of the principal's personnel file, and then decided to notify the principal of the board's intention not to renew his contract. The board advised the principal that he was entitled to review his personal evaluation file and to have written reasons on which the board's decision was based, and to have an informal, private conference with the board or the superintendent. The board then notified the principal of the reasons for termination and granted him an informal private conference. Following that conference, the board terminated the principal's contract and advised him of the reasons why the contract was not being renewed. In doing so, the board complied with the requirements of the South Dakota law.[161]

The court ruled that the principal had a hearing before a fair and impartial tribunal and that the board had followed the statute. The court said:

> It would be a strange practice indeed for a school board to send a teacher a notice of intention of nonrenewal without at least considering the advisability of not renewing the contract, unless, of course, the matter of nonrenewal is to spring pristine to the attention of the board for the first time at the conference held following the notice of intention not to renew. If the requirements of a fair tribunal include the condition that the members of the board must have had absolutely no prior knowledge of the facts that might make it advisable not to renew a teacher's contract and that they must have not discussed the matter and not have formed at least some tentative opinion that the teacher's contract not be renewed prior to the conference with the teacher, then as a practical matter the nonrenewal provisions of the continuing contract law are not available to a school board. We conclude that it is sufficient to meet the requirements of a fair tribunal that the board base its decision upon competent, credible evidence and that there be no evidence of actual bias toward the teacher whose contract is not being renewed.[162]

---

161. *Id.* at 576.
162. *Id.* at 577.

The South Dakota Court concluded:

> The record establishes neither actual bias on the part of the board
> nor the existence of circumstances that lead to the conclusion that
> an unacceptable risk of actual bias or prejudgment inhered in the
> board's procedures; consequently, appellant has not met his bur-
> den of overcoming the presumption that the board acted fairly and
> impartially. *Withrow v. Larkin*, 421 U.S. 35, 95 S. Ct. 1456, *Apoian
> v. State*, 235 N.W.2d 641 (S.D. 1975). *See also Sullivan v. Meade
> Ind. School Dist. No. 101*, 530 F.2d 799 (8th Cir. 1976).[163]

In *Gonzales v. McEuen*,[164] the court considered a claim by students
that the board was not an impartial decision maker. They claimed
overfamiliarity of the board with the case, and also cited the multiple roles
played by the school board counsel and the involvement of the superintendent with the board during and following the hearings. The students alleged that the board had access to the academic and disciplinary records of
the students prior to the expulsion hearings. Relying upon *Withrow* and
Hortonville, the court said that exposure to the evidence was not enough,
nor was a limited combination of investigatory and adjudicatory functions
determinative of malice or personal interest in the outcome. The court
noted:

> A school board would be amiss in its duties if it did not make
> some inquiry to know what was going on in the district for which
> it is responsible. Some familiarity with the facts of the case gained
> by an agency in the performance of its statutory role does not
> disqualify a decision maker. *Hortonville Dist. v. Hortonville Edu-
> cation Association*.[165]

In *Justmann v. Board of Directors*,[166] the Iowa Supreme Court concluded that a board was impartial, even though a board member testified as

163. *Id.* at 578 (quoting Simard v. Board of Educ. of Groton, 473 F.2d 988, 993
(2d Cir. 1973)).

164. Gonzales v. McEuen, 435 F. Supp. 460 (C.D. Cal. 1977).

165. Id. at 464. *See, e.g.,* Swab v. Cedar Rapids Community Sch. Dist., 494 F.2d
353 (8th Cir. 1974).

166. Fairfield Community Sch. Dist. v. Justmann, 476 N.W.2d 335 (Iowa 1991).

a witness in the termination hearing. The board member who testified re-
cused himself, did not listen to the other evidence, and did not participate
in the deliberations or decision.

In *Thie v. Parkersburg Community School District*,[167] the court considered whether a board became biased when it allegedly hired the teacher's
"replacement" before the termination hearing was concluded. When the
termination hearing could not be concluded in the time scheduled, it was
continued for a couple of weeks. In the interim, the board voted to hire an
individual who could be available to replace the teacher, if necessary. The
court accepted the board's explanation, provided on the record at the hearing, that the board had not prejudged the termination, that the board could
use the new teacher as a full-time substitute and still save money, and that
the timing of the hiring was necessary to be certain of obtaining well-
qualified applicants.

2. The Role of Counsel and Administrator

The *Gonzales* court reviewed the multiple roles performed by the school
counsel. The students claimed that the lawyers acted in dual roles at the
expulsion hearing—as prosecutors for the administration and as legal counsel for the board. Counsel admitted they advised the board prior to the
hearings about its obligations regarding these expulsions but denied they
advised the board during the proceedings. The court concluded that the
confidential relationship between the lawyers for the district and the members of the board, reinforced by the advisory role played by the lawyers for
the board, created an unacceptable risk of bias, bearing in mind that board
members are subject to personal liability.[168] The superintendent's role during the expulsion hearings involved the superintendent acting as secretary
to the board on one occasion and, by statute, acting as the chief adviser to
the board and also as the chief of the prosecution team. The record showed
that the superintendent was present with the board for approximately 45
minutes during its deliberations on the issue of expelling the students. The
school district maintained that the superintendent did not participate in the
deliberations. The court said: "Whether he did or did not participate, his

---

167. Parkersburg Community Sch. Dist. v. Thie (Iowa Ct. App. 1994).
168. Gonzales v. McEuen, 435 F. Supp. at 465. *See* THE SCHOOL ATTORNEY: A PRAC-
TICAL GUIDE TO EMPLOYING SCHOOL DISTRICT LEGAL COUNSEL (Edgar H. Bittle ed. 1986);
Weissman v. Board of Educ., 547 P.2d 1267, 1276 (Colo. 1976); State *ex rel.*
Wasilewski v. Board of Sch. Dir. of Milwaukee, 111 N.W.2d 198, 211 (Wis. 1961).

presence to some extent might operate as an inhibiting restraint upon the freedom of action and expression of the Board." The court concluded that the process was fundamentally unfair and raised the presumption of bias.[169]

The rule of necessity and the separation of functions ordinarily should protect the board's ability to act as decision maker and to have advisers such as the superintendent or the school district counsel to assist in the hearing. However, in those instances, superintendent and counsel should be diligent to maintain the separation of function and to not participate in the investigation or prosecution of the case before the board. In some instances, it may be desirable to have separate counsel represent the administration and the board.

3. The Board as the Decision Maker

It is the function of the board to determine, through its own independent judgment, what penalty to assess. When a board merely confirms the principal's judgment and hears the recommendation but does not hear the facts, there is not substantial due process.[170]

In *Hall v. Marion School Dist. No. 2*,[171] the court determined that the board failed to act as an impartial arbiter. *Hall* involved a teacher termination in which the superintendent had sent several memoranda to the school board detailing his efforts to get rid of the teacher in response to the teacher's public criticism of both the board and the superintendent.[172] The court held that the superintendent had become "the eyes and ears" of the board, that the board's failure to reprimand the superintendent after he ran an ad in response to plaintiff's criticism "evidenced [the board's] bias against Hall, and that

---

169. Gonzales v. McEuen, 435 F. Supp. at 465; *see also* Vukadinovich v. Board of Sch. Trustees, 978 F.2d 403 (7th Cir. 1992) (fact that school board's private lawyer presided over hearing did not create bias where she did not counsel administration or participate in board deliberations); Lamb v. Panhandle Community Sch. Dist. No. 2, 826 F.2d 526 (7th Cir. 1987) (combination of an advisory function with hearing participants prosecutorial or testimonial functions does not create a per se facially unacceptable bias of risk); Larsen v. Oakland Community Sch. Dist., 416 N.W.2d 89 (Iowa Ct. App. 1987) (board member previously on committee to observe teacher was not evidence of any member-based decision to terminate other than on the evidence presented at the hearing).

170. Gaylord v. Board of Educ., Unified Sch. Dist. No. 218, 794 P.2d 307 (Kan. App. 1990); Lee v. Macon County Bd. of Educ., 490 F.2d 458, 459–60 (5th Cir. 1974).

171. Hall v. Marion Sch. Dist. No. 2, 31 F.3d 183 (4th Cir. 1994).

172. *Id.* at 191.

[the superintendent] exerted such a strong influence over the board, that effectively [the superintendent's] decisions became the board's decisions."[173]

Consequently, the court determined that the board was not a mutual and detached arbiter. The court noted, however, that ex parte knowledge of the dispute will not automatically render the board biased.[174] "Mere familiarity with the facts of a case does not render a decision maker impermissibly biased."[175]

It is for the board of education to make the decision in those situations when statutes direct the board to do so.[176] In 1995, the Supreme Court held the Gun-Free School Zones Act[177]unconstitutional, as exceeding Congress's power under the Commerce Clause.[178] As it read at the time, the statute "made it a federal offense 'for any individual knowingly to possess a firearm at a place that the individual knows, or has reasonable cause to believe, is a school zone.'"[179] After *Lopez*, Congress amended the statute to include its findings as to how the presence of guns in school zones affects interstate commerce.[180] In addition, the statute now contains a jurisdictional requirement that prohibits only knowing possession of "a firearm *that has moved in . . . interstate or foreign commerce*" in a school zone.[181] The amended Gun-Free School Zones Act has been upheld as a constitutional exercise of Congress's commerce power.[182]

173. *Id.*
174. *Id.*
175. *Id.* at 192.
176. 18 U.S.C. § 922(q)(2)(A) (2000). *See* Hortonville Joint Sch. Dist. No. 1 v. Hortonville Educ. Ass'n, 426 U.S. 482 (1976); Norbeck v. Davenport Community Sch. Dist., 545 F.2d 63 (8th Cir. 1976); Conley v. Bd. of Educ., 123 A.2d 747 (Conn. 1956); Moravek v. Davenport Community Sch. Dist., 262 N.W.2d 797 (Iowa 1978); Schneider v. McLaughlin Indep. Sch. Dist. No. 21, 241 N.W.2d 574 (S.D. 1976).
177. 18 U.S.C. § 922(q)(2)(A) (2000).
178. United States v. Lopez, 514 U.S. 549 (1995).
179. *Id.* at 551 (quoting 18 U.S.C. § 922 (q)(1)(A) (1988 ed., Supp. V)).
180. *See* 18 U.S.C. § 922(q)(1) (2000).
181. *Id.* § 922(q)(2)(A) (emphasis added).
182. *See, e.g.*, United States v. Danks, 221 F.3d 1037, 1039 (8th Cir. 1999).

Threats and Threatening Communications at School

8

James C. Hanks
Danielle Jess Haindfield

A. INTRODUCTION

Threats and threatening communications have become increasingly prevalent in our schools today. With studies showing that a detailed and specific threat to use violence is one of the most reliable indicators that a student is likely to commit a violent act,[1] and with the series of school shooting sprees in Kentucky, Arkansas, Colorado, and California lingering in the minds of Americans, it is not hard to understand why schools are asking themselves: How can we deal with threats that occur at school, and what can we do to prevent such threats from occurring in the first place?

Since a student's speech or writing can invoke certain constitutional rights, school officials must stop and analyze their position before acting. Part of this analysis involves discerning between a harmless joke or figure of speech and a "true

---

1. *See* K. Dwyer, National School Psychologists Association, *quoted in* SCHOOL POLICY LEGAL INSIDER at 3 (Dec. 1998).

threat."[2] This chapter will address how to analyze specific threats and discuss what actions school officials can legally take in response to threatening communications.

B. WHAT IS A THREAT OR A THREATENING COMMUNICATION?

A threat is "an expression of intent to do harm or act out violently against someone or something."[3] A threat can be verbal, written, symbolic, or even a gesture—for example, motioning with one's hands as though strangling or shooting another person.

Threats can be classified into four categories: direct, indirect, veiled, or conditional.[4] "A direct threat articulates a specific act against a particular target in a straightforward, clear, and explicit manner so there can be no misunderstanding";[5] for example, "I am going to plant explosives in the school cafeteria." An indirect threat, on the other hand, tends to be vague, unclear, and ambiguous.[6] "The plan, the intended victim, the motivation, and other aspects of the threat are masked or equivocal: 'If I wanted to, I could kill everyone at this school!' While violence is implied, the threat is phrased tentatively—'If I wanted to'—and suggests that a violent act could occur, not that it will occur."[7]

A veiled threat is one that strongly implies but does not explicitly threaten violence:[8] "This school would be better off without you around anymore." While this statement clearly hints at a possible violent act, it leaves it up to the potential victim to interpret the message and define it as a credible threat.[9]

A conditional threat is the type often seen in cases of blackmail. It warns that a violent or other unwanted act will occur unless certain de-

2. Lisa L. Swem, *Preventing Threats of Violence in Schools from Turning into a Tragedy,* 1999 SCHOOL LAW IN REVIEW, at 1-1 (NSBA 1999).

3. National Center for Analysis of Violent Crime, *Threats Assessment Intervention Model by NCAVC,* at http://www.grps.k12.mi.us/~studentservices/threatsassessment.pdf (hereinafter NCAVC).

4. *Id.*

5. *Id.*

6. *Id.*

7. *Id.*

8. *Id.*

9. *Id.*

mands or conditions are met;[10] for example, "If you don't give me 'x,' I will put a bomb in the school."

C. THREAT ASSESSMENTS

The best way for school officials to begin identifying, managing, and eventually preventing threats and threatening communications is to conduct a routine review of every potential threat and/or threatening situation. This process, known as "threat assessment," was first created by the U.S. Secret Service as a mechanism for investigating threats against the President of the United States and other protected individuals.[11] Recently, the U.S. Secret Service teamed with the U.S. Department of Education to modify its threat assessment process so that it could be utilized by school personnel, law enforcement, and others with protective responsibilities in our nation's schools.[12]

1. Factors in Threat Assessment

There are three critical factors involved in conducting a threat assessment. All of these factors deal with understanding the context from which the threat was made. The first factor requires that specific, plausible details about the alleged threat be ascertained.[13] These details can be discovered through witness or victim interviews; document examination; discussions with counselors, teachers, or other school personnel; or personal observation. The details may include the identity of the alleged speaker or victim(s); potential reason(s) for the making of the threat; the means and method by which the threat is to be carried out; the date, time and location where the threatened act will occur; and concrete information about plans or preparations that have been made to carry out the threat.[14]

The second factor involves determining the emotional content of the threat.[15] By determining this, one can get an important clue into the threatener's mental state.[16]

---

10. *Id.*
11. U.S. Secret Service and U.S. Department of Education, Threat Assessment in Schools: A Guide to Managing Threatening Situations and to Creating Safe School Climates (Washington, D.C., May 2002) at iii.
12. *Id.*
13. NCAVC, *supra* note 3.
14. *Id.*
15. *Id.*
16. *Id.*

The third factor deals with understanding precipitating stressors.[17] These stressors are viewed as incidents or circumstances that can trigger the making of a threat, even though the precipitating stressor may have no direct relevance to the content of the threat.[18] An example may include a student who had a fight with a parent before going to school. This argument may set off an emotional chain reaction leading to the student threatening another student that day at school.[19]

2. Levels of Risk

Another important component of a threat assessment is determining the actual risk posed by the threat, or in other words, the probability or likelihood that the threat will come to fruition. Generally, the more direct and detailed a threat is, the more serious the risk of it being acted upon. The levels of risk in a threat assessment can be categorized from low to high.[20] A low-level threat poses a minimal risk to the victim and public safety in general.[21] Typically, a low-level threat is not only vague and indirect, but its content is implausible and lacks realism, often suggesting that the perpetrator is unlikely to carry out the threat.[22]

A medium-level threat could logistically be carried out; however, not all the pieces of the threat line up and it does not appear entirely realistic.[23] A medium-level threat is clearly more thought out than a low-level threat, but typically the terms of the threat are general in nature and there are no strong indications that preparatory steps have been taken to actually carry out the threat.[24]

High-level threats appear to pose an immediate and significant threat to the health and safety of the named victim or the public in general.[25] A high-level threat is direct, specific, and realistic, and information suggests that the threatener has taken concrete steps toward carrying out the threat.[26]

---

17. *Id.*
18. *Id.*
19. *Id.*
20. *Id.*
21. *Id.*
22. *Id.*
23. *Id.*
24. *Id.*
25. *Id.*
26. *Id.*

A high-level threat will almost always require immediate law enforcement contact and intervention.

In most cases, the distinction between the levels of the threat may not be obvious, and there may be overlap between the categories. What is important is that schools be able to recognize and act on the most serious threats and address all other threats appropriately and in a timely fashion.[27]

3. Implementing a Threat Assessment Program

Threat assessment policies and programs work best when incorporated into an overall school violence prevention strategy and when developed and implemented collectively by local school officials with members of the student body and community as a whole.[28] A proposed course of action for implementing a threat assessment program in a school district is as follows:

1. School board approves the development of a process to evaluate and respond to threatening communications and situations.[29]
2. School creates a planning team to develop or further refine a process to identify, assess, and manage threatening communications and situations.[30] Members of this team should be selected from throughout the community. Team members could include students, parents, board members, administrators, law enforcement representatives, school legal counsel, school psychologists, or other mental health workers.
3. The planning team determines what policies, procedures, rules, regulations, or processes should be revised or created.[31] Specifically, the team determines the status and current effectiveness of the following: (a) information-sharing agreements or policies, (b) existing policies on threats and threatening communications, (c) existing policies regarding the role of law enforcement in school, (d) existing proactive approaches used to create and maintain safe

---

27. *Id.*
28. U.S. SECRET SERVICE & U.S. DEPARTMENT OF EDUCATION, *supra* note 11 at 5–6.
29. Public Entity Risk Institute, *EXTRA: Creating a Safe and Connected School Climate*, *at* http://www.riskinstitute.org/periscope.asp?article_id=1062.
30. *Id.*
31. *Id.*

and respectful school climates and situations, and (e) existing policies on e-mail and Internet usage.[32]

4. School administrators, teachers, law enforcement officials, and other members of the community should be provided with the opportunity to review and comment on any revised policies or recommended processes created by the planning team.[33]

5. School board reviews and acts upon the planning team's recommended changes.[34]

6. After school board approval, the administration and other proper agencies will implement the new threat assessment program and corresponding policies and procedures.[35]

D. HOW SHOULD SCHOOLS LEGALLY RESPOND TO THREATS AND THREATENING COMMUNICATIONS?

Regardless of whether a threat assessment is completed by a threat assessment team as part of a comprehensive threat assessment policy/program or by an administrator contemplating the context of a situation for five minutes, the next questions are, what can the school legally do to respond to the threat, and what legal risks might the school face if it disciplines the student based solely upon the content of the communication?

A recent U.S. Secret Service report that analyzed 37 school shootings highlighted the fact that caring adults—teachers, coaches, counselors, and school administrators—can have a positive affect on troubled students and can play a vital role in preventing threatening communications and subsequent acts of violence in schools.[36] Therefore, school officials should be cognizant of any threatening communications made by students and should promptly respond to any such threats that suggest a student may be contemplating violence either to him- or herself or to others.

---

32. *Id.*
33. *Id.*
34. *Id.*
35. *Id.*
36. *Preventing School Shootings: A Summary of a U.S. Secret Service Safe School Initiative Report*, NAT'L INST. JUSTICE J. (July 21, 2002), *at* http://ericcass.uncg.edu/virtuallib/violence/violencebook.html.

At the same time, however, public school students have a constitutional right to free speech under the First Amendment, and schools must follow due process procedures before certain disciplinary action may be taken against a student. Several school districts have been forced to defend themselves in court for disciplining students who engaged in speech that school officials considered potentially disruptive or dangerous, but that the students themselves claimed was constitutionally protected.[37] Therefore, as one commentator has noted, school officials face a difficult dilemma: "Should they respond to a student's speech that may be an indication of future violence and risk a lawsuit? Or should they scrupulously respect a student's right to free speech, even speech that may be a warning sign of impending violence?"[38]

In an effort to balance student rights with school responsibilities, the courts have been forced to wrestle with significant constitutional questions involving free speech and due process. Not surprisingly, the rulings from these courts are varied and generally result from judicial scrutiny of the specific facts of each case.

1. Free Speech Rights

In the school context, there are two bases in which a student's threatening speech will not be protected by the First Amendment—if the speech is determined to be a "true threat"[39] or if the speech justifies a "reasonable suspicion" by school officials that it may "substantially disrupt the school environment."[40]

a. *True Threat Inquiry*

As a general rule, the First Amendment prohibits governmental actors from dictating what persons may see, read, speak, or hear.[41] However, certain categories or modes of expressions, such as obscenity, defamation, and

---

37. Richard Fossey, *How Should Schools Respond to a Student's Violent Speech: Guidance from Two Federal Courts*, ELA NOTES 14 (Fourth Quarter 2003).

38. *Id.*

39. Watts v. United States, 394 U.S. 705, 708, 22 L. Ed. 2d 664, 89 S. Ct. 1399 (1969).

40. Tinker v. Des Moines Indep. Cmty. Sch. Dist., 393 U.S. 503, 512–13, 21 L. Ed. 2d 731, 89 S. Ct. 733 (1969).

41. Ashcroft v. The Free Speech Coalition, 535 U.S. 234, 152 L. Ed. 2d 403, 122 S. Ct. 1289, 1399 (2002).

fighting words, have been viewed by the courts as having such slight social value that First Amendment protection is not warranted.[42] In *Watts v.
United States*, the U.S. Supreme Court first recognized that threats of violence that constitute "true threats" fall within those categories of speech
that are not protected by the ambit of the First Amendment.[43] The Court in
Watts, however, did not set forth a particular definition of a "true threat"
that distinguishes an unprotected threat from constitutionally protected
speech.[44] Thus, the lower courts have been left to discern for themselves
when a statement triggers the government's interest in preventing the disruption and fear of violence associated with a threat.[45]

The federal courts of appeals have collectively created an objective
test that helps determine whether a statement is a "true threat" falling outside First Amendment protection. This test focuses on "whether a reasonable person would interpret the alleged threat as a serious expression of an
intent to cause a present or future harm."[46] The views of the federal courts
diverge, however, when trying to determine from whose viewpoint the
statement should be determined—in other words, there is still a debate
over whether this objective standard views the nature of the alleged threat
from the perspective of a reasonable recipient or a reasonable speaker.[47]

Regardless of whose viewpoint is used to determine the threatening
nature of a statement, there are certain factors in each case that the courts
will consider in determining whether an expression or speech is a "true

---

42. R.A.V. v. City of St. Paul, 505 U.S. 377, 382, 120 L. Ed. 2d 305, 112 S. Ct.
2538 (1992); Chaplinsky v. New Hampshire, 315 U.S. 568, 571-72, 86 L. Ed. 1031,
62 S. Ct. 766 (1942).

43. Watts v. United States, 394 U.S. 705, 708, 22 L. Ed. 2d 664, 89 S. Ct. 1399
(1969).

44. *See e.g.*, Doe v. Pulaski County Special Sch. Dist., 306 F.3d 616, 622 (8th
Cir. 2002); Demers v. Leominster Sch. Dep't, 263 F. Supp. 2d 195 (D. Mass. 2003).

45. *Id.*

46. *See* United States v. Fulmer, 108 F.3d 1486, 1490–91 (1st Cir. 1990).

47. *Compare Doe*, 306 F.3d at 622–23 (viewing the alleged threat from the viewpoint of a reasonable recipient); United States v. Malik, 16 F.3d 45, 49 (2d Cir.), *cert.
denied*, 513 U.S. 968, 130 L. Ed. 2d 347, 115 S. Ct. 435 (1994) (same); *and* United
States v. Maisonet, 484 F.2d 1356, 1358 (4th Cir. 1973) (same) *with* United States v.
Orozco-Santillan, 903 F.2d 1262, 1265 (9th Cir. 1990) (viewing the alleged threat
from the speaker's viewpoint); United States v. Welch, 745 F.2d 614, 620 (10th Cir.
1984) (same); *and* Mahaffey v. Aldrich, 236 F. Supp. 2d 779, 784 (E.D. Mich. 2002)
(citing United States v. Lineberry, 7 Fed. Appx. 520, 2001 U.S. App. LEXIS 5856
(6th Cir. 2001)) (same).

threat." These factors include: (1) the context in which the alleged threat was made; (2) the actions of the speaker and the reaction of those who heard the alleged threat; (3) whether the person who made the alleged threat communicated it directly to the object of the threat; (4) whether the speaker had a history of making threats against the person purportedly threatened; and (5) whether the recipient had a reason to believe that the speaker had a propensity to engage in violence.[48]

b. Tinker *Analysis*

It has been clearly established that students do not "shed their constitutional rights to freedom of speech or expression at the schoolhouse gate."[49] However, public school officials have been granted substantial deference in determining what speech is appropriate in order to control the conduct and educational environment of the school.[50] In *Tinker v. Des Moines Independent Community School District*, the U.S. Supreme Court held that schools can punish student conduct or speech if the school has a "reasonable suspicion" that the conduct or speech will "materially and substantially interfere with the requirements of appropriate discipline in the operation of the school" and may otherwise "substantially disrupt the school environment."[51]

Consequently, under the *Tinker* analysis, speech that might not otherwise meet the technical threshold of "true threat" may nonetheless be unprotected speech under the Constitution if the speech has a substantial likelihood of causing disruption to the learning process and school environment.[52] Many courts have held that threats and threatening communications directed at students or teachers in the school setting materially and substantially interfere with the school activities and the operation of the school. Additionally, most courts that have utilized the *Tinker* standard with regard to threatening communications have held that threats are unlike those categorized as silent, passive, expression of opinion, or unaccompanied by disorder or disturbance that the students in *Tinker* represented

---

48. T.W. v. School District of Philadelphia, 2000 U.S. Dist. LEXIS 5945 (E.D. Penn. 2003); *Doe*, 306 F.3d at 623.

49. *Tinker*, 393 U.S. at 506.

50. Hazelwood Sch. Dist. v. Kuhlmeier, 484 U.S. 260, 266, 98 L. Ed. 2d 592, 108 S. Ct. 562 (1988) ("A school need not tolerate students' speech that is inconsistent with its basic educational mission, even though the government could not censor similar speech outside the school.").

51. *Tinker*, 393 U.S. at 509, 512–13.

52. Swem, *supra* note 2, at 1–2.

when they silently protested the Vietnam War by wearing black armbands to school.[53]

In *S.G. v. Sayreville*,[54] the Third Circuit upheld the three-day suspension of a 5-year-old kindergarten student for saying, "I am going to shoot you" while playing cops and robbers outside at recess.[55] Applying *Tinker* and placing significant importance on the young age of the student making the threatening statement, the court held that "school officials could reasonably believe they were acting within the scope of their permissible authority in deciding that the use of threatening language [by kindergarten students] at school undermines the school's basic educational mission."[56] The reasonableness of the school's decision in this case was also predicated on the fact that, at the same school, there had been three previous incidents involving children who threatened to shoot someone or who claimed to have a gun, and the fact that two weeks before the incident in question there was a nationally publicized case in which a 6-year-old shot another 6-year-old child at an elementary school in Michigan.[57]

In *Demers v. Leominster School Department*, a student with a discipline and substance abuse history drew a picture at school of explosives surrounding the school, students hanging out of windows, and the superintendent pointing a gun at his head with explosives at his feet.[58] The school suspended the student and the student sued, alleging a violation of his First Amendment right to free speech.[59] Citing *Tinker*, the court held that it would have been unthinkable for the school not to have acted in this case, and that "a reasonable interpretation of the law would allow a school official to prevent potential disorder or disruption to school safety, particularly in the wake of increased school violence across the country."[60]

Other courts have not viewed the *Tinker* standard as providing much latitude for school districts to suppress speech in an effort to maintain order and safety at school.[61] This is particularly true when the allegedly

---

53. *See e.g.*, *Demers*, 263 F. Supp. 2d at 202.
54. S.G. v. Sayreville, 333 F.3d 417 (3d Cir. 2003).
55. *Id*. at 423.
56. *Id*.
57. *Id*.
58. *Demers*, 263 F. Supp. 2d at 198–99.
59. *Id*. at 199.
60. *Id*. at 203.
61. *See, e.g.*, *Mahaffey*, 236 F.2d at 786. *But compare* J.S. v. Bethlehem Area School District, 757 A.2d 412 (Pa Commw. Ct. 2000).

threatening speech is created or communicated off school grounds, such as via a Web site.[62] In *Mahaffey v. Aldrich*, a school district suspended a student after the school learned of a Web site to which the student had contributed.[63] The Web site listed people who the student wished would die and also created a mission whereby readers were told to stab someone for no reason. According to the student, the Web site was created "just for laughs."[64] Utilizing *Tinker*, the court held that the school could only punish the student for his speech on the Web site if that speech "substantially interfered with the work of the school or impinged upon the rights of other students."[65] Applying this standard to the facts of the case, the court found that the student did not communicate the statements on the Web site to anyone and that there was no evidence in the record to prove there was any disruption to the school or campus activity as a result of the creation of the Web site.[66] Therefore, the court ruled that the school's actions against the student violated his First Amendment rights.[67]

2. Due Process Considerations

Once a school official has assessed and analyzed a threatening communication and has determined that the speech is a "true threat," or justifies a reasonable suspicion that the speech may substantially disrupt the school environment, the question then is, what sanctions may or should the school take against the student for the threatening speech, and what due process considerations must be followed?

The Supreme Court, in *Goss v. Lopez*,[68] recognized a student's legitimate entitlement to a public education as a property interest that is protected by the due process clause and that may not be taken away for misconduct without proper adherence to minimum due process procedures.[69] The key procedures for minimum due process are notice and an opportunity to be heard.[70] Short suspensions of 10 days or less require that the student receive oral or written notice of the charges against him or her,

---

62. *Id.*
63. *Mahaffey*, 236 F.2d at 781–82.
64. *Id.*
65. *Id.* at 784.
66. *Id.* at 786.
67. *Id.*
68. Goss v. Lopez, 419 U.S. 565, 42 L. Ed. 2d 725, 95 S. Ct. 729 (1975).
69. *Id.* at 574.
70. *Id.* at 581.

an explanation of the evidence against him or her, and an opportunity to tell his or her side of the story.[71] This exchange of information can be informal for short suspensions and may occur immediately after the incident.[72] For longer suspensions and expulsions, the notice of the charges and evidence should be in writing and should be presented to the student in advance of a more formalized hearing.[73]

In *S.G.v. Sayreville*, the court held that the due process rights of the 5-year-old male student were not violated when, outside the presence of his parents, the school principal questioned the boy about allegedly threatening speech he engaged in during recess.[74] The principal had attempted to locate the parents before talking with the boy but could not reach them, and the principal wanted to question the student as soon after the incident as possible.[75]

During the principal's discussion with the boy, the student admitted he was "playing guns" and that he had made a statement regarding shooting a gun.[76] The court held that this discussion between the principal and student was enough opportunity for the student to present his side of the story and the fact that the parents were not present did not negate this fact.[77] The court upheld the school's decision to suspend the boy for three days.[78]

For due process purposes, notice should also include giving students clear and advance notice of prohibited conduct in the student handbook or conduct code.[79] For example, a school's code of conduct should clearly outline the school's position on threatening behavior and should identify the type of threatening behavior that could subject a student to disciplinary consequences and should identify what those consequences may be. Additionally, if a school intends to impose disciplinary sanctions for passive as well as active conduct regarding threats, the code of conduct or handbook provisions should clearly place students on notice that such passive behavior may also be subject to discipline.[80]

71. *Id.*
72. *Id.* at 582.
73. *Id.*
74. *Sayreville*, 333 F.3d at 424.
75. *Id.*
76. *Id.*
77. *Id.*
78. *Id.*
79. Swem, *supra* note 2, at 1–4.
80. *Id.* (citing Goldwire v. Clark, 507 S.E.2d 209 (Ga. Ct. App. 1998)).

It is imperative that, if a school has due process procedures in place for violations of the school's handbook policies or code of conduct rules, the school follow these procedures. Failure to follow prescribed rules can open a school up to potential liability. In *Mahaffey v. Aldrich,* the court held that a due process hearing afforded to a student who was expelled for a semester for allegedly created a threatening Web page using school computers violated the student's due process rights because the school chose not to follow its own hearing procedures, which were created for analyzing violations of the school's code of conduct.[81] Instead, the school chose to follow procedures set out in a separate protocol.[82] Additionally, at the hearing, the student's counsel attempted several times to cross-examine witnesses but was denied the opportunity to do so, and the student's counsel was also not allowed to call school employees as witnesses.[83]

The previous discussion of recent cases helps to illustrate the legal issues that courts consider when analyzing student speech that could be construed to be a threat. The preceding analysis suggests the following format for the review of threats:

1. In order to sanction a student's allegedly threatening speech, the school should analyze and ascertain whether that threat is either a "true threat" or speech that justified a "reasonable suspicion" that it may "substantially disrupt the school environment";
2. If the school is uncertain whether a student's speech is constitutionally protected, it should consult legal counsel or other professionals for help and guidance; and
3. If it is determined that the speech is not constitutionally protected, the school should sanction such speech pursuant to the guidelines outlined in its policies and procedures and in accordance with constitutionally required due process.

E. PROACTIVE WAYS TO CREATE A SAFE AND CONNECTED SCHOOL CLIMATE

Threat assessment and disciplinary responses to threatening communications should be considered as only part of an overall strategy to prevent such behavior and reduce school violence in general. The threat assess-

---

81. *Mahaffey,* 236 F. Supp. 2d at 788.
82. *Id.*
83. *Id.*

ment process by itself is unlikely to have a lasting effect in reducing threatening behavior and the problem of targeted school violence unless and until that process is implemented within the larger context of working toward a safe and secure learning environment.[84]

The following are major components and tasks for school officials to work toward in the creation of a safe/connected school climate:[85]

1. Assess the school's emotional climate.
2. Emphasize the importance of listening in schools.
3. Break the "code of silence" by letting people know that reporting suspicious or threatening behavior is positive action.
4. Take steps to prevent and intervene in bullying.
5. Empower students and others by involving all members of the school community in planning, creating, and sustaining a school culture of safety and respect.
6. Develop connections and ongoing relationships between adults and students and ensure that every student feels that he or she has a trusting relationship with at least one adult at school.
7. Create mechanisms for developing and sustaining safe school climates.

F. CONCLUSION

In dealing with threats and threatening communications, it is important not only to promptly react to such behavior through threat assessment and disciplinary action where warranted, but also to be proactive in trying to prevent such threatening communications in the first place. The best way to prevent such threatening communication is to create a safe and nurturing environment for students at school.

---

84. U.S. SECRET SERVICE & U.S. DEPARTMENT OF EDUCATION, *supra* note 11, at 11.
85. Public Entity Risk Institute, *EXTRA: Creating a Safe and Connected School Climate, at* http://www.riskinstitute.org/periscope.asp?article_id=1062; U.S. SECRET SERVICE & U.S. DEPARTMENT OF EDUCATION, *supra* note 11, at 6.

Disciplining the Violent Student with Disabilities

9

Ann Majestic
Carolyn Waller
Julie Devine

A. INTRODUCTION

For years after the tragedy at Columbine High School, the media spotlight on school safety issues continues. School safety concerns have prompted legislation at both the state and federal levels that places stiff penalties on students who commit acts of violence in school. At the federal level, Congress has passed legislation requiring schools that receive federal funds to institute a mandatory 365-day suspension for any student who brings a gun to school.[1] Many states have gone further by expanding the list of offenses that could lead to a 365-day suspension or expulsion. California legislation includes a laundry list of possible expulsion offenses, including threats to cause physical injury, intentional use of force or violence, and intentional defiance of school officials.[2] North

---

1. THE GUN-FREE SCHOOLS ACT, 20 U.S.C. § 8921 (1994).
2. *See* CAL. EDUC. CODE § 48900(a)–(o).

155

Carolina legislation includes 365-day suspensions for bomb threats and, after the anthrax scare of October 2001, for making false threats of terror.[3]

Although school disciplinary rules apply to all students, students with disabilities are provided with special statutory protections. The Individuals with Disabilities Education Act (IDEA),[4] the federal law that mandates a "free and appropriate education" for students with disabilities, places significant limitations on the ability of school officials to suspend disabled students for longer than 10 days. Provisions of the IDEA relating to discipline are intended to ensure that school districts do not exclude disabled students from school because of behaviors that are a result of their disabilities. Congress wanted to prevent school districts from "warehousing" special education students or "neglectfully shepherding" them through the school system until they drop out. There was a special concern that schools would improperly exclude children with emotional or behavioral disabilities.[5]

The IDEA, originally passed in 1975 and significantly amended in 1997, is designed to ensure that students with disabilities receive a "free and appropriate public education." Each child who is found eligible for services receives an Individualized Education Program (IEP), which is intended to serve the child in the least restrictive environment. The IEP is created by a multidisciplinary team (IEP team), which includes a special education teacher, a general education teacher, a representative from the local educational agency, someone who can interpret and explain evaluation data, the parent or guardian, and, if appropriate, the child.[6] The IDEA provides parents of disabled children with a variety of procedural protections in the identification and evaluation of children with disabilities and in the creation and implementation of the IEP.

In the context of school discipline, the IDEA provides protections for children who display behaviors that are manifestations of their disabilities and prevents a change in placement without the proper procedures.[7] One of the most powerful protections for children with disabilities is the "stay-put" or pendency provision, which prevents a change in placement if due process proceedings are pending. Under this provision, if a parent or guard-

---

3. *See* N.C. GEN. STAT. § 115C-391(d4).
4. 20 U.S.C. § 1415 *et seq.*
5. Honig v. Doe, 484 U.S. 305, 309 (1988) (citing the congressional statistics).
6. 20 U.S.C. § 1414(d)(1)(B).
7. 20 U.S.C. § 1415(k)(4).

ian initiates due process proceedings outlined in the IDEA to contest some aspect of his or her child's special education, including a long-term suspension, the child remains in the current educational setting while the case is pending. This allows parents to effectively veto a proposed change in placement, like a long-term suspension, until the issue of placement is resolved. If all forums are used, this process could, and sometimes does, last several years.

There are, however, some exceptions to the stay-put provisions when disciplining dangerous students. Under the original IDEA, the only way for school districts to avoid the stay-put provision in a suspension case was to seek an injunction in state or federal court to obtain a change in placement.[8] The 1997 Amendments to the IDEA, along with the accompanying regulations, have created some narrow exceptions to the stay-put provisions and created alternative methods for removing dangerous students with disabilities from school.

Section 504 of the Rehabilitation Act of 1973 also provides protections for disabled students who are suspended or expelled from school. Section 504 prohibits discrimination on the basis of disability in the implementation of educational programs.[9] Section 504 has requirements similar to those under the IDEA for disciplining students with disabilities, including limitations on the length of the suspension and protections for children whose behaviors are a manifestation of their disabilities. Although there are many similarities between the two laws, there are also some differences. In general, if a school district follows the requirements for disciplining a child with a disability under the IDEA, it will meet the requirements of Section 504 for purposes of disciplinary action.

This chapter will discuss how and when school officials may discipline a student with a disability who has engaged in violent or dangerous behavior. It will focus on the discipline requirements under the IDEA and conclude with a discussion of the differences between the IDEA and Section 504 regarding discipline.

B. THE USE OF SHORT-TERM SUSPENSIONS

Short-term suspensions, or those for 10 days or less, do not trigger the same protections for disabled students as longer removals from school.

---

8. *See* Honig v. Doe, 108 S. Ct. 592 (1988).
9. 29 U.S.C. § 706 *et seq.*

The IDEA allows school officials to suspend children with disabilities from school for up to 10 days, even if the parents object, if the discipline is "appropriate and is administered consistent with the treatment of nondisabled children."[10] School officials cannot, however, remove a child with a disability for more than a total of 10 days in a school year without triggering the IDEA procedural protections. If a series of short-term suspensions results in a "change in placement," the procedural protections of the IDEA are triggered, and school officials must follow the procedural steps required for a long-term suspension or expulsion, as described below.

1. Defining a Change in Placement Due to a Pattern of Exclusion

To determine if there has been a "change in placement" or pattern of exclusion of a disabled child due to a series of suspensions exceeding 10 school days, the IDEA regulations direct that the length of each removal, the total amount of time that the child is removed, and the proximity of the removals to one another be considered.[11] The focus of this provision of the IDEA, it appears, is on the impact the removals are likely to have on the child's education program. For example, a total of 15 days of suspension consisting of four days in September, five days in December, and six days in March probably would not constitute a change of placement because the total number of days does not exceed 10 by very many and there are several months separating each suspension. The same three short-term suspensions (four, five, and six days) all occurring within a six-week period, on the other hand, would probably amount to a change of placement because of the significant disruption in the child's education. If a child is removed for portions of the school day (such as a half day), these portions are generally included in determining whether there has been a change in placement or whether the child has been suspended for a total of more than 10 days.[12]

---

10. Assistance to States for the Education of Children with Disabilities and Early Intervention Program for Infants and Toddlers with Disabilities, 64 Fed. Reg. 12,415 (1999).

11. *Id.*

12. Assistance to States for the Education of Children with Disabilities and the Early Intervention Program for Infants and Toddlers with Disabilities, 64 Fed. Reg. 12,406, 12,619 (1999).

a. *Change in Place versus Change in Placement*

The law does not define an "educational placement," so precisely defining a change in placement can be difficult. Generally, a change in location from one school to another is not considered a change in placement, although a move from a neighborhood school to an alternative school may be considered a change in placement.[13] The critical issue is not the physical location of the student's program, but whether the student experienced a material modification to the delivery of services on his or her IEP.[14] Given this definition, a suspension of over 10 days is not automatically considered a change in placement.[15]

C. IN-SCHOOL SUSPENSIONS

The classification of an in-school suspension varies based on the specific circumstances. Comments in the Federal Register indicate that an in-school suspension would not be considered a "change in placement" or count toward the 10-day limit as long as:

> the child is afforded the opportunity to continue to appropriately progress in the general curriculum, continue to receive the services specified on his or her IEP, and continue to participate with nondisabled students to the extent they would have in their current placement.[16]

Given this definition, determining whether an in-school suspension should be counted as a change in placement is a fact-based inquiry. One

---

13. *See, e.g.,* Concerned Parents & Citizens for the Continuing Education at Malcolm X v. The New York City Bd. of Educ., 629 F.2d 751 (2d Cir. 1980).

14. Richmond County Sch. Sys., 32 IDELR 84 (SEA Ga. 1999). *See also* Bd. of Educ. of Cmty. High School Dist. No. 218 v. Ill. State Bd. of Educ., 103 F.3d 545, 548 (7th Cir. 1996) (defining "change in placement"); Kaelin v. Grubbs, 682 F.2d 595 (6th Cir. 1982) (finding that a change in placement occurred when a child was expelled); School Bd. of the County of Prince William, Va. v. Malone, 762 F.2d 1210 (4th Cir. 1985) (finding that explusion reflects change in placement).

15. *See, e.g.,* Parents of Student W. v. Puyallup School Dist. No. 3, 31 F.3d 1489, 1495 (9th Cir. 1994).

16. Assistance to States for the Education of Children with Disabilities and the Early Intervention Program for Infants and Toddlers with Disabilities, 64 Fed. Reg. 12,406, 12,619 (1999).

hearing officer in Iowa found that significant time spent in "crisis intervention" outside of the classroom could not be classified as a suspension because it was a critical part of the child's educational program.[17] In an Indiana case, the Department of Education, Office of Civil Rights (OCR) found that the in-school suspension was not a change in placement because the student received services pursuant to his IEP and behavior plan while he was placed in in-school suspension.[18]

D. BUS SUSPENSIONS

Whether a bus suspension is considered a change in placement depends on whether or not bus transportation was a part of the IEP. If bus service is part of the IEP, a suspension from the bus is considered a change in placement unless the local school district provides alternative transportation.[19] If bus service is not a part of the IEP, a child with a disability can be suspended from the bus according to the same procedures as children without disabilities. The school system should examine, however, whether the behavior on the bus is similar to behavior in the classroom that is addressed in the IEP or behavioral intervention plan for the child. This determination will allow the school system to assess whether special transportation should be considered as a related service for the child.[20]

E. THE USE OF LONG-TERM SUSPENSIONS AND EXPULSIONS

When a special education student faces a suspension longer than 10 days, or if a series of short-term suspensions of the student will result in a change of placement, rigorous procedural protections of the IDEA must be followed.

1. Parental Notice Requirement

Prior to implementing a long-term suspension, expulsion, or any other change in placement for a special education student, administrators must notify parents of the decision and of the procedural safeguards afforded

---

17. Mason City Cmty. School Dist. and Northern Trails Area Educ. Agency, 39 IDELR 25 (SEA Iowa 2003).
18. Jay School Corp. (Ind.), 37 IDELR 97 (OCR 2002).
19. *Id.*
20. 64 Fed. Reg. 12,621, 12,619 (1999).

under the IDEA. School officials must provide this notice on the date of the decision to take the action.[21] In other words, when a school administrator notifies parents of a recommendation for long-term suspension or expulsion, the administrator must also provide parents with full and complete notice of their procedural rights under the IDEA. This notice must comply with general notice requirements of the IDEA, including a disclosure of the decision to suspend or expel the student and the basis for that decision, a statement of other options considered and rejected, notice of the parents' or guardians' right to file for due process, and information about possible sources for assistance in understanding their procedural rights under the IDEA.[22]

2. Manifestation Determination

When the suspension of a special education student will result in a change of placement, the IEP team must determine whether the student's misbehavior is a manifestation of his disability. This process is referred to as a manifestation determination review. A manifestation determination must be made as soon as possible but no later than 10 *school* days after (a) any single suspension lasting more than 10 days, or (b) any series of suspensions exceeding 10 cumulative days that results in a disciplinary change of placement.[23] A manifestation determination, therefore, is not required after a three-day suspension for a child with a disability, but if the same child is suspended for eight days later that same year, and this results in a "change in placement," as described above, the school must hold a manifestation determination.

To determine whether the behavior is a manifestation of a child's disability, the IEP team must consider all relevant information, including: (1) evaluation and diagnostic results; (2) observations of the child; (3) the child's IEP and placement; and (4) parental input.[24] In addition, the team must determine whether, in relation to the behavior subject to disciplinary action:

1. the child's IEP and placement were appropriate, and special education and related services, supplementary aids and services, and

---

21. 20 U.S.C. § 1415(k)(4)(A)(1).
22. 34 C.F.R. §§ 300.503(b)(1)–(7).
23. 20 U.S.C. § 1415(k)(4)(A)(ii); Reg. 300.523(a).
24. 20 U.S.C. § 1415(k)(4)(C)(1).

behavior intervention strategies were provided consistent with the child's IEP and placement;

2. the disability impaired the child's ability to understand the impact and consequences of the behavior; and
3. the disability impaired the child's ability to control the behavior.[25]

If the child's disability includes an inability to control his or her impulses, this does not mean that the child's improper behavior will always be considered a manifestation of his or her disability. In a Georgia case, the parents of an eleventh-grader argued that their son's suspension for bringing a knife to a school football game was improper because it was a manifestation of his attention deficit disorder (ADD).[26] The administrative law judge acknowledged that ADD is often accompanied by impatience, an inability to delay responses, and a lack of conscious thought. He held, however, that the behavior was not a manifestation of the student's ADD because the student admitted to bringing the knife to the game to protect a friend. The administrative law judge found that this showed conscious planning, inconsistent with ADD.[27] Similarly, the U.S. District Court in Maine found that there was no evidence that selling drugs at school was a manifestation of a child's impulsivity problems. The school district showed that the student understood school rules, his actions took place over several hours, and his actions involved not one single decision but many individual ones.[28]

Some school officials fear that misbehavior by a child with an emotional disability will always be considered a manifestation of that disability. There are ways, however, to analyze the student's specific behaviors to determine if they are a result of the child's emotional or behavioral disability. In a Maine case, a hearing officer reviewed a manifestation determination of a child with an emotional disturbance who brought a gun to school and hid it on school grounds. The incident involved a number of small, individual decisions about bringing the gun to school, hiding it outside of the school, and refusing to tell officials where he had hidden it. The hearing officer found that this series of events showed that the student made a conscious,

---

25. 20 U.S.C. § 1415(k)(4)(C)(ii).
26. Carroll County School Sys., 39 IDELR 30 (SEA Georgia 2003).
27. *Id.*
28. Farrin v. Maine School Admin. Dist. No. 50, 165 F. Supp. 2d 37, 52 (D. Maine 2001).

willful, and planned decision to bring the gun to school.[29] The hearing officer determined that the student was acting deliberately, and therefore the behavior was not a manifestation of his emotional disturbance.[30]

In determining what is a manifestation of a child's disability, the IEP team must consider all of the child's disabilities, and not just the primary disability that serves as the child's classification for purposes of the IDEA. In a Wisconsin case, the school district argued that the IEP team only had to consider the primary disability that made the student eligible for special education, which was a learning disability.[31] The court held that the IEP team also had to consider the fact that the child's evaluation indicated that she exhibited behavioral and attentional problems, emphasizing that the IEP team was not limited to considering only her learning disability.[32]

If the IEP team determines that the misbehavior *was not* a manifestation of the child's disability, the administration may initiate disciplinary procedures applicable to all children. The school district, however, must continue to provide the special education student with services, as described below. This may include creating some kind of "expulsion" IEP.

If the IEP team finds that the child's behavior *was* a manifestation of the disability, the child may not be suspended and the child's placement may not be changed except through the IEP process.[33] If the IEP team subsequently meets and determines that a change in placement is appropriate, but the parents object, the parents may file for due process proceedings and trigger the stay-put provision. If this occurs, the child remains in his current placement until the legal dispute is resolved, unless the parents consent to a change or the placement is changed through court action as described below. Again, the definition of a "change in placement" becomes vital at this point. As described above, a change of placement is not automatic if a child is moved from one setting to an alternative setting. If this change in placement follows disciplinary action, however, courts may scrutinize the school district's actions more closely.[34]

---

29. School Admin. Dist. #35, 36 IDELR 249 (SEA Maine 2002).
30. *Id.*
31. Richland Sch. Dist. v. Thomas P., 2000 U.S. Dist. LEXIS 15162 (W.D. Wis. 2000).
32. *Id.* at *24.
33. 20 U.S.C. § 1415(k)(4).
34. Assistance to States for the Education of Children with Disabilities and the Early Intervention Program for Infants and Toddlers with Disabilities, 64 Fed. Reg.12,406, 12,619 (1999).

3. Functional Behavioral Assessments and Behavioral Intervention Plans

A functional behavioral assessment (FBA) and behavioral intervention plan (BIP) must be completed for a special education student who is suspended for more than 10 days in a school year. Within 10 *business* days after 10 cumulative days of suspension, the school district must convene an IEP meeting to develop a functional behavioral assessment to analyze the behavior problem. A behavior intervention plan must then be developed as soon as practical based on the assessment. If the child already has a behavioral intervention plan, the IEP team must review the plan and modify it as necessary to address the behavior.[35]

The specific components of an FBA and a BIP are not identified in federal law or regulations.[36] At a minimum, it appears that an FBA must analyze the student's behavioral problem to assist in designing an intervention plan. The intervention plan, or BIP, should, according to an Iowa hearing officer:

1. be based on assessment data;
2. be individualized to meet the child's unique needs;
3. include positive behavior change strategies; and
4. be consistently implemented as planned and its effects monitored.[37]

In this case, the hearing officer held that the BIP was appropriate because there was assessment data from a private evaluation, the behavior modification program (a token economy) was individualized to the needs of the child, there were ample opportunities to acknowledge and encourage positive behavior, and the school monitored the child's progress through the "point" records and IEP goal updates.[38] In a New York case, the State Review Officer found that a child's functional behavior assessment was

---

35. 20 U.S.C. § 1415(1)(B); 34 C.F.R. § 300.520(b).
36. Allan G. Osborne, *Education Law and Policy: Discipline of Special Education Students under the Individuals with Disabilities Education Act,* 29 FORDHAM URB. L. J. 513, 529 (2001); Cynthia A. Dieterich & Christine J. Villani, *Functional Behavioral Assessment: Process Without Procedure,* 2000 BYU EDUC. & L.J. 209, 210 (2000).
37. Mason City Community Sch. Dist. and Northern Trails Area Educ. Agency, 39 IDELR 25 (SEA Iowa 2003) (quoting 36 IDELR 50, SEA Iowa 2001).
38. *Id.*

inappropriate because there was "virtually no discussion of the boy's behavioral needs."[39] Instead, the student's resource-room teachers met with him to review the support services he was receiving. The State Review Officer found that this could only be considered a part the process of understanding the dimensions of the boy's behavioral problems and was not a legally sufficient functional behavioral assessment.[40]

F. DISCIPLINING CHILDREN WHO HAVE NOT BEEN IDENTIFIED AS HAVING A DISABILITY

Students with disabilities who do not have IEPs may also have protections under the IDEA if the school district had knowledge of the child's disability before the suspension. If the school had knowledge that the student was disabled prior to the disciplinary incident, the student cannot be subject to long-term suspension or expulsion until an evaluation is completed and a manifestation determination is conducted. Thus, if the school district had knowledge of the child's disability, all IDEA protections must be applied. If, however, a manifestation determination is held and the IEP team finds that the behavior was not a manifestation of the disability, then the child may be suspended to the same extent as a nondisabled student.

A school district is deemed to have knowledge that a child has a disability if:

1. the parent of the child has expressed concern in writing (or orally if the parent is not able to write);
2. the child's behavior or performance demonstrates the need for services;
3. the parent has requested an evaluation; or
4. the child's teacher or other personnel has expressed concern about the behavior or performance of the child to school personnel involved in the special education referral system.[41]

If a school district determined in the past that an evaluation was not necessary, or conducted an evaluation and found that the child was not eligible, it would not be deemed to have knowledge of a disability for

---

39. Board of Educ. of the Akron Central School Dist., No. 98-20 (N.Y. 1998), *available at* www.sro.nysed.gov/98-20.htm.

40. *Id.*

41. 34 C.F.R. § 300.527 (b).

purposes of a disciplinary action.[42] In Arkansas, a hearing officer found that the school district could not be deemed to have knowledge that the student had a disability prior to the suspension, where he had been previously evaluated for special education services and found ineligible.[43] The hearing officer noted that the student's behavior prior to his expulsion for a drug violation did not raise any "red flags."[44]

In a recent federal district court decision from Massachusetts, the parents of a student challenged her removal from school while her special education evaluation was pending. They alleged that because the school knew that the student had failed all of her classes the previous year, and because her school health record indicated that she was medicated for attention deficit disorder, the school was on notice that the student likely suffered from a learning disability. The court agreed, finding that the school district had sufficient information at the time it expelled the student that she was a child with a disability. As a result, the court found that the district violated the stay-put provisions of the IDEA by removing the student while it conducted an evaluation.[45]

In contrast, if the events supposedly imputing knowledge to the school district are in the distant past, a district is less likely to be deemed to have knowledge. In a California case, a student was suspended for talking with several classmates about "shooting and blowing up people" at school and recording "suicidal and homicidal ideas" in a notebook. The hearing officer upheld his suspension because he was not identified as having special needs and the district had no knowledge of his disability. The fact that the student had been referred for anger management five years earlier in another school district, and the fact that there had been no behavior or performance issues raised in the interim five years, persuaded the hearing officer that the district had no knowledge of a disability.[46]

Even if a child has a diagnosed condition, the school district is not automatically deemed to have knowledge of it. In a Missouri case, the parents of a high school student claimed that the school district should have had knowledge that their son, who was under a doctor's care for

---

42. 34 C.F.R. § 300.527(c).

43. Cabot School Dist., 34 IDELR 78 (SEA Ark. 2000).

44. *Id.*

45. S.W. v. Holbrook Pub. Schs., 2002 U.S. Dist. LEXIS 17770 (D.C. Mass. Sept. 20, 2002).

46. Alvord Unified School Dist., 34 IDELR 279 (SEA Cal. 2001).

ADHD, had a disability.[47] There was no evidence that the parents expressed any concerns about a disability to the school district or requested a special education evaluation. The school district also introduced the testimony of teachers and other personnel indicating that the child did not need a special education evaluation. In fact, the child was making steady progress in school. The hearing officer found that the suspension for threatening a child with a knife could stand, and that the school district could not be held responsible for knowledge of a disability before the weapons incident.[48]

If the school district did *not* have knowledge of the disability before the disciplinary measures, the school district can impose the same disciplinary measures as it would for a child without a disability.[49] If a request for an evaluation is made while the child is suspended or expelled, the school district must complete the evaluation in an expedited manner. Until the evaluation is completed, the child can remain in the setting determined by school officials, which can include suspension or expulsion without services.[50] If, after the evaluation, the child is deemed eligible for special education services, the school district must provide services.[51]

G. UNILATERAL REMOVAL FOR WEAPONS AND DRUG OFFENSES

If a child "carries a weapon to school" or possesses or uses illegal drugs, or sells or solicits the sale of a controlled substance while at school or at a school function, the school district may unilaterally change the child's placement to an "appropriate interim alternative educational setting" for the same amount of time that a child without a disability would be subject to discipline, but for not more than 45 calendar days. This is true even if the parents disagree, challenge the decision with a due process hearing, or request that the stay-put rules apply.[52]

The statutory language covers instances in which the child is found to have a weapon that was obtained while at school as well as when the

---

47. Francis Howell R-III School Dist., 37 IDELR 89 (SEA Missouri 2001).
48. *Id.*
49. 34 C.F.R. § 300.527(d).
50. 34 C.F.R. § 300.527(d)(2)(i).
51. 34 C.F.R. § 300.527(2)(d)(iii).
52. 20 U.S.C. § 1415(k)(1)(ii)(1); 20 U.S.C. §1415(k)(7).

student "carries a weapon to school or to a school function."[53] For the purposes of this regulation, a "weapon" is also defined quite broadly as: a device, instrument, material, or substance, animate or inanimate, that is used for, or is readily capable of, causing death or serious bodily injury, except that such term does not include a pocket knife with a blade of less than two and a half inches in length.[54] Hearing officers seem reluctant to expand this definition any further. One hearing officer found that a paper clip, even when used to cut the neck of another student, is not a weapon, absent a showing by the district that the student "used the paper clip at issue to inflict death or serious bodily injury.[55] Another hearing officer refused to find that a pencil was a weapon.[56]

1. Placement at the End of 45 Days

Although students can be unilaterally placed in an interim alternative educational setting for weapons and drug offenses regardless of their stay-put placement, this alternative placement is only for 45 days. If there is a disagreement between the parents or guardians and school district about the child's placement following the 45 days, the stay-put rules apply to the school the child attended *before* the interim alternative placement. If school personnel believe that it is dangerous for the child to be returned to this placement, the school district may request an expedited hearing with a hearing officer or seek an injunction in court to prevent the child from attending the school. To extend the alternative placement, the school district will be required to establish that the child is dangerous, as described below.[57]

H. REMOVAL FOR DANGEROUSNESS

If a disabled child's behavior was a manifestation of his disability, the school system may *not* unilaterally change the placement of a student based on dangerousness alone, absent a weapons or drugs violation. If a school dis-

---

53. U.S. Dep't of Educ., Office of Special Education Programs, *Special Education Q & A's Written by the Experts, available at* http://www.ideapractices.org/qanda/qanda.php?showCat=33&showSub=36#24.

54. 18 U.S.C. § 930(g)(2); *see also* 34 C.F.R. § 300.520(d)(3), which provides that the above-referenced section of the U.S. Code provides the definition of "weapon" to be used in regard to this provision of the IDEA.

55. Anaheim Union High Sch. Dist., 32 IDELR 129 (SEA Cal. 2000).

56. Independent School Dist. #831, 32 IDELR 163 (SEA Minn. 1999).

57. 20 U.S.C. §§ 1415(k)(7)(B), (C).

trict believes that it is unsafe for the child to return to school pending the outcome of due process proceedings, the district may seek a decision by a hearing officer or an injunction in state or federal court. If, however, the child's behavior was not a manifestation of his or her disability, the child may be disciplined in the same manner as a child without a disability (but he or she must continue to receive some services, as described below).

1. Removal for Dangerousness via an Administrative Hearing

A school system may request an expedited administrative hearing to place a dangerous student in an Interim Alternative Educational Setting (IAES). If the school system can demonstrate that the student is dangerous to him- or herself or others, then a hearing officer may order that the student be placed in an IAES for up to 45 calendar days.[58]

The 1997 amendments to the IDEA allow a hearing officer to determine whether the child meets the dangerousness standard and can be removed to an IAES. In an administrative hearing about whether a child should be removed for dangerousness, the parents or guardians must have an opportunity to be heard.[59] To demonstrate dangerousness, the school system must show by substantial evidence the following:

1. Maintaining the child's current placement is substantially likely to result in injury to the child or others;
2. The school undertook reasonable steps to minimize the likelihood of harm, including use of supplementary aids and services;
3. The current IEP is appropriate; and
4. The interim alternative educational setting allows the child to participate in the general curriculum and continue to progress on IEP goals and receive related services.[60]

School districts must make a strong and specific showing to meet the dangerousness standard. One school district was denied its request to place a child in a 45-day alternative placement despite a finding that it had made reasonable efforts to minimize the likelihood of harm. It was noted that many of the child's behaviors were verbal rather than physical, including

58. 20 U.S.C. § 1415(k)(2).
59. 64 Fed. Reg. 12,621 (1999).
60. 20 U.S.C. § 1415(k)(2).

"abusive language, defiance of authority, profanity [and] verbal threats." Other problem behaviors included kicking a student and unintentionally stabbing a fellow student with a pencil.[61] The hearing officer held that there was not "substantial evidence" that keeping the child in his current placement was "substantially likely to result in injury to the child or to others."[62]

Similarly, a hearing officer in Arkansas held that the child's behaviors did not rise to the level of dangerousness to warrant an immediate removal from the school.[63] The twelfth-grade student was diagnosed with ADHD, oppositional defiant disorder, conduct disorder, solitary aggressive type, and mild mental retardation with severe deficits in receptive and expressive language. The court found that the school district did not make the appropriate interventions, and that the child's behaviors, which were mostly complaints about being disrespectful but also included a fight with another student and a verbal threat against the school resource officer, did not justify his removal from school pending the outcome of his due process hearings.[64]

In contrast, a hearing officer in Massachusetts held that there was sufficient evidence to place a second-grade student in an interim alternative setting.[65] The child's behaviors included pushing over furniture, threatening to get a weapon and "get even" with his teacher, running into the street outside of the school, kicking and punching his teacher (which resulted in her requiring medical treatment for abrasions and contusions), pushing and punching fellow students, and throwing himself to the ground and hitting his head on the floor. The school district showed that it attempted to intervene by consulting with a behavioral specialist and a one-on-one assistant. Based on this record, the hearing officer granted the school district's petition to place the student in a school for behaviorally disturbed students as an interim alternative placement.[66]

2. The Use of an Injunction

As an alternative to seeking a 45-day interim placement for a dangerous student through a hearing officer, a school district may seek an injunction

61. Independent Sch. Dist. 831, 32 IDELR 163 (SEA Minn. 1999).
62. *Id.*
63. Altheimer Sch. Dist., 38 IDELR 149 (SEA Ark. 2003).
64. *Id.*
65. Boston Public Schools, 34 IDELR 102 (SEA MA 2001).
66. *Id.*

in state or federal court to remove a child with a disability from school. According to the U.S. Supreme Court's decision in *Honig v. Doe*, the court can order a change in a disabled student's placement if maintaining the student in his current placement is "substantially likely to result in serious injury to the child or others."[67] A court may consider a district's request for a temporary restraining order (TRO) without hearing any evidence from the parents or guardians. If the school district presents sufficient evidence to convince the court that there will be irreparable harm if the change in placement is not granted and that the district is likely to prevail at the due process hearing, the court may grant the temporary order.[68] The parents or guardians will, however, have the opportunity to be heard at a preliminary hearing, which must be held within 10 days of when the TRO is granted.

Prior to the 1997 amendments, there were no statutory exceptions for removing a dangerous child if the parent or guardian exercised the pendency rights and there was a dispute about the placement. In 1988, the U.S. Supreme Court held in *Honig v. Doe* that a state or federal judge can order a change in a disabled student's placement if maintaining the student in his current placement is "substantially likely to result in serious injury to the child or to others."[69] In 1994, the Eighth Circuit in *Light v. Parkway C-2 School District* further delineated the *Honig* standard by creating a two-part test to determine whether a student with a disability can be removed from his or her school placement through an injunction in court.[70] First, the school district must show that "maintaining the child in his or her current placement is substantially likely to result in injury either to himself or herself, or to others."[71] The Eighth Circuit rejected the parents' contention that to be removed, a child must intend to cause injury, indicating that "a child's capacity for harmful intent plays no role in this analysis." There is also no requirement that a child inflict serious harm before he or she can be deemed likely to injure him or herself or others.[72] Part two of the test requires the school district to show that it "has made reasonable efforts to accommodate the child's disabilities so as to minimize the likelihood that the child will injure herself or others."[73]

---

67. Honig v. Doe, 108 S. Ct. 592 (1988).
68. 64 Fed. Reg. 12,621 (1999).
69. *See* Honig v. Doe, 108 S. Ct. 592 (1988).
70. Light v. Parkway C-2 School Dist., 41 F.3d 1223 (8th Cir. 1994).
71. *Honig, supra* note 5 at 328.
72. *Light, supra* note 70 at 1230.
73. *Id.* at 1228.

Some districts may prefer obtaining an injunction in court to remove a dangerous child because there is not a 45-day limit on the removal (which applies if the dangerous child is removed by an order of a hearing officer). A potential downside to filing for injunctive relief is that courts may only grant such injunctions in "near-emergency situations," especially in light of the remedies available through the administrative process.[74] In a case from the U.S. District Court in Missouri, a student threatened school officials and students, including threatening to make a teacher "black and blue," threatening to place an explosive device in the principal's car, and repeatedly throwing and violently pushing furniture and other objects. The district court found that this was not enough of a threat of physical injury to warrant an injunction.[75]

Courts have tended to grant these injunctions when the child has a severe disability and the school district has been able to document both the child's aggressive and violent behaviors and the school's interventions. In the *Light* case, the child had multiple mental disabilities, behavioral disorders, conduct disorders, pervasive developmental delay, certain features of autism, language impairment, and organic brain syndrome. The child exhibited many aggressive and disruptive behaviors, such as:

> biting, hitting, kicking and poking persons, throwing objects, and turning over furniture. School records document that in the two years prior to her suspension [the child] committed eleven to nineteen aggressive acts per week, with a mean of fifteen per week. Her daily tally of aggressive acts ranged from zero to nine, with a mean of three per day. Of these incidents, approximately thirty required the attention of the school nurse.[76]

In *Light*, the court granted an injunction because the school district was able to document the child's dangerousness as well as its interventions.

In contrast, a district court rejected a school district's request for a TRO to remove a middle-school student with a learning disability where it cited only six incidents over a five-month period, and only three of the

---

74. Clinton County R-III School Dist. v. CJK, 896 F. Supp. 948 (W.D. Mo. 1995).
75. *Id.*
76. *Light, supra* note 70 at 1225.

incidents involved physical touching.[77] The school district claimed that the student hit another student, "assaulted two classmates, punching them in the face," and "shoved" the principal against a wall. The school district could not show, however, that any preventive measures were attempted. The district court held that the student's behavior did not justify the "extraordinary relief" of a temporary restraining order enjoining him from attending his current school placement.[78]

Similarly, a district court in Pennsylvania refused to grant a preliminary injunction for a middle-school student with a learning disability who cut the hand of a student with a single-blade razor.[79] Although a district judge granted a TRO in the case, the judge hearing the preliminary injunction found there was no record of any other misconduct or disciplinary referrals regarding the child, and "virtually no preventive or ameliorative measures have been employed."[80] In a similar case in California, a district court found that fighting with another student and bringing a gun to school were insufficient for a temporary restraining order.[81]

Some courts have used the standard for a preliminary injunction (Federal Rule of Civil Procedure 65), in conjunction with the *Honig* standard, to determine when to issue an injunction in cases regarding the placement of a dangerous child with a disability. A federal district court in Florida held that using the standard for a preliminary injunction was consistent with *Honig* and the IDEA.[82] The court analyzed whether the school district was substantially likely to prevail on the merits, whether the school district would suffer irreparable harm, whether the injury to the school district would outweigh the injury to the child, and whether it serves a public purpose.[83] After analyzing these factors, the court issued the preliminary injunction. The school district, however, was able to show documentation of 43 instances of aggressive behavior and the efforts to accommodate the child.[84]

---

77. Phoenixville Area School Dist. v. Marquis B., 25 IDELR 452 (E.D. Penn. 1997).
78. *Id.*
79. School Dist. of Philadelphia v. Stephan M., 25 IDELR 506 (E.D. Penn. 1997).
80. *Id.*
81. M.P. by D.P. v. Governing Bd. of the Grossmont Union High Sch. Dist., 858 F. Supp. 1044 (S.D. Cal. 1994).
82. School Board of Pinellas County, Fla. v. J.M., 957 F. Supp. 1252, 1257–58 (M.D. Fla. 1997).
83. *Id.* at 1258–59.
84. *Id.*

A federal district court in Texas also used the test for a preliminary injunction after it had concluded that the child "constitutes a severe and ongoing threat of imminent danger to himself and others."[85] The child in the case had been diagnosed as having a psychotic disorder and the school had documented numerous incidents of maladaptive behaviors, including threats to kill himself and others and attempts to jump out of windows.[86]

3. Requirements for an Interim Alternative Educational Setting

When a student is unilaterally removed to an interim alternative setting (IAES) for a drugs or weapons offense, the IEP team must determine the appropriate setting. If the removal is for dangerousness, the hearing officer must determine the appropriate setting. In either event, the IAES must be one where the child can continue to participate in the general curriculum, to receive the special services and modifications as listed in the IEP, and to work toward the goals of the IEP. The educational program at the alternative site must also include services or modifications designed to address the behavior that led to the child's placement in the IAES.[87] A hearing officer in Kansas held that placement in an IAES was appropriate for an elementary school student who was exhibiting aggressive and violent behavior. Even though the student might not deal well with the new placement because transitions were very difficult for him, the hearing officer found that the placement would allow him to participate in the general education curriculum and continue to receive services and modifications on his IEP. The hearing officer found that the substantial likelihood that the child would injure himself or others overrode the concerns about changing the child's placement.[88]

Homebound instruction as an alternative setting may not always be considered appropriate. In a case from Illinois, a child with ADD and a behavior disorder was suspended for verbal threats regarding the Columbine shootings three days after the shootings.[89] He was suspended and

---

85. Texas City Indep. Sch. Dist. v. Jorstad, 752 F. Supp. 231, 238 (S.D. Tex. 1990).
86. *Id.* at 233, 234.
87. 20 U.S.C. § 1415(k)(3).
88. Unified Sch. Dist. #259, 38 Individuals with Disabilities Education Law Report (IDELR) 234 (SEA Kan. 2003).
89. Community Consol. Sch. Dist. #93 v. John F., 33 IDELR 210 (N.D. Ill. 2001).

received nine and a half hours of tutoring and one and a half hours of social work therapy over the course of the 22 days he was receiving homebound services. The court found these services lacking because the homebound placement failed to address the student's social and emotional needs—he had no opportunity to practice interacting with peers or to work on his communication skills.[90]

4. Other Court Involvement

Involving law enforcement is another potential avenue of removing a dangerous student from school. School officials have the freedom—and in some states the obligation—to report criminal activity to local law enforcement authorities.[91] The IDEA regulations make this point clear:

> Nothing in this part prohibits an agency from reporting a crime committed by a child with a disability to appropriate authorities or to prevent State law enforcement and judicial authorities from exercising their responsibilities. . . .[92]

Such reporting does not trigger the procedural safeguards of the IDEA. In practical terms, this means that school officials may notify law enforcement without first notifying parents or otherwise complying with the procedural requirements of the IDEA.[93] If a student is unable to attend school for more than 10 days as a result of the district's notification to law enforcement, at least one hearing officer has held that this has no triggering impact on IDEA procedural protections, and there is no obligation to call an IEP meeting.

The Office of Civil Rights has held that a school district did not violate the IDEA or Section 504 when it called a school resource officer for assistance when a violent student would not leave the school premises after he was suspended for fighting. This is true even though the child was later arrested by juvenile justice authorities.[94] Similarly, making a report that leads to the child's detention by juvenile authorities does not consti-

---

90. *Id.*
91. *See, e.g.,* Bensalem Township Sch. Dist., 32 IDELR 26 (SEA Penn. 1999) (finding that the school district has an obligation under the IDEA to report crimes).
92. 34 C.F.R. § 300.529.
93. *See* Joseph M. v. Southeast Delco School Dist., 2001 U.S. Dist. LEXIS 2994 (E.D. Penn. 2001).
94. Citrus County Sch. Dist., 34 IDELR 67 (OCR 2000).

tute a cessation of services, in the nature of an expulsion, because IDEA requires states to provide appropriate special education to all eligible children regardless of their location, which includes children in state custody.[95]

Likewise, involving the family court probably does not trigger IDEA protections. The New York State Court of Appeals held that school district officials may initiate a Person In Need of Supervision (PINS) case in family court without triggering the procedural safeguards of the IDEA regarding a change in placement.[96] The court emphasized that not all PINS proceedings contemplate a change in school placement, and that school officials did not seek to change the child's placement by filing the petition.[97]

5. Providing Services During Removal

When school administrators *do* remove a special education student from the classroom for more than 10 days, services must continue. For example, if a child's behavior is not a manifestation of his or her disability, and the child is long-term suspended, the school district must continue to provide services. The text of the IDEA requires schools to provide a "free and appropriate public education" to students who are suspended. The proposed regulations, however, provide that such education is not required during the first 10 days of suspension in a school year.[98] For subsequent suspensions, the IEP team must determine what services are necessary to allow the student to continue appropriate progress in the general curriculum and to achieve the child's IEP goals.[99]

If a student is removed from school on a long-term basis, the IEP team determines the services that must be provided to ensure a free and appropriate public education. The IDEA regulations note that:

> the extent to which instructional services need to be provided and the type of instruction to be provided would depend on the length of the removal, the extent to which the child has been removed

---

95. Northside Independent Sch. Dist., 28 IDELR 1118 (SEA Tex. 1998). *See also* Joseph M. v. Southeast Delco Sch. Dist., 2001 U.S. Dist. LEXIS 2994 (E.D. Pa. 2001) (holding that the school's referral of the child to juvenile court did not violate the IDEA).

96. *In re* Beau II, 2000 N.Y. Int. 0108 (Oct. 19, 2000).

97. *Id.*

98. 34 C.F.R. § 300.520.

99. 34 C.F.R. § 300.121(d).

previously, and the child's needs and educational goals. For example, a child with a learning disability who is placed in a 45-day placement will likely need far more extensive services in order to progress in the general curriculum and advance appropriately toward meeting the goals of the child's IEP than would a child who is removed for only a few days, and is performing at grade level.[100]

In a Maine case regarding an "expulsion IEP," the parents argued the IEP plan was inappropriate because it lacked art, computer, and physical education instruction.[101] The eighth-grade student was expelled for selling drugs at school. The IEP team decided that selling drugs was not a manifestation of his learning disability. While he was expelled, he received two hours per day of at-home instruction in his core courses and two hours per week of specialized reading instruction. The U.S. District Court in Maine found that the "expulsion IEP" was appropriate, and that the exclusion of art, computer, and physical education did not prevent the student from obtaining the credits or skills he would need to graduate.[102] The court noted that the IDEA requires that the child is able to "progress" in the general curriculum, but not necessarily participate in all of it.[103]

L. SUSPENSION OF "504" STUDENTS

As it applies to public schools, Section 504 of the Rehabilitation Act of 1973 prohibits discrimination on the basis of disability in the implementation of educational programs.[104] In general, Section 504 and the IDEA have been interpreted to provide the same protections to students with disabilities facing suspension or expulsion. Both the Office of Special Education and Rehabilitative Services (OSERS) and the Office for Civil Rights have expressed concern that Section 504 and the IDEA be interpreted in such a way as to avoid inconsistent obligations on the part of states and school districts.[105] There are a few ways, however, that students who obtain services pursuant to the IDEA receive more protections re-

---

100. 64 Fed. Reg. 12,623 (1999).
101. Farrin v. Maine Sch. Admin. Dist. No. 59, 165 F. Supp. 2d, 37, 53 (D. Maine 2001).
102. *Id.*
103. *Id.*
104. 29 U.S.C. § 706, *et seq.*
105. Education of the Handicapped Law Report (EHLR) 202:395 (OSEP 1987).

garding discipline than students who obtain accommodations pursuant to Section 504 only.

Like all students, including children who qualify for services under the IDEA, students with Section 504 accommodation plans may be suspended for up to 10 days in a school year in the same manner as general education students.[106] In addition, like the IDEA student, whenever the 504 student is recommended for a suspension that will result in a change in placement (that is, any long-term suspension or any series of short-term suspensions that result in a change of placement), a manifestation determination must be conducted and the student may not be suspended if it is determined that his misbehavior was a manifestation of his disability.[107] The 504 regulations do not specify, however, who must make this manifestation determination. Other placement decisions regarding accommodations under 504 must be made by "a group of persons, including persons knowledgeable about the child, the meaning of the evaluation data, and the placement options."[108] Presumably, these same criteria apply to making a decision to change a student's placement because of a suspension. There is not an explicit requirement that the parent be involved in the manifestation determination meeting.[109]

The most important distinction from the IDEA comes when there is a determination that the student's behavior is not a manifestation of his or her disability. At that point, the 504 student may be disciplined to the same extent as a regular education student, and, unlike the IDEA, there is no obligation to continue educational services to the student while he is suspended.[110]

M. CONCLUSION

The requirements and procedures for disciplining students with disabilities reflect the dual and sometimes conflicting goals of keeping schools safe and ensuring that students with disabilities are not improperly ex-

---

106. Honig v. Doe, 108 S.Ct. 592 (1988). *See also* 34 C.F.R. § 104.35 (a).

107. *See* OCR Staff Memorandum, 16 EHLR 491 (OCR 1989) (stating that a manifestation determination must be conducted prior to suspending a 504 student for more than 10 days). *See also* 34 C.F.R. § 104.35(a).

108. 34 C.F.R. §104.35(c).

109. *See* OCR Staff Memorandum, 16 EHLR 491 (OCR 1989).

110. *See, e.g.*, Knox County (Tenn.) School Dist., 26 IDELR 762 (OCR 1997).

cluded from school. If students with disabilities are truly dangerous, school districts have the ability to remove them from their school settings. School districts must take care, however, to follow all of the procedures outlined in the IDEA and document both the students' behaviors and the schools' interventions.

Discipline of Students for Off-Campus Conduct

10

Lisa L. Swem

A. INTRODUCTION

A school district's authority to discipline students for conduct occurring away from school premises has been the subject of litigation since the mid-nineteenth century.[1] Courts will extend that authority to off-campus conduct *if* school officials can demonstrate that the student's conduct has a direct and immediate effect on school discipline or the school's general safety and welfare.[2]

---

1. *See, e.g.,* Douglas v. Campbell, 116 S.W.211 (Ark. 1909) (student disciplined for being drunk in public during the Christmas holidays); Magnum v. Keith, 95 S.E.1 (Ga. 1918) (school rule permitted expulsion for attending motion pictures or social events on nights other than Friday or Saturday); Sherman v. Charlestown, 62 Mass. 160 (1859) (student expelled for "notorious immoral propensities" for allegedly working as a prostitute); Lander v. Seaver, 32 Vt. 114 (1859) (teacher's whipping of student in front of the teacher's home was justified because the student was disrespectful).

2. *See generally* Daniel E. Feld, Annotation, *Right to Discipline Pupils for Conduct Away from School Grounds or Not Immediately Connected with School Activities*, 53 A.L.R. 3d, 1124 (1973 ed. and 2003 supp.).

Court decisions result in rulings both for and against schools. As might be expected, the factually intensive nature of these decisions is significant. Nonetheless, while the facts and results differ, the analytical focus remains fairly consistent: How does the student conduct relate to the school?[3] Courts do not give tacit approval to school discipline for off-campus conduct that is criminal or "dangerous." School officials must continue to meet their burden of connecting the conduct to the operations of the school. Expressive conduct that has First Amendment speech protections must clear even higher hurdles.

B. CRIMINAL OR DANGEROUS CONDUCT

A powder-puff football game involving more than 50 students from Glenbrook North High School in Illinois concluded with a hazing ritual involving significant violence. Senior girls hit, kicked, and smeared foul substances (including excrement and paint) on the junior girls. Although this event took place on a Sunday at a local forest preserve, school officials responded with disciplinary proceedings against the senior girls. The legal actions challenging the school's discipline were not successful.[4] The trial judge found "patently absurd" the argument that the school could not respond to this off-campus behavior. Rather, the court found a nexus between the school and the student's conduct because "attendance at Glenbrook North was central to the event, and class standing essential to the roles played."

In *Giles ex rel. Giles v. Brookville Area School District,*[5] a Pennsylvania court ruled that a student could be expelled for selling drugs even though the actual exchange occurred off school property. The agreement, however, was made on school property. Similarly, in *Howard v. Colonial*

---

3. Courts generally hold that a student's interest in extracurricular activities is not constitutionally protected because participation is a "privilege" to which no property or liberty interest attaches. Accordingly, schools have greater discretion to impose disciplinary consequences to participants in extracurricular activities whose offending conduct occurs off campus. *See, e.g.,* Bush v. Dassel-Cokato Bd. of Educ., 745 F. Supp. 562 (D. Minn. 1990); Farver v. Board of Ed. of Carroll County, 40 F. Supp. 2d 323 (D. Md. 1999); L.P.M. and J.D.T. v. School Bd. of Seminole County, 753 So. 2d 130 (Fla. App. 2000); Jordan v. O'Fallon Twp. High Sch. Dist. No. 203, 706 N.E.2d 137 (Ill. App. 1999).

4. Gendelman v. Glenbrook North High School, et al., U.S. Dist. LEXIS 8508 (N.D. Ill. May 21, 2003).

5. 669 A.2d 1079 (Pa. Commw. Ct. 1995), *app. denied,* 679 A.2d 231 (Pa. 1996).

School District,[6] the court upheld a student expulsion for off-campus sale of cocaine. The court held that the presence of a drug dealer at school would have a detrimental impact on the health, safety, and welfare of the school's students.

Courts have also overturned discipline to students who engaged in off-campus drug activities. In *Labrosse v. St. Bernard Parish School Board,*[7] the court ruled that a student could not be expelled for off-campus drug possession when the school rule was limited to on-campus possession. In *Packer v. Board of Education of the Town of Thomaston,*[8] the court invalidated a student's expulsion for possessing marijuana in his car trunk after school hours and off school grounds. School officials failed to demonstrate "some tangible connection" of this conduct to the operation of the school.

In *Nicholas B. v. School Committee of Worcester,*[9] the court upheld a student's expulsion for an off-campus assault of another student because the assault "was a continuation of improper conduct that occurred on school grounds." School officials established that the assault was planned that day at school and was an extension of a student confrontation. Similarly, in *Porter v. Board of School Directors of Clairton School District,*[10] the court upheld discipline to a student who assaulted another student off school grounds after an argument that began at a school basketball game.[11] On the other hand, in *Robinson v. Oak Park and River Forest High School,*[12] the court found no evidence of material disruption of school activities when a board expelled a student for striking another student off school grounds after school hours.

---

6. 621 A.2d 362 (Del. Super. Ct. 1992).

7. 483 So. 2d 1253 (La. App. 1986).

8. 717 A.2d 117 (Conn. 1998).

9. 587 N.E.2d 211 (Mass. 1992).

10. 445 A.2d 1386 (Pa. Commw. 1982),

11. *See also* Pollnow v. Glennon, 757 F.2d 496 (2d Cir. 1984), *aff'g* 594 F. Supp. 220 (S.D. N.Y. 1984) (upholding discipline to student who assaulted his friend's mother at her home during the spring school vacation); Smith v. Little Rock Sch. Dist., 582 F. Supp. 159 (E.D. Ark. 1984) (shooting and killing a fellow student away from school); Doe v. Superintendent of Schools of Stoughton, 2002 WL 989467 (Mass., May 16, 2002) (although felony charge alone does not justify suspension, the discipline was upheld because student's presence at school "would have a substantial detrimental effect on the general welfare of the school"); R.R. v. Board of Educ. of the Shore Reg'l High Sch. Dist., 263A.2d 180 (N.J. Super. 1970) (upholding student's expulsion for off-campus stabbing).

12. 571 N.E.2d 931 (Ill. App. 1991).

C. EXPRESSIVE ACTIVITY

The U.S. Supreme Court first articulated the standards of student First Amendment speech rights in *Tinker v. Des Moines Independent Community School District*.[13] Striking down the school's rule prohibiting students from wearing black armbands to protest the Vietnam War, the Supreme Court held that students are accorded First Amendment speech rights unless their conduct or speech "materially disrupts class work or involves substantial disorder or invasion of the rights of others. . . ."[14] The Court emphasized, however, that "undifferentiated fear or apprehension of disturbance is not enough to overcome the right to freedom of expression."[15]

The Supreme Court clarified the "material and substantial disruption standard" in *Bethel School District No. 403 v. Fraser*,[16] when it upheld a three-day suspension to a student who used sexually explicit metaphors in a speech delivered to the student body. The Court concluded, "[I]t is a highly appropriate function of a public school education to prohibit the use of vulgar and offensive terms in public discourse."

While courts frequently analyze off-campus expressive activity by applying *Tinker* and *Fraser*, neither case involved off-campus conduct. The facts in *Tinker* and the Court's reference to the "special characteristics of the school environment" suggest that the Court was only addressing on-campus expression when it held that students and teachers do not "shed their constitutional rights to freedom of speech or expression at the schoolhouse gate."[17] Moreover, while the student speech in *Fraser* also occurred on campus, Justice Brennan noted that if the student "had given the same speech outside of the school environment, he could not have been penalized simply because government officials considered his language to be inappropriate; the Court's opinion does not suggest otherwise."[18]

Courts applying *Tinker* to the discipline of students for authoring or distributing "underground" publications have reached varied results.[19]

---

13. 393 U.S. 503 (1969).
14. *Id.* at 513.
15. *Id.* at 508.
16. 478 U.S. 675 (1986).
17. *Id.* at 506.
18. 478 U.S. at 688 (Brennan, J., concurring) (citation omitted).
19. *Compare* Thomas v. Board of Educ. of Granville Cent. Sch. Dist., 607 F.2d 1043 (2d Cir. 1979) (*Tinker* not applied because underground newspaper not distributed at school); Shanley v. Northeast Indep. Sch. Dist., 462 F.2d 960 (5th Cir. 1972)

In *Thomas v. Board of Education of Granville Central School District*,[20] the Second Circuit Court of Appeals noted that a court's "willingness to defer to the schoolmaster's expertise in administering school discipline rests, in large measure, upon the supposition that the arm of authority does not reach beyond the school gate." The court added: "While these activities are certainly the proper subjects of parental discipline, the First Amendment forbids public school administrators and teachers from regulating the material to which a child is exposed after he leaves school each afternoon."[21] In ruling that school officials violated the First Amendment for suspending the students who published a satirical newspaper that "was conceived, executed, and distributed outside the school," the Second Circuit concluded that "our willingness to grant school officials substantial autonomy within their academic domain rests in part on the confinement of that power within the metes and bounds of the school itself."[22] Otherwise, it is the role of parents, not school officials, to respond.[23]

D. OFFENSIVE SPEECH AND THREATS

School officials must distinguish between student speech that is merely offensive and student speech that is truly threatening. Offensive speech that is nonthreatening and not part of the school program receives First Amendment protection.[24] The First Amendment, however, does not protect all off-campus speech.[25]

(underground newspaper distributed outside school that caused no disruption in school could not be subject to the school's disciplinary authority); Boucher v. School Bd. of the Sch. Dist. of Greenfield, 134 F.3d 821 (7th Cir. 1998) (*Tinker*'s substantial disruption standard applies because the article "So You Want to Be a Hacker" was distributed on campus and advocated on-campus activity); Bystrom v. Fridley High Sch. Indep. Sch. Dist. No. 14, 822 F.2d 747 (8th Cir. 1987) (*Tinker* applies because the underground newspaper was distributed at school).

20. 607 F.2d 1043, 1044-45 (2d Cir. 1979).

21. *Id.*

22. *Id.* at 1052.

23. *Id.* at 1050.

24. Texas v. Johnson, 491 U.S. 397, 414 (1989) ("If there is a bedrock principle underlying the First Amendment, it is that the government may not prohibit the expression of an idea simply because society finds the idea itself offensive or disagreeable.").

25. R.A.V. v. City of St. Paul, 505 U.S. 377, 382-90 (1992) (certain areas of speech may "be regulated because of their constitutionally proscribable content").

The school's authority to discipline "offensive" off-campus conduct was reviewed in *Klein v. Smith*.[26] The student was suspended for 10 days for extending "the finger" to a teacher in a restaurant parking lot far from school premises, after school hours, and at a time when neither the teacher nor the student were associated with their respective roles as teacher and student.[27] The court rejected the school's argument that the student's conduct had "sapped their resolve to enforce proper discipline."[28] Even though 62 school officials signed a letter to this effect, the court ruled that their "professional integrity, personal mental resolve, and individual character are [not] going to dissolve, willy-nilly, in the face of the digital posturing of the splenetic, bad-mannered boy."[29]

In *Doe v. Pulaski County Special School District*,[30] a student wrote a letter at home that described how he would rape, sodomize, and kill a female classmate who no longer wished to be his girlfriend. The student's best friend found the letter in the student's bedroom and took it without his knowledge and permission. The friend brought the letter to school and delivered it to the girl, who gave it to the principal. The student was expelled and a lawsuit was filed alleging that the expulsion violated the student's free speech rights. The Eighth Circuit ruled that the communication was not protected speech because it was a "true threat."[31] The court noted that the student expressed his hatred for the girl, referred to her with various profane epithets over 80 times, used the F-word 90 times, and repeatedly expressed his wish to sodomize, rape, and kill the girl.

The litigation history of the *Doe* case demonstrates the difficult analysis inherent with "speech" and off-campus conduct. After a bench trial, the district court ordered the expelled student reinstated, concluding that the

---

26, 635 F. Supp. 1440 (D. Me. 1986).

27. *Id.* at 1441.

28. *Id.* at 1442 n. 4.

29. *Id.* See also Felton v. Fayette School District, 874 F.2d 191 (8th Cir. 1989) (discipline upheld for student making offensive remarks about school employees); *but see* Donavan v. Ritchie, 68 F.3d 14 (1st Cir. 1995) (school could punish student for compiling a "shit list" of people he disliked); Fenton v. Stear, 423 F. Supp. 767 (W.D. Pa. 1976) (student suspension for calling a teacher a "prick" in mall parking lot did not violate the First Amendment).

30. 306 F.3d 616 (8th Cir. 2002) (en banc).

31. *Id.* at 626. *See also William Bird, True Threat Doctrine and Public School Speech: An Expansive View of a School's Authority to Discipline Allegedly Threatening Student Speech Arising Off Campus*, 26 U. ARK. LITTLE ROCK L. REV. 111 (2003).

letter was not a "true threat" and received the First Amendment protection. A divided panel of the appeals court affirmed the district court's decision.[32] The panel decision was vacated and granted en banc review.[33] After en banc rehearing, the court issued a 6-4 decision holding that the school did not violate the First Amendment.[34]

E. CYBERSPACE

How far is cyberspace from *Tinker*'s schoolhouse gate? While the same First Amendment analysis applies to student expressive activity posted to the Internet, the first inquiry must be to determine whether the conduct is indeed "off-campus." While courts typically find that Web sites hosted and created away from school are off-campus speech, a different conclusion results for students who bring their speech on campus (printed or downloaded onto personal Web sites on school computers).

The Supreme Court has ruled that speech on the Internet deserves the highest level of First Amendment protection.[35] Nonetheless, this technology raises free speech questions that our courts have yet to fully address.[36] Of the eight student "cyberspeech" cases reviewed below, only two courts have ruled in the school's favor.

---

32. *See* Doe v. Pulaski County Special School District, 263 F.3d 833 (8th Cir. 2001).

33. Doe v. Pulaski County Special School District, 2001 U.S. App LEXIS 23877 (8th Cir. Nov. 5, 2001).

34. Doe v. Pulaski County Special School District, 306 F.3d 616 (8th Cir. 2002).

35. Reno v. A.C.L.U., 521 U.S. 844, 863 (1997).

36. *See* Clay Calvert, *Off-Campus Speech, On-Campus Punishment: Censorship of the Emerging Internet Underground*, 7 B.U. J. Sci. & Tech. L. 243 (2001); Aaron H. Caplan, *Public School Discipline for Creating Uncensored Anonymous Internet Forums*, 39 Willamette L. Rev. 93 (2003); Leora Harpaz, *Internet Speech and the First Amendment Rights of Public School Students*, 2000 B.Y.U. Educ. & L.J. 123 (2000); David L. Hudson, Jr., *Censorship of Student Internet Speech: The Effect of Diminishing Student Rights, Fear of the Internet and Columbine*, 2000 Det. C.L. Rev. 199 (2000); Robert E. Simpson, Jr., *Limits on Students' Speech in the Internet Age,* 105 Dick. L. Rev. 181 (2001); Jennifer K. Swartz, *Beyond the Schoolhouse Gates: Do Students Shed Their Constitutional Rights When Communicating to a Cyber-Audience?* 48 Drake L. Rev. 587 (2000); Alexander G. Tuneski, *Online, Not on Grounds: Protecting Student Internet Speech*, 89 Va. L. Rev. 139 (2003); Garner K. Weng, *Type No Evil: The Proper Latitude of Public Educational Institutions in Restricting Expressions of Their Students on the Internet*, 20 Hastings Comm. & Ent. L.J. 751 (1998).

In *Beussink v. Woodland R-IV School District,*[37] the court issued a preliminary injunction enjoining the school from suspending a student for his home-created Web site that criticized school administrators and used vulgar language. Applying *Tinker*, the court concluded that the "homepage did not materially and substantially interfere with school discipline." The court added, "[D]isliking or being upset by the content of a student's speech is not an acceptable justification for limiting student speech."[38]

In *Beidler v. North Thurston School District No. 3,*[39] a student was suspended for six months for creating a Web site with reimaged pictures of an assistant principal in a Viagra commercial, in a Nazi book-burning scene, and as a cartoon character having sex. The county superior court reversed the suspension finding that the speech did not meet *Tinker's* substantial disruption standard. The court awarded the student $10,000 in damages and $52,000 in legal fees.[40]

In *Emmett v. Kent School District No. 415,*[41] a student created a Web site as an unofficial home page for his high school. The site contained mock obituaries of some students and allowed visitors to vote on who would "die" next—that iswho would be the subject of the next mock obituary. The student was placed on emergency expulsion (subsequently modified to a suspension) for intimidation, harassment, and disruption to the educational process. The student sued, seeking a preliminary injunction against the school district. Although acknowledging that "school administrators are in an acutely difficult position after recent school shootings in Colorado, Oregon, and other places," the court granted the preliminary injunction because the student's conduct was "entirely outside of the school's supervision or control" and the school presented no evidence that the site constituted a threat of violence.[42]

In *Killion v. Franklin Regional School District,*[43] the student received a 10-day suspension for creating a top-10 list about the athletic director,

37. 30 F. Supp. 2d 1175 (E.D. Mo. 1998).
38. *Id.* at 1180.
39. No. 99-2-00236-6 (Wash. Sup. Ct. July 18, 2000),
40. Lisa Stiffler, *Ex-Student Awarded Damages in His Free Speech Lawsuit: Youth Had Been Punished for Website Spoofing School Administrator,* SEATTLE POST-INTELLIGENCER, Feb. 21, 2001, at B1.
41. 92 F. Supp. 2d 1088 (W.D. Wash. 2000).
42. *Id.* at 1089–90.
43. 136 F. Supp. 2d 446 (W.D. Pa. 2001),

including statements about his appearance and genitalia. The student e-mailed the list from his home computer to friends at their homes. As might be expected, the list eventually made its way to school. The court held that *Tinker* applied regardless of where the speech was created. The school, however, failed to meet the *Tinker* standard because it did not show a reasonably foreseeable material and substantial disruption of school activities. The court commented, "We cannot accept, without more, that the childish and boorish antics of a minor could impair the administrator's abilities to discipline students and maintain control."[44] Moreover, the court found that the school's policy was constitutionally overbroad because it could be (and was) interpreted to punish protected speech without geographical or contextual limitations.

In *Coy v. Board of Education of North Canton City School,*[45] a middle-school student created a Web site on his home computer. The site included student pictures with insulting comments in a section entitled "Losers." The student accessed the Web site while at school and was suspended for violating the student code of conduct relating to obscenity, profanity, disobedience, and inappropriate conduct. A lawsuit followed, alleging that the school violated the student's First Amendment rights. Applying *Tinker,* the court held that summary judgment was not proper because material issues of fact existed as to the basis of the student's discipline. If the discipline was based on the student's misuse of the school computer, the school's action was proper. On the other hand, the discipline would not be proper if it was based on the content of the student's at-home Web site.

In *Mahaffey v. Aldrich,*[46] a student was suspended for his contributions to a Web site titled "Satan's Web Page," which contained various lists, including one titled "People I Wish Would Die." The site also advocated rape, murder, drug use, joining the Ku Klux Klan, and wreaking general havoc. Applying *Tinker,* the federal district court ruled that the suspension violated the student's First Amendment rights absent proof that the Web site caused a disruption to school or that the Web site was created on school property. Although the court concluded that the Web site's content was repugnant, its content was protected by the Constitution because it did not constitute a "true threat."

---

44. *Id.* at 456.
45. 205 F. Supp. 2d 791 (N.D. Ohio 2002).
46. 236 F. Supp. 2d 779 (E.D. Mich. 2002),

The two cases reviewed below held for the school. In *J.S. v. Bethlehem Area School District,*[47] the court affirmed the permanent expulsion of an eighth-grade student who created a Web site titled "Teacher Sux," which contained derogatory comments about teachers and the principal. In addition to insulting comments and epithets, the site solicited responses to the question "Why should [a specific teacher] die?" and "Take a look at the diagram and the reasons I gave, then give me $20.00 to help pay for the hitman." The site also included an image of the teacher decapitated with blood dripping from her neck. Although holding that the Web site was not a "true threat" and was protected by the First Amendment, the court applied *Tinker* and *Bethel* to conclude that the student's conduct caused a material and substantial disruption to the school.[48]

In *Porter v. Ascension Parish School Board,*[49] the court upheld disciplinary action taken against two brothers for violent drawings that they created. The drawings, made two years earlier by Adam, were in a sketch pad that Andrew took to school. One of the drawings depicted a person holding a torch next to the gasoline-soaked high school as well as a missile aimed at the school and a student throwing a brick at the principal. The drawing also included racial epithets and vulgarity. In granting the school defendants' motion to dismiss, the court rejected the argument that the drawing was protected speech. The court found the Columbine tragedy significant to its analysis. The court also rejected the argument that one of the brothers could not be disciplined for the drawing because he sketched it at home and never intended that it be viewed by students or school officials. Instead, the court ruled that the student's intentions "[d]o not and should not matter," because the drawing was in fact communicated to others who perceived it as a threat that would be carried out.[50]

F. CONCLUSION

School-imposed discipline (typically suspension or expulsion) is not the only recourse for addressing off-campus conduct. Alternative approaches remain available, including parental involvement and notice to the Internet

---

47. 807 A.2d 847 (Pa., 2002), *aff'g* 757 A.2d 412 (Pa. Commw. Ct. 2000).

48. *See also S.L. v. Friends Central School,* 2000 WL 352367 (E.D. Pa. 2000) (discipline upheld for threatening or defaming students or school employees on the Internet).

49. 301 F. Supp. 2d 576 (M.D. La. 2004).

50. *Id.* at 588.

Service Provider, as well as the civil, criminal, and juvenile justice systems. As one federal district court noted: "A student is subject to the same criminal laws and owes the same civil duties as other citizens, and this status as a student should not alter his obligations during his private life away from the campus."[51] A student's offensive conduct directed at school personnel may also provide a basis for various tort claims, including intentional infliction of emotional distress, invasion of privacy, and defamation. State courts have split on whether public school principals and teachers are "public officials" for purposes of defamation law. If so, the public official must prove "actual malice" to recover for defamatory statements about their official conduct.[52] The jurisprudence governing discipline to students for off-campus conduct will continue to develop, particularly in the post-Columbine consciousness that affects decisions that school officials make about student discipline matters.[53]

---

51. Sullivan v. Houston Indep. Sch. Dist., 307 F. Supp. 1328, 1341 (S.D. Tex. 1969).

52. New York Times Co. v. Sullivan, 376 U.S. 254, 270 (1964).

53. The American Civil Liberties Union has actively litigated these cases against schools and maintains a page on its Web site titled "Students' Rights: Off-Campus Conduct," which reports about ACLU litigation on this topic. *Available at* http://www.aclu.org/StudentsRights/StudentsRightslist. *See also* Robert D. Richards and Clay Calvert, *Columbine Fallout: The Long-Term Effects on Free Expression Take Hold in Public Schools,* 83 B.U. L. Rev. 1089 (2003); David L. Hudson, Jr., *Fear of Violence in Our Schools: Is "Undifferentiated Fear" in the Age of Columbine Leading to a Suppression of Student Speech?* 42 Washburn L. J. 79 (2002).

Antiterrorism Planning in the Schools: Practical and Legal Considerations*

11

Heather K. Brickman
Sara E. Groom

A. INTRODUCTION

The word "terrorism" became commonplace in our head-lines, at the water cooler, and at the dinner table on September 11, 2001. However, the concept of terrorism is not new to the school community. School boards, administrators, and teachers have faced differing degrees of terrorism for many years. Jonesboro- and Columbine-like shootings, as well as other student attacks, have taken place at schools across the country. In fact, for years before school violence became a subject of public discourse, schools experienced attacks on teachers by students and parents, and witnessed parents attacking each other at athletic events.

* This chapter is based upon the authors' article "Planning for a Terrorist Attack on Schools: Practical and Legal Considerations," as first published in *Inquiry and Analysis* (2003), a publication of the National School Boards Association Council of School Attorneys, and is reprinted with permission. The authors wish to extend great thanks to Stephanie E. Jones for her contributions to this article.

193

Now, in the post–September 11 era, schools face broader threats of terrorism. In the past, school crisis management plans commonly focused on evacuation in the event of a gas leak or a fire. Today, schools must be prepared to address biological, chemical, and radiological attacks. Administrators must be prepared for car bombings, suicide attacks, and armed intruders, and know their responsibilities and liabilities related to a potential terrorist attack.[1] As an educational community, we must support and educate each other to ensure that we are ready to act when a crisis occurs. This chapter explores practical and legal requirements of school safety planning to assist school administrators in this task.

B. COMPONENTS OF SAFETY PLANNING

Safety planning requires a thorough assessment of risks and the development of prevention, preparedness, and response strategies. The resulting strategies for prevention may manifest themselves in physical changes to the facilities as well as general school district curricula and policies. Preparedness and response strategies are compiled and set forth in a crisis management plan.

The federal Safe and Drug-Free Schools and Communities Act requires districts that receive funding under the Act to give assurances to the state that they have adopted crisis management plans.[2] Additionally, many state laws require schools to develop crisis management plans or engage in safety assessments. Federal and state funding for planning, however, is scarce. Unfortunately, the lack of funding does not negate the necessity of preparing for a crisis situation.

In May 2003, the U.S. Department of Education released the model document *Practical Information on Crisis Planning: A Guide for Schools and Communities*.[3] This guide was designed to help school administrators create and implement individualized school crisis management plans. The Department of Education strongly suggests that each school district address safety planning in the following four phases: (I) Prevention/Mitiga-

1. U.S. Department of Education, *Emergency Planning for America's Schools* (March 2003), *available at* http://www.ed.gov/news/pressreleases/2003/03/0305-emergencyplan.pdf.

2. 20 U.S.C. § 7114.

3. U.S. Department of Education, *Practical Information on Crisis Planning: A Guide for Schools and Communities* (May 2003), *available at* http://www.ed.gov/admins/lead/safety/emergencyplan/crisisplanning.pdf.

tion; (II) Preparedness; (III) Response; and (IV) Recovery. Each phase is explored in detail below.

1. Phase I: Prevention and Mitigation

During Phase I, schools should conduct safety assessments of each school building. Such assessments should include a survey of school grounds to identify hazards to the school community, including the adequacy of lighting, entrances, and exits; a review of past safety audits or plans; coordination of crisis plans with local businesses, emergency personnel, administration, faculty, staff, and parents; a review of policies for all potential school visitors (including contractors and delivery drivers); a review of communication policies between school districts and local agencies; and a review of traffic patterns to and from schools to ensure that routes are secure and able to be closed if needed. Some state boards of education have created safety assessment audit documents to guide school districts in conducting safety self-assessments.[4]

2. Phase II: Preparedness

After conducting a safety assessment, school administrators should proceed to Phase II to plan and prepare for various crisis situations. A crisis management plan should contain site plans for each building, including both floor plans and elevations. Windows should be marked on each floor plan and show elevation to correspond with each other. Every access to a building, including windows, doors, and ventilation shaft openings, should be clearly marked to allow first responders and S.W.A.T. teams access to intruders or trapped victims in the building. All power and communication access points should be marked as well, including control panels, shutoff valves, and building access points for electric, water, gas, telephone, and cable lines. To ensure that all pertinent information is included, the site plans should be developed in conjunction with local police, fire, and emergency personnel. Final copies of the site plans should be maintained in the main office of every district building, in the homes of key administrators, and in the local police and fire department offices. All staff should receive annual in-service training on the contents of the plan.

---

4. Illinois State Board of Education, *Safe at School: A Resource Manual for Self-Assessment, Planning and Training to Improve School Safety* (Feb. 1999), *available at* http://www.isbe.state.il.us/safeschools/PDF/SafeSchool.pdf.

A chain of command and communication should be established within the crisis management plan. To avoid confusion in the event the top building administrator is unavailable or incapacitated, a second and third in command for each school building should be appointed in advance. Parent and media liaisons also should be designated. Districts must develop procedures for communication with students, faculty, and staff inside the building and the parents, public safety officials, and media outside the building. Districts must plan and organize a method of communication within the building to notify occupants of the nature and seriousness of the situation and the proper response, if one is needed. Codes may be devised to communicate via intercom with staff during a crisis. Alternate communication plans should be developed to ensure effective communication if traditional forms of communication are destroyed. Each person responsible for addressing the outside world should know his or her duties and responsibilities. All staff should know who is allowed to speak with parents or the media, and staff should understand that no one other than those appointed should make statements.

The crisis management plan should include a detailed set of instructions and action plans for each crisis situation. Schools should conduct drills to practice responding to different scenarios. Administrators should ensure that safety equipment is regularly inspected. Finally, necessary information regarding safety, evacuation, and secondary contact information should be furnished to emergency personnel, community leaders, and parents/guardians.

3. Phase III: Response

Once school administrators have completed Phases I and II, they need to develop a crisis response procedure. Phase III should include planning for a command center for responding to emergencies, multiple evacuation routes, and meeting places for every type of crisis. The response procedure should permit no one on the scene of a crisis until law enforcement certifies that the scene is safe to the public. Once evacuated, students must not be allowed back on school grounds. A location for media, parents, and administrators to gather also should be identified. All evacuation and meeting locations should be in reasonable proximity to the respective school buildings, but at a safe distance to minimize risk of injury from stray gunshots or emanating chemical fumes. In securing meeting places, schools should contact local churches, libraries, grocery stores, community centers, or other facilities that may be able to accommodate a large number of students. Schools should not assume they have permission to evacuate to a certain facility, or that a chosen facility has sufficient occupancy, unless some agreement is reached between the school and facility, even if informal.

Schools should be prepared to contact parents and the public in the event of a crisis to disseminate timely information. The crisis management plan should contain directions for connecting parents with their children once the threat or crisis is under control. Not only should the plan address how a school will inform parents of a crisis and where to find their children, it should also address how the school intends to verify that the person claiming to be a student's parent has the legal right to pick that child up from an evacuation point.

4. Phase IV: Recovery

Once the preparedness and response phases of the crisis management plan are developed and functional, school administrators should turn their attention to preparing for the aftermath of an emergency. The school district should have a plan to return to the business of teaching and learning as soon as possible after a crisis. As part of crisis response training, the administration may wish to provide staff training in assessment of emotional needs of students and colleagues to assist in determining intervention needs at a time of crisis. School counselors, with the help of administrators, should identify and approve teams of credentialed mental health workers to be on call to provide services to staff and students.[5] The school district may arrange with the local department of public health, mental health, or social services to have social workers and psychologists standing by in the event of a crisis. Advance agreements with local mental health agencies or private entities are advisable.

C. LEGAL IMPLICATIONS

One challenging aspect of school antiterrorism planning is consideration of the legal implications attendant to antiterrorism and other violence prevention and response policies. Districts must be mindful of current federal and state laws that may affect the legality of these plans. For example, in the areas of student discipline and the release of student records, districts

5. U.S. Department of Education, *Emergency Planning for America's Schools* (March 2003), *available at* http://www.ed.gov/emergencyplan.

must abide by federal legislation, such as the Gun Free Schools Act, Individuals with Disabilities Education Act, U.S.A. PATRIOT Act, and Family Educational Rights and Privacy Act, as well as state privacy and disclosure laws. Districts and their legal counsel also should be attuned to constitutional implications when crafting general policies and procedures on topics impacting school safety, such as student searches, reciprocal reporting agreements with law enforcement, student or visitor profiling, and student expulsion.

1. FERPA

The federal Family Educational Rights and Privacy Act (FERPA) prohibits the disclosure of student records without consent, unless the nature of the disclosure falls within special enumerated categories. In crisis situations, for example, the Act allows nonconsensual disclosure of educational records or personally identifiable, nondirectory information from educational records to appropriate parties when it is necessary to protect the health or safety of the student or other individuals.[6] The U.S. Department of Education has consistently interpreted this exception to be limited to specific situations of imminent danger or immediate need for information from a student's record in order to avert serious threats to the safety or health of the school community.[7]

Nonconsensual disclosure of health information in the circumstances of smallpox, anthrax, or other terrorism-related attacks are examples in which the safety and health exemption of FERPA would apply.[8] Under this exception, all disclosures must be narrowly tailored to the emergency and made only to appropriate parties who can directly assist, such as law enforcement officials, public health officials, and trained medical personnel.[9] School administrators also must remember that if they disclose such information, they must abide by FERPA's recordkeeping requirements.[10]

---

6. U.S. Department of Education, *Recent Amendments to Family Educational Rights and Privacy Act Relating to Anti-Terrorism Activities*, at 3 (Apr. 12, 2002); 34 C.F.R. 99.36 (a) and (c).

7. U.S. Department of Education, *Recent Amendments to Family Educational Rights and Privacy Act Relating to Anti-Terrorism Activities*, at 3 (Apr. 12, 2002).

8. *Id.*

9. *Id.* at 4.; 20 U.S.C. § 1232g; 34 C.F.R. § 99.36 (a).

10. U.S. Department of Education, *supra* note 7, at 4; 34 C.F.R. § 99.32.

Additionally, pursuant to FERPA, and when authorized by state law, state and local officials may make nonconsensual disclosures of education records to the juvenile justice system when necessary to the system's ability to effectively serve, prior to adjudication, the student whose records are released.[11] In order to do this, school administrators must secure, in writing, from the officials and/or authorities to whom such information is disclosed, verification that the juvenile authorities will not disclose such information to any other party except as provided under state law without the prior written consent of the student or parent.[12] It is advisable that the parameters of such information exchanges between school districts and law enforcement authorities be set forth in agreements for the reciprocal reporting of information.

FERPA is a records release statute and, thus, does not apply when school personnel disclose information about a student's suspicious activity or behavior gleaned from their own personal observation.[13] For example, a teacher may overhear a student verbally threaten to perform a school shooting or bombing, or observe the student acting with unusual aggression. The teacher's report to federal, state, or local law enforcement units regarding such observed conduct is not subject to FERPA.

2. Students' Due Process Rights

In developing school safety or antiterrorism policies, administrators must be mindful of a student's constitutional due process rights. Policies on random or mass student searches and screenings or student expulsion, for example, must meet applicable due process standards, with particular attention to implementation where actual violence did not occur, such as instances of threats or suspicious behavior. Use of video and audio recording devices and metal detectors should comply with basic due process notice requirements as well as any restrictions under state law. All policies must comport with applicable nondiscrimination laws under federal and state statutes. Policies, whether formal or informal, that contemplate profiling certain students or groups for risk assessment should be scrutinized. School districts also must be attentive to student groups who may be at risk for retaliatory actions by other students. For example, many schools

---

11. 20 U.S.C. § 1232g (b)(1)(E)(i)–(ii).
12. *Id.*
13. U.S. Department of Education, *supra* note7, at 4.

have been sensitive to reactionary behavior by students toward specific ethnic student populations after recent national terrorist events.

3. Discipline and Behavior Intervention Policies

Schools should use their discipline policies to prevent student attacks. A comprehensive and consistently enforced discipline policy can help a school identify those students who exhibit aggressive behavior. Behavior intervention and aggressive behavior management policies, including those specifically targeting the prevention of bullying behavior, serve as useful tools in conjunction with the exercise of discipline or standing alone. In implementing all such policies, school districts must comply with state and federal laws governing the discipline and behavior management of students, from the basic notions of constitutional due process applicable to all students to the complex procedural steps set forth in laws and regulations governing the education of disabled students.

4. Search Procedures

The key to legally valid student search procedures and policies is compliance with constitutional boundaries. Although courts have held that school districts possess broad discretion to search students and their belongings, searches must be in accordance with a nonarbitrary policy, and the scope of a search must be reasonable and appropriate in light of the purpose. Administrators and school lawyers must be mindful of constitutional issues, but must balance these legal considerations with the public-policy dictates of student safety.

5. State Law

Many state legislatures have addressed legal issues surrounding antiterrorism and safety planning in the schools. Laws enacted in the 1990s advising or requiring school safety assessments and mandating minimum expulsion periods for violent student behavior are now being joined by laws addressing subtler aspects of safety planning, such as protecting plans from disclosure under state sunshine laws. For example, Illinois recently passed legislation amending its Freedom of Information Act to exempt from mandatory disclosure any construction-related technical documents, vulnerability assessments, security measures, and response policies or plans to the extent disclosure would compromise security or the effectiveness of safety measures.[14] Other Illinois legislation exempts from open meeting requirements discussions regarding security procedures and the use of personnel and equipment to respond to an actual, threatened, or reasonably potential danger to the safety of employees, students, staff, or public property.[15] School boards and lawyers should familiarize themselves with the records and meetings exemptions applicable to safety and security matters in their states and ensure that board policies are updated to comport with current law.

6. District Liability

Finally, school lawyers should inform school boards and administrators that the failure to prepare for or respond appropriately to a terrorist attack or other emergency situation may result in lawsuits against the district similar to the lawsuits brought against school officials in the aftermath of the Columbine High School violence in 1999. While schools and school administrators generally benefit from local governmental immunities and will not be subject to civil liability in most circumstances unless their actions were wanton or willful, defending these lawsuits will be costly. School board administrators should consult with their lawyers when creating, developing, or implementing new school safety policies to minimize unnecessary liability to their district.

7. Other Resources for Safety Planning

Many resources are available for crisis planning in addition to the resources provided by the Department of Education. The U.S. Bureau of Alcohol, Tobacco, Firearms, and Explosives, in conjunction with the U.S. Department of Education, released an interactive CD-ROM to local educational agencies and public school systems containing a program to help school administrators and state and local public safety officials better prepare for bomb threats against the nation's schools.[16] They also created an interactive Web site to explain and help local officials implement the program.[17] The American Red Cross issued a Homeland Security Advisor System

---

14. 5 ILCS 140/7 (ll) (as enacted by P.A. 93-422).
15. 5 ILCS 120/2(c)(8).
16. A copy of the CD-ROM may be ordered at http://www.threatplan.org/.
17. Access this Web site at www.threatplan.org.

detailing the actions they recommend schools to take during the five different homeland security risk-of-attack levels.[18]

Additionally, many state agencies have worked with state boards of education or other educators to develop similar models or school safety workshops. For example, in Illinois, the Illinois Emergency Management Agency and the Illinois State Board of Education developed a School Emergency Planning Guide.[19] This document includes sample plans for response to natural and technological disasters as well as civil disturbances (including bomb threats, demonstrations and riots, and terrorism). State boards of education and other education, law enforcement, and safety entities are sponsoring various safe school workshops, including topics such as the impact of terrorism and war on school security and crisis preparedness planning, school safety and the law, and updating school emergency plans. For more information in your state, contact your state board of education or emergency planning/management agency.[20]

D. CONCLUSION

School administrators face many challenges in developing and implementing antiterrorism and school safety plans. The investment of time, the number of entities involved, and the legal ramifications can appear daunting. It is critical, however, that such planning continue to evolve. School administrators, together with federal and state agencies, school lawyers, district staff, parents, and the community, must work toward the goal of compre-

---

18. American Red Cross, *Homeland Security Advisory System Recommendations: Schools* (Aug. 2002), *available at* http://www.redcross.org/static/file_cont1412_lang0_631.pdf.

19. Illinois Emergency Management Agency, *School Emergency Planning Guide* (1999), *available at* http://www.state.il.us/IEMA/Prep/schlplgd.htm.

20. The following is a list of state model or operational district safety/crisis management plans that can be reviewed in implementing, revising, or updating management plans: (1) U.S Department of Education, *at* http://www.ed.gov/admins/lead/safety/emergencyplan/index.html?exp=0; (2) Michigan Association of School Boards, *at* http://www.masb.org/pdf/crisisplan.pdf; (3) North Carolina's Critical Incident Response Kit Project, *at* www.ncdjjdp.org/cpsv/cirk/cirk.htm); (4) Arizona Department of Education, *at* http://www.ade.az.gov/health-safety/health/ schoolsafety/plansresources.asp; (5) Virginia Department of Education, *at* http://www.fcps.k12.va.us/DOC/support/index.htm; (6) Fairfax County Public Schools, *at* www.fcbs.edu/DOC/support; and (7) Montgomery County Public Schools, *at* www.mcps.k12.md.us/info/ emergency/.

hensive safety planning, integrating curriculum, policy, and crisis management. Although the practical and legal considerations related to school safety planning are myriad, the risk of heightened violence on school property renders these issues a priority for schools across the country. With forethought and commitment, schools can be prepared to prevent and respond effectively to potential terrorist attacks and crisis situations.

Appendix A:
Selected Educational Resources

WEB SITES

American Academy of Pediatrics Violence Prevention Resources
www.agp.org/advocagy/violence.htm

American Association of School Administrators
www.aasa.org

Center for Effective Collaboration and Practice
http://www.air-dc.org/cecp/default.htm

Center for the Prevention of School Violence
http://www.ncsu.edu/cpsv/

Committee for Children On Youth Violence Prevention Program
http://www.cfchildren.org/violence.htm

Education Commission of the States' Information Clearinghouse summary
of federal and state laws concerning zero-tolerance/gun control
http://www.esc.org/

ERIC Pathway on Youth Violence
http://eric-web.tc.columbia.edu/pathways/youth_violence/

National Alliance for Safe Schools
http://www.safeschools.org

National Association of Attorneys General
www.keepschoolssafe.org

National Association of School Psychologists
http://www.naspweb.org

National Education Association's Safe, Secure and Healthy Schools
http://www.nea.orp,,/resource/safe.html

National School Boards Association
www.nsba.org

National Schools Safety Center
www.nsscl.org

Safe Schools Coalition
www.ed.mtu.edu/safe

U. S. Department of Education Early Warning Signs
www.ed.gov/offices/OSERS/OSEP/earlywrn.html

U. S. Department of Education, Safe and Drug Free Schools
www.ed.gov/offices/OESE/SDFS

U. S. Department of Justice Office of Juvenile Justice
http://ojjdp.ncjirs.org/

PUBLICATIONS

A. Troy Adams, *The Status of School Discipline and Violence*, 567 The
Annals of The American Academy of Political and Social Science 140

A. Adler, *A Rationale for Teaching Conflict Resolution,* West Palm Beach,
Fla.: School District of Palm Beach County (1993)

American Academy of Pediatrics, *Raising Children to Resist Violence*,
available at http://www.aap.org

Annual Report on School Safety, 1998
www.ed.jzoy/pubs/annschoolrgpt98/intro.html

R. V. Barnett, A. Alder, J. Easton, and K. P. Howard, *An Evaluation of Peach Education Foundation's Conflict Resolution and Peer Mediation Program,* School Business Affairs 29–39 (July 2001)

R. V. Barnett and G. D. Israel, *Striving for School Safety: Reporting Crime and Violence in Public Schools,* School Business Affairs 66(7), 26–33 (2000)

Blueprints for Violence Prevention
www.colo.edu/cspv/blueprints

B. T. Blythe, *Creating Your School's Crisis Management Team,* School Business Affairs 16–18

California School Boards Association, *Governing Board Strategies to Combat School Violence,* California School Boards Association, 3100 Beacon Boulevard, P.O. Box 1660, West Sacramento, CA 95691 916/371–4691, ext. 3038

California School Boards Association, *Legal Guidelines for Curbing School Violence,* 800/706–6722

California School Boards Association, *Violence in the Schools: How America's School Boards Are Safeguarding Your Children,* 800/706–6722

B. Cain, *Standardized Dress: Where Angels (and School Boards) Fear to Tread,* School Business Affairs 39–43 (June 2002)

Common Sense Urged Over "Zero Tolerance," Education Reporter, No. 136, 5 (May 1997)

Creating Safe and Drug-Free Schools: An Action Guide
www.ed.gov/offices/OESE/SDFS/actguid/index.html

R. L. Curwin and A. N. Mendler, *Zero Tolerance for Zero Tolerance,* Phi Delta Kappan 81(2), 119–20 (1999)

W. DeJong, *School-Based Conflict Resolution. Give Educators More Credit,* Journal of Health Affairs 13(4), 163–64 (1994)

L. J. Dolan, S. G. Kellam, C. H. Brown, L. Werthamer-Larsson, G. W. Rebok, L. S. Mayer, J. Laudolff, J. S. Turkkan, C. Ford and L. Wheeler, *The Short-Term Impact of Two Classroom-Based Preventive Intervention Trials on Aggressive and Shy Behaviors and Poor Achievement,* Journal of Applied Developmental Psychology 14, 317–45 (1993)

Drug Strategies, *Safe School, Safe Students: A Guide to Violence Prevention Strategies* www.drugstrategies.org; 1445 M Street NW, Suite 480, Washington, D.C. 20037, 202/663–6090

Early Warning, Timely Response: A Guide to Safe Schools www.ed.gov/offices/OSERS/OSEP/earlywrn.html

M. Easterbrook, *Taking Aim at Violence,* Psychology Today 32(4), 52–57 (1999)

Daniel Flannery, *Improving School Violence Prevention Programs Through Meaningful Evaluation* http://eric-web.tc.columbia.edu/digests/dig32.html

M. Greene, *Learning About School Violence: Lessons for Educators, Parents, Students, and Communities,* New York: Peter Lang Publishing (2001)

D. C. Grossman, H. J. Neckerman, T. D. Koepsell, P. Y. Liu, K. N. Asher, K. Beland, K. Frey and F. P. Rivara, *Effectiveness of a Violence Prevention Curriculum Among Children in Elementary School,* Journal of the American Medical Association 277(20), 1605–11 (1997)

Harvard University, *Opportunities Suspended: The Devastating Consequences of Zero Tolerance and School Discipline Policies* [Report of

the Advancement Project and the Civil Rights Project]
http://www.law.harvard.edu/civilrights/conferences/zero/zt-report2.html

J. D. Hawkins, E. Von Cleve, and R. F. Catalano, *Reducing Early Childhood Aggression: Results of a Primary Prevention Program,* Journal of the American Academy of Child & Adolescent Psychiatry 30, 208–17 (1991)

T. J. Ilg, *An Alternative Approach to Zero Tolerance Policies,* School Business Affairs 43–48 (2001)

Indicators of School Crime and Safety, 1999 www.nces.ed.gov/pubs99/19999057.pdf

D. W. Johnson and R. T. Johnson, *Why Violence Prevention Programs Don't Work—And What Does,* Educational Leadership, 52(5), 63–67 (1995)

D. W. Johnson and R. T. Johnson, *Reducing School Violence Through Conflict Resolution Training,* NASSP Bulletin 80(579), 11–18 (1996)

T. L. Kandakai, J. H. Price, S. K. Telljohann and C. A. Wilson, *Mothers' Perceptions of Factors Influencing Violence in Schools,* Journal of School Health 60(5), 189–95 (1999)

E. Karres, *Violence-Proof Your Kids Now: How to Recognize the 8 Warning Signs and What to Do About Them,* Berkeley, Cal.: Conari Press (2000)

M. Kennedy, *The Changing Face of School Violence,* American School and University 71 (11), 6–9 (1999)

Manual to Combat Truancy
www.ed/gov/pubs/Truan

J. McGee, C. DeBernardo, *The Classroom Avenger: A Behavioral Profile of School-Based Shootings,* Forensic Examiner, May/June 1999

Mentoring: A Proven Delinquency Prevention Strategy www.ncjrs.org/ pdffiles/164834.pdf

National Association of Secondary School Principals, *Civil Rights Implications of Zero Tolerance Programs* [Statement on Civil Rights Implications of Zero Tolerance Programs Before the U.S. Commission on Civil Rights] http://38.202.153.34/news/05-02-01.html

National Center for Education Statistics, *Violence and Discipline Problems in U.S. Public Schools: 1996–97* (March 1998) http://nces.ed.gov/ pubs98/Violence

National Educational Service, *Safe Schools: A Handbook for Violence Prevention* http://www.nes.org/res/safeschools.html

National Longitudinal Study of Adolescent Health www.cpc.unc.edu/ addheath/

Kirk Neil, *When Is Safe, Safe Enough?* School Business Affairs 4–7 (June 2002)

K. E. Powell, L. Muir-McClain, and L. Halasyamani, *A Review of Selected School-Based Conflict Resolution and Peer Mediation Projects,* Journal of School Health 65(10), 426–31 (1995)

Preventing Crime: What Works, What Doesn't, What's Promising www.ncjrs.org/works

M. A. Raywid and L. Oshiyama, *Musings in the Wake of Columbine: What Can Schools Do?* Phi Delta Kappan 81(6), 444–49 (2000)

William Reisman, *The Memphis Conference: Suggestions for Preventing and Dealing with Student Initiated Violence,* 515/961–4814

Safeguarding Our Children: An Action Guide www.ed.gov/admins/lead/ safety/actguide/

School Shooter: A Threat Assessment Perspective (Sept. 2000) www.fbi.gov/librtga/school/school2.pd

W. Schwartz, *An Overview of Strategies to Reduce School Violence,* ERIC Clearinghouse on Urban Education Digest, No. 115, 1-7 (1996)

A. Shanker, *Zero Tolerance* (January 26, 1997) http://www.aft.org/stand/previous/1997/012697.html

Sharing Information: A Guide to the Family Educational Rights and Privacy Act and Participation in Juvenile Justice Programs www.ncjrs.org/jigen.htm

R. Skiba and R. Peterson, *The Dark Side of Zero Tolerance: Can Punishment Lead to Safe Schools?* Phi Delta Kappan, 80(5), 372–76, 381–82 (1999)

M. G. Tebo, *Zero Tolerance, Zero Sense,* ABA Journal 86(4), 40–46, 113 (2000)

The Busy Citizen's Discussion Guide: Violence in Our Communities www.cpn.gov/SCRC/Violence short.html

Threat Assessment in Schools: A Guide to Managing Threatening Situations and to Creating Safe School Climates www.ed.gov/offices/OESE/SDFS

P. H. Tolan and N. G. Guerra, *What Works in Reducing Adolescent Violence: An Empirical Review of the Field,* Boulder: Colorado Center for the Study and Prevention of Violence (1994)

C. C. Williams and J. J. Heinrich, *Comprehensive Threat Assessment Plan for Schools and Communities: Cooperation + Collaboration in Communities = Safe and Secure School Environments,* School Business Affairs 8–12 (June 2002)

CURRICULUM GUIDES

For curriculum guides that target potentially violent behavior, contact the Iowa Center for Law and Civic Education, Drake University Law School, Des Moines, IA 50311, 515/271–4960.

Appendix B:
Selected Legal Resources

Thomas R. Baker, *Tinkering with "Tinker": The Third Circuit's Overbreadth Test for School Anti-Harassment Codes,* 164 Ed. Law Rep. 527 (July 4, 2002)

Gayle Tronvig Carper, Merry Rhodes, and Steven Rittenmeyer, *In Search of Klebold's Ghost: Investigating the Legal Ambiguities of Violent Student Profiling,* 174 Ed. Law Rep. 793 (May 22, 2003)

Robert C. Cloud, *Federal, State, and Local Responses to Public School Violence,* 120 Educ. L. Rep. 877 (1997)

Todd A. DeMitchell, *Security with the Schoolhouse Gate: An Emerging Fundamental Value in Educational Policy Making,* 120 Ed. Law Rep. 379 (1977)

R. A. Griffin, *Using Legal Tools to Confront Student Violence and Misconduct,* School Business Affairs 33–37 (Jan. 2001)

William Haft, *More Than Zero: The Cost of Zero Tolerance and the Case for Restorative Justice in Schools,* 77 Denv. U.L. Rev. 795

David A. Harris, *The Stories, The Statistics, and the Law: Why "Driving While Black" Matters,* 84 Minn. L. Rev. 264 (1999)

Cherry Henault, *Zero Tolerance in Schools,* 30 J. L. & Educ. 547 (2001)

Milton Heumann and Lance Cassak, *Profiles in Justice? Police Discretion, Symbolic Assailants and Stereotyping,* 53 Rutgers L. Rev. 911 (2001)

213

Margaret-Ann Howie, *Digital Discipline: Off-campus Student Conduct, the First Amendment and Web Sites,* NSBA, School Law in Review (3-1) 2001

Alicia Insley, *Suspending and Expelling Children From Educational Opportunity: Time to Reevaluate Zero Tolerance Policies,* 50 Am. U.L. Rev. 1039

J. Kevin Jenkins and John Dayton, *Students, Weapons, and Due Process: An Analysis of Zero Tolerance Policies in Public Schools,* 171 Ed. Law Rep. 13 (January 2, 2003)

R. Jones, *Schools and the Law—Legal Trouble Spots and How to Avoid Them,* American School Board Journal 187(4), 24–30 (2000)

Ann L. Majestic and Jonathan A. Blumberg, *Legal and Policy Issues in Curbing Violence in Schools,* NSBA, School Law in Review (1-1) 1994

Troy Y. Nelson, *If Clothes Make the Person, Do Uniforms Make the Student?: Constitutional Free Speech Rights and Student Uniforms in Public Schools,* 118 Educ. L. Rep. 1 (1997)

James Peden, *Through a Glass Darkly: Educating With Zero Tolerance,* 10 Kan. J. L. & Pub. Pol'y 369

T. Pickrell, *Zero Tolerance Isn't Zero Thinking,* ABA Journal 30(1), 12 (Winter 2000)

Eric W. Schulze and J. T. Martinez, *Into the Snakepit: Section 1983 Liability Under the State-Created Danger Theory for Acts of Private Violence at School,* 104 Ed. Law Rep. 539 (1995)

Cary Silverman, *School Violence: Is It Time to Hold School Districts Responsible for Inadequate Safety Measures?* 145 Ed. Law Rep. 535 (2000)

Douglas Stewart and Charles Russo, *Maintaining Safe Schools,* 151 Ed. Law Rep. 363 (2001)

Nadine Strossen, *Keeping the Constitution Inside the Schoolhouse Gate: Students' Rights Thirty Years After* Tinker v. Des Moines Independent Community School District, 48 Drake L. Rev. 445 (2000)

W. Stuart Stuller, *Hate Speech and the Public Schools,* School Law in Review (7-1) 2000

Lisa L. Swem, *Preventing Threats of Violence in Schools from Turning into a Tragedy,* School Law in Review (1-1) 1999

Ihsan K. Taylor, *Majority of Dade Schools Back Uniforms for Students,* Education Week, April 30, 1997, at 3

R. Craig Wood and Mark D. Chestnutt, *Violence in U.S. Schools: The Problems and Some Responses,* 97 Ed. Law Rep. 619 (1995)

Table of Cases

217

Board of Curators of the University of Mo. v. Horowitz, 435 U.S. 78, 85–89 (1978)   102 n.16, 122 n.106

Board of Educ. of Ft. Madison Community Sch. Dist. v. Youel, 282 N.W.2d 677 (Iowa 1979)   127 n.123

Board of Educ. of Indep. Sch. Dist. No. 92 of Pottawatomie County v. Earls, 122 S. Ct. 2559 (2002)   36 n.16

Board of Regents v. Roth, 408 U.S. 564, 573 (1972)   103 n.21

Boehn v. University of Pa. Sch. of Veterinary Med., 573 A.2d 575, 579 (Pa. Super. Ct. 1990)   100 n.2

Boner v. Eminence R-1 Sch. Dist., 55 F.3d 1339 (8th Cir. 1995)   116 n.82

Booher v. Hogans, 468 F. Supp. 28, 32, *aff'd without opinion*, 588 F.2d 830 (6th Cir. 1978)   101 n.7

Borger v. Bisciglia, 888 F. Supp. 97 (E.D. Wis. 1995)   108 n.46, 110 n.51

Borschel v. City of Perry, 512 N.W.2d 565 (Iowa 1994)   103 n.24

Boucher v. School Bd. of the Sch. Dist. of Greenfield, 134 F.3d 821 (7th Cir. 1998)   55 n.71, 184 n.20

Bowman v. Parma Bd. of Educ., 44 Ohio App. 3d 169, 542 N.E.2d 663 (Ohio Ct. App. 1988)   87 n.3

Bradstreet v. Sobol, 630 N.Y.S.2d 486 (Supp. 1995)   104 n.32

Briggs v. Board of Dirs. of Hinton Cmty. Sch. Dist., 282 N.W.2d 740, 743 (Iowa 1979)   127 n.124

Brouillette v. Board of Directors of Merged Area IX, 519 F.2d 126, 128, 129 (8th Cir. 1975)   116 n.82; 119 nn.92, 94; 131 n.147; 132 n.149

Broward County Sch. Bd. v. Ruiz, 493 So. 2d 474, 477 (Fla. Dist. Ct. App. 1986)   3 n.10

Brown v. Bd. of Educ. of the Glen Cove Public Schools, 700 N.Y.S.2d 58 (N.Y. App. Div. 1999)   2 n.4

Brown v. Georgia Dep't of Revenue, 881 F.2d 1018 (11th Cir. 1989)   100 n.3; 103 n.24; 116 n.82; 118 n.90

Brown v. Indep. Sch. Dist., 763 F. Supp. 905 (S.D. Tex. 1991)   5 n.15

Bundick v. Bay City Ind. Sch. Dist., 140 F. Supp. 2d 735, 739 (2001)   53 n.46

Bush v. Dassel-Cokato Bd. of Educ., 745 F. Supp. 562 (D. Minn. 1990)   182 n.3

Bystrom v. Fridley High Sch. Indep. Sch. Dist. No. 14, 822 F.2d 747 (8th Cir. 1987)   184 n.20

Parkersburg Community Sch. Dist. v. Thie (Iowa Ct. App. 1994) 137 n.167

Patchogue-Medford Congress of Teachers v. Board of Educ., 505 N.Y.S.2d 888 (N.Y. App. Div. 1986), *aff'd,* 510 N.E.2d 325 (N.Y. 1987) 112 n.58

Paul v. Davis, 424 U.S. 693, 710 (1976) 7 n.25

Peck v. Siau, 65 Wash. App. 285, 827 P.2d 1108 (Wash. Ct. App. 1992) 89

Pegram v. Nelson, 469 F. Supp. 1134, 1139 (M.D.N.C. 1979) 104 n.32

People v. D., 315 N.E.2d 466 (N.Y. 1974) 114 n.74

People v. Dukes, 151 Misc. 2d 295, 580 N.Y.S.2d 850 (1992) 42 n.40

People v. Pruitt, 278 Ill. App. 3d 194, 214 Ill. Dec. 974, 662 N.E.2d 540 (Ill. App. 1 Dist. 1996) 41 n.34

People v. Ward, 233 N.W.2d 180 (Mich. Ct. App. 1975) 114 n.74

Pesce v. J. Sterling Morton High Sch., 830 F.2d 789 (7th Cir. 1987) 105 n.35

Phoenixville Area School Dist. v. Marquis B., 25 IDELR 452 (E.D. Pa. 1997) 173 n.77

Plough v. West Des Moines Community Sch. Dist., 70 F.3d 512, 515 (8th Cir. 1995) 130 n.135, 131 n.141

Plyler v. Doe, 457 U.S. 202, 221 (1982) 104 n.28

Pollnow v. Glennon, 757 F.2d 496 (2d Cir. 1984), *aff'g* 594 F. Supp. 220 (S.D. N.Y. 1984) 183 n.11

Pulido v. Dennis, 888 S.W.2d 518 (Tex. App.—El Paso 1994) 6 n.21

R.A.V. v. City of St. Paul, 505 U.S. 377, 382-90, 120 L. Ed. 2d 305, 112 S. Ct. 2538 (1992) 148 n.42, 185 n.25

R.R. v. Board of Educ. of the Shore Reg'l High Sch. Dist., 263A.2d 180 (N.J. Super. 1970) 183 n.11

Randi W. v. Muroc Joint Unified School District, 14 Cal. 4th 1066, 929 P.2d 582 (Cal. 1997) 86

Ray v. Antioch Unified Sch. Dist., 107 F. Supp. 2d 1165 (N.D. Cal. 2000) 13 n.51

Regents of the Univ. of Minn. v. NCAA, 422 F. Supp. 1158, 1161 (D. Minn. 1976), *rev'd on other grounds,* 560 F.2d 352 (8th Cir. 1977) 105 n.33

Reno v. A.C.L.U., 521 U.S. 844, 863 (1997) 187 n.35

Rock Island Indep. School Dist. No. 907 v. County Bd. of Sch. Trustees, 423 S.W.2d 665 (Tex. Civ. App. 1968) 128 n.127

Rosa R. v. Connelly, 889 F.2d 435, 439 (2d Cir. 1989) 29 n.99, 118 n.92

Index

D

Books from the American Bar Association
Section of State and Local Government Law

ABCs of Arbitrage, 2002 Edition
Tax Rules for Investment of Bond Proceeds by Municipalities
Frederic L. Ballard, Jr.

Concentrates on tax-exempt bonds issued by a municipality and the market for taxable bonds issued by a corporation or by the federal government. *2002, 7 x 10, 385 pages, paper*
PC: 5330078   *SLGL member price: $119.95*   *Regular price: $134.95*

Case Dismissed: Taking Your Harassment Prevention Training to Trial
Mindy H. Chapman, Carol M. Merchasin, Jeff Polisky

A team of training experts for Seyfarth Shaw at Work show you how to deliver harassment training in ways that are legally sound, fun and interactive. *2003, 7 x 10, 284 pages, paper*
PC: 5330081   *SLGL member price: $69.95*   *Regular price: $85.00*

Court-Awarded Attorneys' Fees: Examining Issues of Delay, Payment and Risk
Russell E. Lovell, II, Editor

Provides an in-depth examination of the history, process and structure of these fees. *1999, 6 x 9, 275 pages, paper*
PC: 5330070   *SLGL member price: $69.95 $17.50   Regular price: $79.95 $17.50*

Current Trends and Practical Strategies in Land Use Law and Zoning
Patricia E. Salkin, Editor

A compilation of significant trends in land use law, featuring landmark court decisions from the U.S. Supreme Court, federal district courts and state high courts. *2004, 6 x 9, 242 pages, paper*
PC: 5330082   *SLGL member price: $69.95*   *Regular price: $94.95*

Ethical Standards in the Public Sector
A Guide for Government Lawyers, Clients and Public Officials
Patricia E. Salkin, Editor

A compilation of essays, articles, and research intended to help government lawyers, their clients, and other public officials focus on some of the ethical considerations that arise in the practice of law in the public sector.
1999, 7 x 10, 319 pages, paper
PC: 5330067   *SLGL member price: $74.95*   *Regular price: $84.95*

Freedom of Speech in the Public Workplace
A Legal and Practical Guide to Issues Affecting Public Employment
Marcy S. Edwards, Jill Leka, James Baird, Stefanie Lee Black

Includes discussions about how the First Amendment applies to the speech of public employees, how race, sex, sexual preference, and religion are affected by the First Amendment and what issues are relevant when public functions are privatized. *1998, 7 x 10, 158 pages, paper*
PC: 5330063   *SLGL member price: $64.95 $16.25   Regular price: $74.95 $16.25*

From Sprawl to Smart Growth
Successful Legal, Planning, and Environmental Systems
Robert H. Freilich, Editor

Discusses how states and local governments can control sprawl, maintain urban areas, enlarge their quality of life through new urban and mixed use developments, and increase the economic development base through transportation

Hot Topics in Land Use Law: From the Comprehensive Plan to Del Monte Dunes
Patricia E. Salkin and Robert H. Freilich, Editors

This book combines an array of land use articles from *The Urban Lawyer* with specially commissioned essays. Covers a broad range of issues that are changing the way land use law and zoning are practiced and interpreted in the courts.
2000, 6 x 9, 223 pages, paper
PC: 5330069   *SLGL member price: $64.95 $15.00   Regular price: $74.95 $15.00*

How to Litigate a Land Use Case: Strategies and Trial Tactics
Larry J. Smith, Editor

A step-by-step guide from the earliest days of a land use controversy to the delivery of the oral argument in an appellate court. *2000, 6 x 9, 426 pages, paper*
PC: 5330073   *SLGL member price: $64.95 $37.50   Regular price: $74.95 $37.50*

School Violence: From Discipline to Due Process
James C. Hanks, Editor

A comprehensive review of major legal issues relating to school violence. The book provides important and useful guidance for dealing with these very timely issues. *2004, 6 x 9, 256 pages, paper*
PC: 5330083   *SLGL member price: $49.95   Regular price: $59.95*

Sexual Harassment in the Public Workplace
Benjamin E. Griffith, Editor

Provides an in-depth analysis of the most current caselaw, and information on how to try and defend sexual harassment cases. *2001, 6 x 9, 312 pages, paper*
PC: 5330074   *SLGL member price: $75.00   Regular price: $90.00*

Sword & Shield Revisited, Second Edition: A Practical Approach to Section 1983
Mary Massaron Ross, Editor

Provides an understanding of the framework of Section 1983 and takes you beyond the basic issues to the comprehensive information to assist you in your practice. *1998, 695 pages, 6 x 9, paper*
PC: 5330064   *SLGL member price: $75.00 $18.75   Regular price: $85.00 $18.75*

Taking Sides on Takings Issues: Public and Private Perspectives
Thomas E. Roberts, Editor

Compiles and contrasts the public and private perspectives on the most controversial issues in takings law.
2002, 6 x 9, 600 pages, paper
PC: 5330077   *SLGL member price: $75.95   Regular price: $90.00*

Taking Sides on Takings Issues: The Impact of Tahoe-Sierra
Thomas E. Roberts, Editor

Offers a comprehensive analysis of the blockbuster takings case, *Tahoe-Sierra Preservation Council v. Tahoe Regional Planning Agency*. *2003, 6 x 9, 109 pages, paper*
PC: 5330079   *SLGL member price: $29.95   Regular price: $34.95*

Trends in Land Use Law from A to Z: Adult Uses to Zoning
Patricia E. Salkin, Editor

Includes information on *Palazzolo v. State of Rhode Island,* the short decision handed down by the U.S. Supreme Court in the *Olech* case, and the issues that arise when land use law meets the First Amendment.
2001, 6 x 9, 504 pages, paper
PC: 5330075   *SLGL member price: $75.00   Regular price: $110.00*

For more information on these books, please call (800) 285-2221 or visit our web site at *www.ababooks.org*